Praise for *This Bridge Called My Back*

"*This Bridge Called My Back* . . . dispels all doubt about the power of a single text to radically transform the terrain of our theory and practice. Twenty years after its publication, we can now see how it helped to untether the production of knowledge from its disciplinary anchors—and not only in the field of women's studies. *This Bridge* has allowed us to define the promise of research on race, gender, class and sexuality as profoundly linked to collaboration and coalition-building. And perhaps most important, it has offered us strategies for transformative political practice that are as valid today as they were two decades ago."

—Angela Davis,
University of California, Santa Cruz

"*This Bridge Called My Back* . . . has served as a significant rallying call for women of color for a generation, and this new edition keeps that call alive at a time when divisions prove ever more stubborn and dangerous. A much-cited text, its influence has been visible and broad both in academia and among activists. We owe much of the sound of our present voices to the brave scholars and feminists whose ideas and ideals crowd its pages."

—Shirley Geok-lin Lim,
University of California, Santa Barbara

"This book is a manifesto—the 1981 declaration of a new politics 'US Third World Feminism.' No great de-colonial writer, from Fanon, Shaarawi, Blackhawk, or Sartre, to Mountain Wolf Woman, de Beauvoir, Saussure, or Newton could have alone proclaimed this 'politic born of necessity.' This politic denies no truths: its luminosities drive into and through our bodies. Writers and readers alike become shape-shifters, are invited to enter the shaman/witness state, to invoke power differently. 'US Third World Feminism' requires a re-peopling: the creation of planetary citizen-warriors. This book is a guide that directs citizenry shadowed in hate, terror, suffering, disconnection, and pain toward the light of social justice, gender and erotic liberation, peace, and revolutionary love. *This Bridge* . . . transits our dreams, and brings them to the real."

—Chela Sandoval,
University of California, Santa Barbara

This Bridge Called My Back

Fortieth Anniversary Edition

Celia Herrera Rodríguez, *Omecihuatl*, 1979
Watercolor on fiberglass paper, 22" × 30"
Destroyed in fire in 1982

This Bridge Called My Back

writings by
radical women of color

Fortieth Anniversary Edition

Edited by
Cherríe Moraga
and
Gloria Anzaldúa

Cover art designed by Amane Kaneko

Published by State University of New York Press, Albany

For information, contact State University of New York Press, Albany, NY
www.sunypress.edu

Library of Congress Cataloging-in-Publication Data

This bridge called my back : writings by radical women of color / edited by
    Cherríe L. Moraga and Gloria E. Anzaldúa. — Fortieth anniversary edition.
        pages cm
    Includes bibliographical references and index.
    ISBN 978-1-4384-8827-1 (hardcover : alk. paper)
    ISBN 978-1-4384-8828-8 (pbk. : alk. paper)
    1. Feminism—Literary collections. 2. Women—United States—Literary
collections. 3. American literature—Minority authors. 4. Minority women—
Literary collections. 5. American literature—Women authors. 6. Radicalism—
Literary collections. I. Moraga, Cherríe, editor. II. Anzaldúa, Gloria, editor.

PS509.F44T5 2015
810.8'09287—dc23   2014039109

10 9 8 7 6 5 4 3 2 1

para

> *Elvira Moraga Lawrence y*
> *Amalia García Anzaldúa*
> *y para todas nuestras madres*
> *por la obediencia y*
> *la insurrección*
> *que ellas nos enseñaron.*

for

> *Elvira Moraga Lawrence and*
> *Amalia García Anzaldúa*
> *and for all our mothers*
> *for the obedience and rebellion*
> *they taught us.*

Contents

Artwork   xiii

Enough Is Enough: Preface to the Fortieth Anniversary Edition   xv
Cherríe Moraga

Acts of Healing   xxiii
Gloria Anzaldúa and The Gloria E. Anzaldúa Literary Trust

Catching Fire: Introduction, 2015   xxv
Cherríe Moraga

Foreword to the First Edition, 1981   xxxvii
Toni Cade Bambara

The Bridge Poem   xli
Kate Rushin

La Jornada: Preface, 1981   xliii
Cherríe Moraga

Introduction, 1981   li
Cherríe Moraga and Gloria Anzaldúa

I

Children Passing in the Streets
The Roots of Our Radicalism

When I Was Growing Up   5
Nellie Wong

on not bein   7
mary hope whitehead lee

For the Color of My Mother   10
Cherríe Moraga

I Am What I Am   12
Rosario Morales

Dreams of Violence   14
Naomi Littlebear Morena

He Saw   16
Chrystos

II

Entering the Lives of Others

Theory in the Flesh

Wonder Woman   20
Genny Lim

La Güera   22
Cherríe Moraga

Invisibility Is an Unnatural Disaster:
Reflections of an Asian American Woman   30
Mitsuye Yamada

It's in My Blood, My Face—My Mother's Voice, the Way I Sweat   36
Anita Valerio

"Gee You Don't Seem Like an Indian from the Reservation"   41
Barbara Cameron

". . . And Even Fidel Can't Change That!"   48
Aurora Levins Morales

I Walk in the History of My People   53
Chrystos

III

And When You Leave, Take Your Pictures with You

Racism in the Women's Movement

And When You Leave, Take Your Pictures with You   60
Jo Carillo

Beyond the Cliffs of Abiquiu   62
Jo Carillo

I Don't Understand Those Who Have Turned Away
from Me   65
Chrystos

Asian Pacific Women and Feminism   68
Mitsuye Yamada

"—But I Know You, American Woman"   73
Judit Moschkovich

The Black Back-Ups   78
Kate Rushin

The Pathology of Racism:
A Conversation with Third World Wimmin   81
doris davenport

We're All in the Same Boat   87
Rosario Morales

An Open Letter to Mary Daly   90
Audre Lorde

The Master's Tools Will Never Dismantle
the Master's House   94
Audre Lorde

IV

Between the Lines

On Culture, Class, and Homophobia

The Other Heritage   104
Rosario Morales

The Tired Poem: Last Letter from a Typical
(Unemployed) Black Professional Woman   106
Kate Rushin

To Be Continued . . .   109
Kate Rushin

Across the Kitchen Table: A Sister-to-Sister Dialogue   111
Barbara Smith and Beverly Smith

Lesbianism: An Act of Resistance   126
Cheryl Clarke

Lowriding through the Women's Movement   136
Barbara Noda

Letter to Ma   138
Merle Woo

I Come with No Illusions   146
Mirtha N. Quintanales

I Paid Very Hard for My Immigrant Ignorance   148
Mirtha N. Quintanales

Earth-Lover, Survivor, Musician   155
Naomi Littlebear Morena

V

Speaking in Tongues

The Third World Woman Writer

Speaking in Tongues:
A Letter to Third World Women Writers   163
Gloria Anzaldúa

Millicent Fredericks   173
Gabrielle Daniels

In Search of the Self as Hero: Confetti of Voices on
New Year's Night—a Letter to Myself   176
Nellie Wong

Chicana's Feminist Literature: A Re-vision through
Malintzin/or Malintzin Putting Flesh Back on the Object   181
Norma Alarcón

Ceremony for Completing a Poetry Reading   190
Chrystos

VI

El Mundo Zurdo

The Vision

Give Me Back   197
Chrystos

La Prieta   198
Gloria Anzaldúa

A Black Feminist Statement   210
Combahee River Collective

The Welder   219
Cherríe Moraga

O.K. Momma, Who the Hell Am I?
An Interview with Luisah Teish   221
Gloria Anzaldúa

Brownness   232
Andrea Canaan

Revolution: It's Not Neat or Pretty or Quick   238
Pat Parker

No Rock Scorns Me as Whore   243
Chrystos

Appendix

Afterword: On the Fourth Edition   249
Cherríe Moraga

Foreword to the Second Edition, 1983   253
Gloria Anzaldúa

Refugees of a World on Fire:
Foreword to the Second Edition, 1983   255
Cherríe Moraga

Counsels from the Firing . . . past, present, future:
Foreword to the Third Edition, 2001   261
Gloria Anzaldúa

Biographies of Contributors   267

Biographies of the Original Contributors, 1981   277

Credits   283

Artwork

Omecihuatl, 1979   frontispiece
Celia Herrera Rodríguez

Mattie Looks for Steven Biko, 1985   2
Hulleah Tsinhnahjinnie

Portrait of the Artist as the Virgin of Guadalupe, 1978   18
Yolanda M. López

The Liberation of Aunt Jemima, 1972   56
Betye Saar

New Country Daughter/Lebanese American, 1981   100
Happy/L.A. Hyder

Aveugle Voix, 1975   160
Theresa Hak Kyung Cha

Los desaparecidos en el cielo, 1977   194
Liliana Wilson

Untitled (Body Tracks), 1974   246
Ana Mendieta

Enough Is Enough

Preface to the Fortieth Anniversary Edition

Cherríe Moraga

The phenomenon of a forty-year-old *This Bridge Called My Back* may be best understood as a document of the living legacy of forebearers bound not by blood, but by the *bridge* of intracultural women of color consciousness—the living breadth of which far exceeds the pages and geographies of this book. A certain collective ancestral spirit has sustained this collection through its many pauses in production, including the untimely death of coeditor Gloria Anzaldúa in 2004. Along with her, we remember each of the contributors who have joined Gloria as ancestor: Audre Lorde, Toni Cade Bambara, (la Boricua) Rosario Morales, Barbara Cameron (Lakota), and the power that is Pat Parker.

A few days before this writing, Hawaiian sovereignty activist and writer-warrior Haunani-Kay Trask joined this pantheon of sisters. One week earlier, a Chicana foremother of *Bridge*, Betita Martínez, also passed at the age of ninety-six. With the proximity of their departures, the word "sisterhood" resonates more deeply in me than it has in a long time. As foremothers, they become our accessible relations. I turn to them in this writing.

What might be the collective message of *This Bridge Called My Back* in 2021? What would the chorus herein of the twenty-nine writers—sisters of the yam, of the rice, of the corn, of the plantain[1]—say to young people today? I am confident of one thing: it would refuse the seduction of a return to the "normal." COVID opened our eyes to what we, as people of color, queer and trans, elder and disabled, immigrant and

Native, have known all along: the hierarchical structure of privilege in this world determines who gets to live and who dies. The "normal" is what got us here inside the numbing heart of the disproportionate numbers of our loss.

I go to the subtitle of *Bridge* for direction: "Writings by *Radical* Women of Color." We named this work "radical" toward the uncompromised excavation of the root of our oppression y la raíz de nuestra liberación.

"When did globalization begin?" my students ask. (It is a creative writing class.)

I answer. "About five hundred and thirty years ago."

Philosopher María Lugones (1944–2020) reminds us that with that first 1492 moment of European contact with América,[2] no honest encounters between worlds ever truly happened. No good-faith transactions of ways and means; no genuine "free trade"; no routes shaped simply by the currents of curious footsteps, followed by an equitable exchange of shining stones for seeds that might grow a sustainable future.

From the moment of that initial meeting with Europe, none of us were ever fully allowed to witness the human face of whiteness before "whiteness," before "race" and racism had deformed its beholder. Racism, structurally executed through patriarchy, is the unredeemable and tragic cost of colonization.

As a result, those of us who see ourselves as active (dis)inheritors of colonization are still trying to recover within ourselves a different history of world relation. We imagine free-traveling African and original Américan philosophers; voyagers from near and far, proffering distinct modes of equitable governance, sustainable living, and healing practices. So much has been lost—technologies and teachings, credos y creaciones—and so much needs to be found for the survival and flourishing of remaining peoples, species, mountains, streams, and just daily drinkable water.

We cannot assess the loss without reckoning with true and full histories; the confrontation with, and the insights into, the tragic horror of (neo)colonization as the widening breadth of its bite consumes the planet. I confess it is difficult to bear witness to the logical global consequence of colonization—a way of seeing the world without hope, a world where the virus of greed ultimately wins.

It's everywhere—a cancel culture that binds our tongues, a corporate academy with more insidious methods. The current vernacular is wrought with political implications. One which steals original thought on the daily and quickly commodifies it into jargon; one which turns once good words like "diversity" and "democracy" into generic meaninglessness in an "exceptional" America. We can read too well the sense of entitlement implicit in self-appointed "ally-ships" and the limitations of US Anglocentric antiracist activism that never bothers to look south of the border or even west of the Mississippi to the complex histories of colonization, caste systems, and liberation struggles impacting the whole of América, to this day.

It seems that as we grow older, we encounter fewer and fewer words to describe the depth of what we have come to know. Each day our preguntas se vuelven mas profundas y mas silenciadas.[3] I leaf through the pages of *Bridge* in search of the language that might ignite the words I need to speak for the "we" of *Bridge*.

"The holocaust has already occurred," Chrystos writes. "What follows is only the burning brush. How my heart aches & cries to write these words . . . I will be screaming no no no more destruction in that last blinding light" (245). These are last lines in the final "Vision" section of this book. They may be the most "radical" and instructive words for *Bridge* readers of today. For, if all that we have left in face of the transnational theft of earth's resources and its consequent global warming are: mass incarcerations, the forced dislocation of Indigenous communities, children in cages; starvation in Yemen; Palestine bombed and bombed again; víctimas del feminicidio and los desaparecidos scattered throughout the once fertile milpas of Latin America; while school girls are still being abducted in Nigeria; if worldwide, the poor grow ever poorer and the rich grow richer than ever, if the Colorado river has finally run dry and over one billion sea creatures are "cooked alive" in the Salish Sea during the latest heat wave in the Northwest, if . . . if . . . if . . . then our collective informed resistance in the form of "No" is the *only* justifiable response.

No. No. No. More. Destruction. This is the cry of radical consciencia.

This is three Black women saying "No." No to impunity, no to the murder of Black and Brown folk by the police. This is the birth of the Black Lives Matter movement.

This is Standing Rock, saying "No" to the Dakota Access Pipeline and Indigenous activists blocking Enbridge Energy Line 3 construction in Minnesota.

This is a "Me, Too" movement first voiced by a Black activist from the Bronx, Tarana Burke.

This is Berta Cáceres (Lenca), murdered in 2016, defending her land and water rights in Honduras.

And this is Haunani-Kay Trask, resounding an unequivocal *No*. "We are not American! We will die as Hawaiians! We will never be American!"

This is women of color feminisms spearheading radical action on the ground in virtually every area of anti-globalization and human rights movements, including world poverty, violence against women, and trans liberation. This is intersectionality as living practice.

In the resistant body of that "No" resides an authentic affirmation for a radically altered future. But here may be the hardest truth to swallow: that even in our so-called resistance, we must move through this world differently; we must acknowledge that we are not the center of the universe and must never design to be so. There are whole worlds of knowledge that we are not privy to, here and elsewhere. We are blessed if and when they still exist; for these are the teachers our grandchildren have been waiting for (perhaps unbeknownst to them) to reconstruct a livable planet.

Paradoxically, this knowledge only comes to us if it is not coveted. It cannot be "gotten," taken, owned. It requires a radical transformation of our thinking literally from the ground up that revolves around one fundamental value: *nature and its dwellers are not property*. The same can be said of the knowledges and values systems that promise to repair this planet. They cannot be owned or extracted for profit. We must unlearn the lessons of colonialism even in the act of dismantling it.

What might it mean, to wait actively, to begin to listen attentively to the so-called "nobodies" of the world, the unnoticed in Anzaldúa's "Mundo Zurdo," to those brothers trapped in 115-degree heat waves in Washington State prisons, to teachers with the gift of tongues in revolt that might send us marching into an engaged life of critical consciousness? No short cuts, no more Facebook quarrels, no gossip, but employing language that strives to express what is wholly known in the body. Today I understand the *true* porousness of the border by the Indigenous bodies that insist on breaking through it.

I think this remains the very heart of *Bridge*'s intention: that we have to keep looking to our home grounds to find the road back to values that promise to slow the glacier's meltdown and the spread of the next virus. From that place, we skill-build our weaponry toward what we understand as our calling and our work, the hard connective labor of coalition, compassion, and consciousness in a radically renewed social order of a globalized world.

Recognizing the ephemerality of a lifetime (long and short), my hope is that you, the new or returning reader to *This Bridge Called My Back*, might glimpse the aspirational intention in the lines and lives of each *Bridge* contributor, many writing at the very pinnacle of their own politicization as women of color within the context of a burgeoning feminist of color movement in the late 1970s into the 1980s. My hope is that you might see yourselves and the promise of your own radicalization reflected in their principles, poetry, and passion for change.

Old radical ways and concepts return to me from my own forty-plus years of social and political engagement: consciousness-raising groups, criticism/self-criticism, universities without walls; writing pen-to-page and dating face-to-face. Liberation Theology. Engels's *The Origin of the Family, Private Property and the State*. The Buddhist concept of "relative truth." It seems that each of us moves forward by what touches and stays with us; what agitates us into action.

The world is not an accident as long as we strive to draw meaning from it and in so doing act upon it with courage and grace.

As the years pass, *Bridge* will continue to reflect a longer and living history, even as we, its aging contributors, join the company of our ancestor predecessors. But you, we, are all present in this book—looking back and forward.

And so, I end this writing where we began, with an honoring of our ancestors.

What follows is a short list of women of color activists, writers, and artists[4]—some recognizable to many, some less so. But they *were* there, contributors to *Bridge*'s vision by their own concurrent life practice. And that has got to be enough.

Theresa Hak Kyung Cha (1951–1982). Korean American avant-garde novelist and filmmaker; best known for her 1982 novel, *Dictee*. Cha was raped and murdered one week after her book's publication.

Victoria Mercado (1951–1982). Chicana labor union activist, comunista; died in what was believed to be a politically motivated murder.

Ana Mendieta (1948–1985). Early feminist Cuban American visual and performance artist; sculptor. Her art reflected an intimate relationship with nature, especially that of the landscape of Cuba. Her death was believed to be a domestic homicide.

Mabel Hampton (1902–1989). African American lesbian; a dancer during the Harlem Renaissance; volunteer at the Lesbian Herstory Archives (NYC).

Marsha Gómez (1951–1998). Choctaw/Chicana; a potter of great craft and passion for Madre Tierra; longtime director of Alma de Mujer, a retreat center outside of Austin, and a board member of the Indigenous Women's Network; murdered by her son, suffering schizophrenia.

Ingrid Washinawatok El-Issa/Flying Eagle Woman (1957–1999). Menominee international activist for the sovereign rights and education of Indigenous peoples; was kidnapped and murdered by FARC guerrillas while en route to work with the U'wa People of Colombia.

Sandra Camacho (1960–2004). Nuyorican lesbian feminist women of color organizer; co-coordinator of New York Women Against Rape in the 1980s.

Barbara Christian (1943–2000). Caribbean-born; first Black woman to be granted tenure at UC Berkeley in 1978; produced multiple seminal works on Black women's literatures.

Patsy Mink (1927–2002). Sansei (third-generation) Japanese American; Democratic congresswoman for Hawaii; coauthored Title IX Amendment of the Higher Education Act.

June Jordan (1936–2002). Harlem-born, Jamaican American "Poet for the People"; activist, essayist, and professor with over thirty years of politically engaged, powerfully rendered writings.

Sylvia Rivera (1951–2002). Radical Latina Transgender Rights activist; participated in the Stonewall Uprising; in 2002 the Sylvia Rivera Law Project was founded in her honor.

Octavia Butler (1947–2006). African American science fiction author. *Parable of the Sower* offers a new way to be in the world.

VèVè Amasasa Clark (1944–2007). Clark's scholarship, teaching, and service reflect her passionate commitment to the field of African American and African Diaspora studies.

Paula Gunn Allen (1939–2008). Laguna Pueblo from New Mexico; prolific poet and scholar of Native American Women's Spirituality, most significantly *The Sacred Hoop*.

Elena Avila (1944–2011). New Mexican curandera and spiritual consejera; practitioner of "medicine of the people"; author of *Woman Who Glows in the Dark*.

Yuri Kochiyama (1921–2014). Japanese American lifetime activist in Asian American, Black, and Third World movements, as well as antiwar and Puerto Rican Independence struggles.

Ntozake Shange (1948–2018). Author of the choreopoem *For Colored Girls Who Have Considered Suicide When the Rainbow Is Enuf*. One of the first to speak out as a public writer on violence against Black women within the Black community.

Toni Morrison (1931–2019). Winner of the Nobel Prize for Literature in 1993; author of *Sula, Beloved, Song of Solomon*, and many more works of incomparable beauty and a complex comprehension of Black American lives and histories.

Uzuri Amini Iya Oshogbo (1954–2018). African American lesbian poet and priestess of Oshun, who specialized in healing women survivors of sexual abuse.

Emma Amos (1937–2020). Incomparable and acclaimed African American figurative painter, printmaker, and weaver; arts activist.

Nawal El Saadawi (1931–2021). Egyptian feminist writer, activist, and physician; a prolific writer and advocate for women in the Arab world; especially notable—*Women and Sex* (1969), which was banned in Egypt for almost two decades.

> Also, in acknowledgment of all those unnamed,
> we wish our sisters liberation
> in the wellspring of zero,
> we wish them life.

8 july 2021

Notes

1. Toni Cade Bambara, foreword to the first edition of *This Bridge Called My Back: Writings by Radical Women of Color*, xxxvii, this volume.
2. The accent refers to América North, South, Central and the Caribbean.
3. questions grow deeper and more silenced
4. This list, neither definitive nor representative, contains very abbreviated descriptions but reflects women who came to mind in writing and were also suggested to me by several *Bridge* writers who responded to my inquiry. I encourage you to find out more about their remarkable lives.

Editor's Note

In this edition, we regrettably were not able to secure permission to republish hattie gosset's two essays, which had appeared in earlier editions: "billie lives! billie lives" and "who told you anybody wants to hear from you? you ain't nothing but a black woman." Gratefully, however, we were able to include additional poems by Kate Rushin, which pay tribute to women of color and their work—those "Back-Ups . . . my mama and your mama" (80) who have made our writings and art possible.

Agradecimientos. Thank you to our literary representative, Stuart Bernstein, who was critical to the successful recompilation of the 2015 edition of *Bridge*. After over a decade of being out-of-print, Stuart's good faith, tenacity, and calm heart were foundational to the book's relaunch. Gracias to all of the production and marketing folks at SUNY Press, especially the ever-present patience of Diane Ganeles and her team, and the support of Beth Bouloukos and Kate Seburyamo. We also thank Larin McLaughlin, who made the initial efforts of acquiring *Bridge* for SUNY Press. Additional thanks are in order for the team that helped produce this fortieth anniversary edition. They are: Timothy Stookesberry, Rebecca Colesworthy, Sharla Clute, James Peltz, and Michael Campochiaro.

My gratitude goes, as always, to AnaLouise Keating (of The Gloria E. Anzaldúa Literary Trust) for her continued dedication to Gloria's vision. Finally, deep thanks a mi compañera por vida, Celia Herrera Rodríguez, as daily and righteous witness to our shared labors of love.

Acts of Healing

Gloria Anzaldúa

A lot of women are talking about all this radical stuff, but when it comes to be it will scare the shit out of them.

—Gloria Anzaldúa

Gloria Evangelina Anzaldúa believed that This Bridge *should be published by a large, mainstream press in order to give it visibility, sustainability, and a wide audience. The Anzaldúa Trust is confident that Anzaldúa would be pleased with the additional possibilities this publication promises. As the following previously unpublished material, drawn from a 1983* Bridge *preface draft titled "And not acts of killing but of healing" indicates, Anzaldúa viewed* This Bridge *as part of an ongoing, planetary transformational project.*

—*The Gloria E. Anzaldúa Literary Trust*

Before turning our eyes "forward" let's cast a look at the roads that led us here. The paths we've traveled on have been rocky and thorny, and no doubt they will continue to be so. But instead of the rocks and the thorns, we want to concentrate on the rain and the sunlight and the spider webs glistening on both. Some of you, like us, are up to here with the chorus of laments whose chief chant is "I'm more poor, more oppressed than you," who give suffering and pain more merit than laughter and health. And yes, we intimately know the origins of oppression; it brewed in our beds, tables, and streets; screaming out in anger is a necessary stage in our evolution into freedom, but do we have to dwell forever on that piece of terrain, forever stuck in the middle of that bridge? This land of thorns is not habitable. We carry this bridge inside us, the struggle, the movement toward liberation. No doubt all of us have found by now that you don't build bridges by storming walls—that only puts people's backs up.

Not acts of barging in the door and ramming our ideologies down people's throats but of turning away, walking away from those who are not yet ready to hear us, who perhaps can never hear us. To stand our ground with those who look us in the eye, to wait for that glimmer of recognition to pass between us, to let the force of our being penetrate the other with gentleness. Touching is an act of making love, and if political touching is not made with love no connections, no linkings happen.

We each are our sisters' and brothers' keepers; no one is an island or has ever been. Every person, animal, plant, stone is interconnected in a life-and-death symbiosis. We are each responsible for what is happening down the street, south of the border or across the sea. And those of us who have more of anything—more brains, more physical strength, more political power, more money, or more spiritual energies—must give or exchange with those who don't have these energies but may have other things to give. It is the responsibility of some of us who tap the vast source of spiritual/political energies to help heal others, to put down a drawbridge; at the same time we must depend more and more on our own sources for survival. Ayudar a las mujeres que todavía viven en la jaula dar nuevos pasos y a romper barreras antiguas. (To help women who still live in cages to take new steps, and to break old barriers.)

Catching Fire

Introduction, 2015

Cherríe Moraga

Egypt is burning
bonfires of celebration
ignited with the tinder
of that first
single
enflamed body
Tunisia.

!Sí! !Se puede!
The MeXicana[1] mantra rises to my lips.
We look across oceans
for hope.

When I first began to consider a preface to the 4th edition of *This Bridge Called My Back: Writings by Radical Women of Color,* these opening lines came to me. I wrote them at a moment in history when progressive revolution seemed possible. I remember that February nearly four years ago, watching the late night news, during the eighteen days of revolt in Tahrir Square, scanning the faces of protesters, searching for visual signs of *sisters* amid the fervent masses of men. I spy the hijab; swatches of dark fabric and multicolored pastel blend among the hundreds of thousands. I press my ear to an Al Jazeera radio broadcast, "Hosni Mubarak steps down!" And I hear a woman's voice, "I have worked for this my whole life." She is crying and I am crying because her victory is mine. To view the world today through a feminist of color lens shatters all barriers of state-imposed nationality. *The Egyptian revolution is my revolution!*

The first edition of *This Bridge Called My Back* was collectively penned nearly thirty-five years ago with a similar hope for revolutionary solidarity. For the first time in the United States, women of color, who had been historically denied a shared political voice, endeavored to create bridges of consciousness through the exploration, in print, of their diverse classes, cultures and sexualities. Thirty-five years ago was before Facebook, before Twitter, before cell phones, fax machines, before home computers and the internet. Thirty-five years ago, Egypt, Afghanistan, Nigeria seemed very far away. They are no longer so far.

Over those three and a half decades, the writers herein have grown much older as the proximity of "foreign" nations has grown much closer through technology and globalization, bringing millions of new immigrants to the United States, especially from Western and South Asia and the América just south of us. *Bridge's* original political conception of "US women of color" as primarily including Chinese, Japanese, and Filipina American, Chicana/Latina, Native and African American, has now evolved into a transnational and increasingly complex movement of women today, whose origins reside in Asia, throughout the global south and in Indigenous North America.

The prism of a US Third World Feminist consciousness has shifted as we turned our gaze *away* from a feminism prescribed by white women of privilege (even in opposition to them) and turned *toward* the process of discerning the multilayered and intersecting sites of identity and struggle—distinct and shared—among women of color across the globe. In recent years, even our understanding of how gender and "womanhood" are defined has been challenged by young trans women and men of color. They've required us to look more deeply into some of our fiercest feminist convictions about queer desire and female identity. Thirty-five years later, *Bridge* contributor Anita Valerio is now Max Wolf Valerio. His very presence in this collection attests to the human truth of our evolving lives and the "two spirits" of our consciousness.

Dated as it is, I am honored to re-introduce this collection of 1981 testimonies for the very reason that it is, in fact, *dated*; marked by the hour and place of these writers' and artists' births, our geographies of dislocation and homecoming, the ancestral memory that comes with us, and the politics of the period that shaped us.

El pueblo unido jamás será vencido. The people united will never be defeated.

I believed that once with a profound passion, remembering my youthful political optimism in the 1970s and into the eighties; the progressive political climate that gave birth to *Bridge*; that contagious solidarity among women and people of color movements in the United States and with our camaradas throughout Latin America and the rest of the Third World.[2] And then suddenly, and throughout the ensuing decades, we saw our dreams dashed over and over again:

- the United States' three-decade history of invasion— Grenada, Panama, Kuwait, Afghanistan and Iraq;
- the federal response to the AIDS pandemic and to the disproportionate loss of a whole generation of queer men of color, and of the women of color who died in the wake of that generation;
- the CIA's role in dismantling the Sandinista People's revolution in Nicaragua and the ouster of democratically elected Aristide in Haiti;
- NAFTA's binational betrayal of the Mexican worker and FEMA's betrayal of Katrina-devastated Africa America;
- the endemic alienation of middle-class youth erupting in the tragedies of the Columbine shooting, the Virginia Tech Massacre; and Sandy Hook Elementary;
- the brown children left behind through the Bush administration's "No Child Left Behind";
- the Supreme Court's removal of the ban on political spending by corporations in 2010;
- the gutting of the Voting Rights Act in 2013;
- the rise in anti-abortion violence and the constant erosion of women's right to choose;
- the Tea Party
- the USA Patriot Act;
- and the apartheid state of Arizona.

Assessing the conditions of our lives in the United States since the original publication of *This Bridge Called My Back*, it appears that today our identities are shaped less by an engaged democratic citizenship and more by our role as consumers. The two major crises that the United States experienced within its shores in the previous decade—9/11 and the economic depression—were generated by the same corporate greed that legislates an oil-ravenous and dangerous foreign policy in the Middle East.

And . . . We. Keep. "Buying" it.

Nationally, grassroots feminists continue to be undermined by single-issue liberals who believe that by breaking a class-entitled glass ceiling—"beating the boys at their own game"—there is some kind of "trickle down" effect on the actual lives of working-class and poor women and children. This is the same "trickle down" of our share of corporate profit, secured by tax benefits for the wealthy, that has yet to land on our kitchen tables, our paychecks, or our children's public school educations. Social change does not occur through tokenism or exceptions to the rule of discrimination, but through the systemic abolishment of the rule itself.

Is this the American Dream deferred?

What *does* happen to a "dream deferred"?

Does it explode, as Langston Hughes suggests?

Egypt exploded.

And, now what?

Entering the second decade of the 21ˢᵗ century, political currents begin to shift. We witness Twitter-instigated town square rebellions and WikiLeaks assumes the role of an international free press. Progressive movements—those "rolling rebellions" of the Middle East and North Africa—roll across the ocean to break onto US shores in a way that my 1981 twenty-something imagination could never have foreseen.[3]

In response to the federal government's "bailout" betrayal of its citizens, the Occupy movement and its slogan of "we are the 99%" spilled onto Wall Street and onto the Main Streets of this country, spreading the dirtiest five-letter word in "America": C-L-A-S-S. The Emperor's nakedness had been revealed: the United States is a class-based society, with an absolutely unconscionable unequal distribution of wealth and resources upheld by our government. For that revelation alone, in that it inspired a critical view of class inequity in this country, I am beholden to the Occupy movement, misnomered as it is.[4] Although women of color and working-class people were not represented there in large numbers, these activists, of some social privilege, publicly (and en masse) acknowledged that they were being bamboozled by their own government. *Just like us.* This is what the "Occupy" movement proffered, the possibility of a one-day aligned oppositional movement.

What would it mean for progressive struggles like Occupy to truly integrate a feminist of color politic in everything from climate change to the dissolution of the World Bank? It is not always a matter of the actual bodies in the room, but of a life dedicated to a growing awareness of who and what is *missing* in that room; and responding to that absence. *What ideas never surface because we imagine we already have all the answers?* Patriarchy and white privilege can so seamlessly disguise ignorances that later become the Achilles heel of many progressive organizations, leading to their demise.

Currently, at a grassroots level, the Climate Change movement is forced to take note, as Native women in Canada wage local and international protests against the tar sands industry. Truly radical environmentalists are beginning to recognize that—without the counsel and active engagement of people of color, whose homes "neighbor" the majority of dumping sites in the United States; without the leadership models of traditional and innovative Indigenous practices of sustainability; and, without the *organized* outcry of mothers, who personally suffer the illness of their children due to environmental contamination—no mass movement to literally "save our planet" can occur.[5]

I was twenty-seven years old when Gloria Anzaldúa and I entered upon the project of *This Bridge Called My Back*. I am now sixty-two. As I age, I watch the divide between generations widen with time and technology. I watch how desperately we need political memory, so that we are not always imagining ourselves the ever-inventors of our revolution; so that we are humbled by the valiant efforts of our foremothers; and so, with humility and a firm foothold in history, we can enter upon an informed and re-envisioned strategy for social/political change in decades ahead.

Bridge is an account of US women of color coming to late 20th century social consciousness through conflict—familial and institutional—and arriving at a politic, a "theory in the flesh" (19), that makes sense of the seeming paradoxes of our lives; that complex confluence of identities—race, class, gender, sexuality—systemic to women of color oppression *and* liberation. At home, amongst ourselves, women of color ask the political question: *what about us?* Which really means: *what about all of us?* Combahee River Collective writes: If Black [Indigenous][6] women were free . . . everyone else would have to be free since our freedom would necessitate the destruction of all the systems of oppression" (217).

We are "third world" consciousness within the first world. We are women under capitalist patriarchy. We can impact United States foreign and domestic policy as union members, as organized domestic and service workers, as community farmers, as sex worker advocates and Native water rights activists, as student protesters and street protesters, as mountain-top mining resisters, as migrant workers and migrant rights workers, as public health care providers, as single mothers *really* raising our kids, and as academics *really* decolonizing young minds. We do all this in concert with women across the globe pursuing the same goals: a shared and thriving existence in a world where our leaders have for the most part abandoned us and on a planet on the brink of utter abandonment.

Is not the United States' delayed and "party-politics" response to the Ebola virus plagued with "exceptionalism" and xenophobia? *Africa is not us*, America lies. But, as women of color, how are we to look away from the mirror of the Monrovian mother sitting stunned and broken by the small heap of crumbled cloth that is her now dead daughter?[7] It is not so far away.

Global warming. Campus rape. "Dead Man Walking while Black" on the Ferguson Streets of the USA. Somehow all these concerns reside within the politic of women of color feminism; for it is a political practice that is shaped first from the specific economic conditions and the cultural context of our own landbase—from the inner-city barrio to the reservation; from the middleamerica suburb to the Purépeha village transplanted to the state of Oregon; and, fundamentally, to a dangerously threatened Earth.

Daily, Indigenous relatives from the south are left splayed and bleeding across the barbed wire of a border, "defended" by United States amory, wielded by border patrol and drug cartels. Anti-immigrant racism fuels Congress's policies of violent discrimination against Raza, funding the "round-up" of undocumented immigrants and sequestering them into "family detention centers." Our own *Bridge* contributor, Mitsuye Yamada (now, 91), could attest to the terrible familiarity of the times, remembering how—nearly seventy-five years ago—she and her family were among the 120,000 Japanese *Americans* forcibly removed from their homes and sent to internment camps during World War II. "Invisibility *Is* an Unnatural Disaster" (30); and visibility, the most effective strategy to quell the rising tide of discrimination.

In 2010, Arizona's anti-immigrant legislation[8] sparked a swelling and ongoing resistance movement, distinguished by the visible participation and leadership of mujeres and undocumented queers. Gay and lesbian guatemaltecas, salvadoreños, mexicanas y más helped force the Immigrant Rights movement into the national public eye through courageous acts of civil disobedience, risking jail and deportation. And they also made publicly evident that "coming out of the closet"/"salir de las sombras" is not a single issue. The Undocuqueer movement reflects the "simultaneity of oppression,"[9] foundational to women of color feminism: that the queer daughters and sons of domestic workers, farmworkers, and day-laborers can fight for their familias' rights, without compromise to the *whole* of their own identities. The political is profoundly personal.

This Bridge Called My Back is less about each one of us and much more about the pending promise inscribed by all of us who believe that revolution—physical and metaphysical at once—is possible. Many women of my generation came to that belief based on the empowering historical conditions of our early years. The African Independence movements of the early 1960s, the Cuban Revolution, the Civil Rights movement, the American Indian, Black Power and Chicano movements, the anti- (Vietnam) war movement, Women's and Gay Liberation—all laid political ground and theoretical framework for a late 1970s feminism of color; as did so much of the concurrent radical literature of the period (*The Wretched of the Earth, Pedagogy of the Oppressed, The Open Veins of Latin America, The Red Stockings Manifesto, The Autobiography of Malcolm X, Bury My Heart at Wounded Knee, The Dialectic of Sex, El Plan Espiritual de Aztlán* . . .).

Ten years before the publication of *Bridge*, the Third World Women's Alliance had already begun publishing its *Triple Jeopardy* newspaper, linking "Racism, Imperialism and Sexism" to domestic worker and welfare rights, the political prisoner movement, the sterilization of Black and Puerto Rican women, reproductive rights, and the liberation of Palestine. In 1981, we were the inheritors of that vision. And it is my hope that the young readers of this fourth edition of *Bridge* will be the inheritors of ours, informed by a twenty-first-century perspective of mind *and* heart.

What brought me to feminism almost forty years ago was "heart." Feminism allowed "heart" to matter. It acknowledged that the oppression we experienced as human beings was not always materially manifested, and that we also suffered spiritually and sexually. Women of color have traditionally served as the gateways—the knowledge-holders—to those profoundly silent areas of expression and oppression: domestic abuse aggravated by poverty, patriarchal strictures that distort the "spirit" of religious practice; false familial hierarchies that deform our children's potential; erotic desire deadened by duty.

Such suffering is experienced by both males and females (not proportionately, but mutually). Women of color feminists see our movement as necessary for the liberation of men of color as well: liberation from war, from greed, from the theft of our neighborhoods, and from men's destructive alienation from women and nature. This is no "stand by your man" liberal feminism, but one that requires intra-cultural conversation and confrontation in order to build an unyielding platform of equity among us. Without the yoke of sexism and queer-phobias, we might finally be able to build a united front against the myriad forms of racism we experience.

In the twenty years that *Bridge* stayed in, and went out of, publication over 100,000 copies were sold. It has also been read by thousands more. Early edition copies, dog-eared and coffee-stained, have been passed from hand to hand, borrowed then borrowed again, and "liberated" from library shelves. Often referred to by its believers as the "bible" of women of color feminism, it has been pirated online for two hundred dollars a copy, reprinted in university course readers (with and without permission), PDF'd and copied, pressing its yellowing pages against the xerox machine glass to capture in print that Kate Rushin "Bridge" poem, that "essay about growing up on the rez" (Barbara Cameron), or "that Asian American woman's letter to her mom" (Merle Woo). So, in many ways, *Bridge* has already fulfilled its original mission: to find its way into "every major city and hole in the wall in this country."[10]

From a teaching perspective, *Bridge* documents the living experience of what academics now refer to as "intersectionality," where multiple identities converge at the crossroads of a woman of color life. The woman of color life *is* the crossroad, where no aspect of our identity is wholly dismissed from our consciousness, even as we navigate a daily shifting political landscape. In many ways *Bridge* catalyzed the reconstitution of Women & Gender and Ethnic Studies programs throughout the country. After *Bridge*, "the race of gender and the gender of race" could no longer be overlooked in any academic area or political organization that claimed to be about Women or Ethnicity. Still, the "holes in walls" of our thinking remain wide and many and there is an abundant amount of "bridging" left to be done.

As I write this, wars rage against women of color nationally and internationally: the epidemic of mass rapes of women in Congo; the brutal slaughter of thousands of women and girls (mostly unreported) in that transnational desert of despair, Juárez, Mexico; the abduction of hundreds of Nigerian school girls into a life of sexual enslavement, as ISIL barters

Yazidi females into forced marriages and religious conversions. Closer to home, the news of rising incidents of sexual assault on college campuses and inside the neocolony of United States reservation system begins to break through a wall of fierce censorship. Native women speak out. It is not always safe to do so.

Even among the community of *Bridge*, the premature (and in some cases, violent) deaths of so many of the book's contributors testify to the undisputable fact of the daily threat to women of color lives. It also speaks to the profound costs of just being us: visible women of color artists and activists suffering disabling illnesses; single mothers and grandmothers, queer women, raising our children's children, while relegated to the margins of our own communities. "Stress" is too benign a term.

With the publication of this fourth edition, we call out the names of the dead. Co-editor Gloria Anzaldúa (1942–2004) is the first to cross our lips, as it was she who held the first kernel of thought for this book in 1979. As the years pass, we will follow Gloria, as Rosario Morales (2011) followed her, and as Gloria followed Barbara Cameron (2002), Toni Cade Bambara (1995), Audre Lorde (1992), and Pat Parker (1989).

The artwork in this collection tells a parallel story. *Bridge*'s opening image "Omecihuatl," by Celia Herrera Rodríguez, depicts the goddess-virgin's face as that of Chicana union activist and lesbian Victoria Mercado, murdered in 1982 in a politically-motivated assault. *Bridge* concludes with a similar refrain in the 1974 image from "Body Tracks," by Cuban-born New York conceptual artist Ana Mendieta, who "fell" from a window to her death in 1985.[11]

In the face of world-wide misogynist atrocities and intimate violences, we cannot escape recurring self-doubts about the actual power of our acts of resistance against global patriarchy. I admit I have long days of doubt. Perhaps it's my age, the knowledge of the lengthening list of sisters/compañeras who've passed, and the sense of my own diminishing years. As so many others have said before me, *I don't imagine I will live to see the revolution.* I smile at the arrogance of this; that we imagine that our work begins and ends with us.

Still, here, in the underbelly of the "first" world, women of color writing is one liberation tool at our disposal. History is always in the making; while women of color and Indigenous peoples remain wordless in the official record. The very *act* of writing then, conjuring/coming to "see," what has yet to be recorded in history is to bring into consciousness what only the body knows to be true. The body—that site which houses the intuitive, the unspoken, the viscera of our being—this is the revolutionary promise of "theory in the flesh"; for it is both the *expression* of evolving political consciousness and the *creator* of consciousness, itself. Seldom recorded and hardly honored, our theory *incarnate* provides the most reliable roadmap to liberation.

So, let then this thirty-five-year-old document, *This Bridge Called My Back*, this living testimony of women of color epiphanies of political awakening, become part of the *un*official and truer record; an archive of accounts of those first ruptures of *consciencia* where we turned and looked at one another across culture, color and class difference to share an origin story of displacement in a nation never fully home to us.

Ultimately, as all people of progressive politic do, we wrote this book for you—the next generation, *and the next one*. Your lives are so vast before you—you whom the popular culture has impassively termed "Millennials." But I think the women of *Bridge* would've simply called you "familia"— our progeny, entrusting you with the legacy of our thoughts and activisms, in order to better grow them into a flourishing planet and a just world.

"Refugees of a world on Fire." This is how I understood US woman of color citizenship in the early 1980s. Perhaps the naming is now more apt than ever. Ours is a freedom movement that has yet to be fully realized, but it was promised among those women in the streets of an enflamed and now smoldering Cairo. It is also promised in the spirit of those young people who may first pick up this collection of poems, protests, and prayers and suddenly, without warning, feel their own consciousness catch fire.

In honor of the legacy of Mahsa Shekarloo.[12]

5 noviembre 2014

Notes

1. "MeXicana" is feminine here in honor of Dolores Huerta, cofounder of the United Farm Workers. She first coined the phrase "¡Sí! ¡Se puede!" ("Yes, we can!") as a call to activism during El Movimiento of the 1960s.

2. As women (people) of color in the United States, we also used "Third World" to align ourselves with countries bearing colonial histories and still suffering their effects, much of today's global south. We saw ourselves as "internally" colonized in the United States.

3. I also could not have imagined how the vision of those popular rebellions would become so sabotaged by the escalation of violent conflict now being visited upon the peoples of the region; the USA having had no small hand in its creation.

4. From a Third World perspective "occupy" is what the colonizer does; that is, he settles on land that does not belong to him. For that reason, we state that Xicanos and other Indigenous peoples live in "Occupied América" (Rodolfo Acuña).

5. The ongoing campaign led by the Mexican Mothers of Kettleman City against the toxic waste dump in their San Joaquin Valley town is a notable example. Also, for more information/reflection on Native-based environmental sustainability, see the writings of Winona LaDuke (Anishinaabekwe [Ojibwe]; visit: www.honorearth.org.

6. Black women are Indigenous women, once forcibly removed from their ancestral homeland. If not in the specifics, the major ideological tenets of the 1977 Combahee River Collective statement can serve today as a treatise for Indigenous women's rights movements globally.

7. Hawa Konneh was her name. The image appeared in *Time*, August 25, 1914.

8. S.B. 1070. One of the harshest and most extensive anti-immigrant bills in the recent history violated the constitutional and human rights of undocumented immigrants, while "racially profiling" anyone who looked like them.

9. Comhahee River Collective.

10. From the 1981 introduction to *Bridge*, reprinted in this volume.

11. There had been strong evidence in and out of court to convict Mendieta's husband, a world-renown artist, of her murder, but he was exonerated. Of Mendieta's "Body Tracks" Celia Herrera Rodríguez writes: "the bloodied hand and arm tracks descending to the ground [are] a reminder that this path is dangerous and many have fallen" (*Bridge*, 3rd edition, 281).

12. My beloved friend Mahsa Shekarloo was an Iranian-American transnational feminist and a Tehran-based activist for the rights of women and children. She was also an editor, and the founder of the online feminist journal *Bad Jens*. In fall 2012, upon the news of her cancer, Mahsa returned from Tehran to her family's home in Oakland. After a two-year struggle, she left this life on September 5, 2014. She was forty-four years old, and the mother of a six-year-old son. An emergent and eloquent writer, Mahsa, and what would have been her future works, will be deeply missed.

Foreword to the First Edition, 1981

Toni Cade Bambara

How I cherish this collection of cables, esoesses, conjurations and fusil missiles. Its motive force. Its gathering-us-in-ness. Its midwifery of mutually wise understandings. Its promise of autonomy and community. And its pledge of an abundant life for us all. On time. That is to say— overdue, given the times. ("Arrogance rising, moon in oppression, sun in destruction"—Cameron.)

Blackfoot amiga Nisei hermana Down Home Up Souf Sistuh sister El Barrio suburbia Korean The Bronx Lakota Menominee Cubana Chinese Puertoriqueña reservation Chicana campañera and letters testimonials poems interviews essays journal entries sharing Sisters of the yam Sisters of the rice Sisters of the corn Sisters of the plantain putting in telecalls to each other. And we're all on the line.

Now that we've begun to break the silence and begun to break through the diabolically erected barriers and can hear each other and see each other, we can sit down with trust and break bread together. Rise up and break our chains as well. For though the initial motive of several siter/riters here may have been to protest, complain or explain to white feminist would-be allies that there are other ties and visions that bind, prior allegiances and priorities that supercede their invitations to coalesce on their terms ("Assimilation within a solely western-european herstory is not acceptable"—Lorde), the process of examining that would-be alliance awakens us to new tasks ("We have a lot more to concentrate on beside the pathology of white wimmin"—davenport).

and a new connection:	US
a new set of recognitions:	US
a new site of accountability:	US
a new source of power:	US

And the possibilities intuited here or alluded to there or called forth in various pieces in flat out talking in tongues—the possibility of several million women refuting the numbers game inherent in "minority," the possibility of denouncing the insulated/orchestrated conflict game of divide and conquer—through the fashioning of potent networks of all the daughters of the ancient mother cultures is awesome, mighty, a glorious life work. *This Bridge* lays down the planks to cross over onto a new place where stooped labor cramped quartered down pressed and caged up combatants can straighten the spine and expand the lungs and make the vision manifest ("The dream is real, my friends. The failure to realize it is the only unreality."—Street Preacher in *The Salt Eaters*).

This Bridge documents particular rites of passage. Coming of age and coming to terms with community—race, group, class, gender, self perversions—racism, prejudice, elitism, misogyny, homophobia, and murder. And coming to terms with the incorporation of disease, struggling to overthrow the internal colonial/pro-racist loyalties—color/hue/hair caste within the household, power perversities engaged in under the guise of "personal relationships," accommodation to and collaboration with self-ambush and amnesia and murder. And coming to grips with those false awakenings too that give us ease as we substitute a militant mouth for a radical politic, delaying our true coming of age as committed, competent, principled combatants.

There is more than a hint in these pages that too many of us still equate tone with substance, a hot eye with clear vision, and congratulate ourselves for our political maturity. For, of course, it takes more than pique to unite our wrath ("the capacity of heat to change the shape of things"—Moraga) and to wrest power from those who have it and abuse it, to reclaim our ancient powers lying dormant with neglect ("i wanna ask billie to teach us how to use our voices like she used hers on that old 78 record"—gossett), and create new powers in arenas where they never before existed. And of course it takes more than the self-disclosure and the bold glimpse of each others' life documents to make the grand resolve to fearlessly work toward potent meshings. Takes more than a rinsed lens to face unblinkingly the particular twists of the divide and conquer tactics of this moment: the practice of withdrawing small business loans from the Puerto Rican grocer in favor of the South Korean wig shop, of stripping from Black students the Martin Luther King scholarship fund fought for and delivering those funds up to South Vietnamese or white

Cubans or any other group the government has made a commitment to in its greedy grab for empire. We have got to know each other better and teach each other our ways, our views, if we're to remove the scales ("seeing radical differences where they don't exist and not seeing them when they are critical"—Quintanales) and get the work done.

This Bridge can get us there. Can coax us into the habit of listening to each other and learning each other's ways of seeing and being. Of hearing each other as we heard each other in Pat Lee's *Freshtones*, as we heard each other in Pat Jones and Faye Chiang, et al.'s *Ordinary Women*, as we heard each other in Fran Beale's *Third World Women's Alliance* newspaper. As we heard each other over the years in snatched time moments in hallways and conference corridors, caucusing between sets. As we heard each other in those split second interfacings of yours and mine and hers student union meetings. As we heard each other in that rainbow attempt under the auspices of IFCO years ago. And way before that when Chinese, Mexican, and African women in this country saluted each other's attempts to form protective leagues. And before that when New Orleans African women and Yamassee and Yamacrow women went into the swamps to meet with Filipino wives of "draftees" and "defectors" during the so-called French and Indian War. And when members of the maroon communities and women of the long lodge held council together while the Seminole Wars raged. And way way before that, before the breaking of the land mass when we mothers of the yam, of the rice, of the maize, of the plantain sat together in a circle, staring into the campfire, the answers in our laps, knowing how to focus . . .

Quite frankly, *This Bridge* needs no Foreword. It is the Afterward that'll count. The coalitions of women determined to be a danger to our enemies, as June Jordan would put it. The will to be dangerous ("ask billie so we can learn how to have those bigtime bigdaddies jumping outta windows and otherwise offing theyselves in droves"—gossett). And the contracts we creative combatants will make to mutually care and cure each other into wholesomeness. And blue-prints we will draw up of the new order we will make manifest. And the personal unction we will discover in the mirror, in the dreams, or on the path across *This Bridge*. The work: To make revolution irresistible.

Blessings,
Toni Cade Bambara

Novelist Bambara and interviewer Kalamu Ya Salaam were discussing a call she made in *The Salt Eaters* through *The Seven Sisters*, a multicultural, multimedia arts troupe, a call to unite our wrath, our vision, our powers.

Kalamu: Do you think that fiction is the most effective way to do this?
Toni: No. The most effective way to do it, is to do it![1]

Note

1. "In Search of the Mother Tongue: An Interview with Toni Cade Bambara,"
   First World Journal (Fall 1980).

The Bridge Poem

Kate Rushin

I've had enough
I'm sick of seeing and touching
Both sides of things
Sick of being the damn bridge for everybody

Nobody
Can talk to anybody
Without me
Right?

I explain my mother to my father my father to my little sister
My little sister to my brother to the white feminists
The white feminists to the Black church folks the Black church folks
To the ex-hippies the ex-hippies to the Black separatists the
Black separatists to the artists the artists to my friends' parents . . .

Then
I've got to explain myself
To everybody

I do more translating
Than the Gawdamn UN

Forget it
I'm sick of it

I'm sick of filling in your gaps

Sick of being your insurance against
The isolation of your self-imposed limitations
Sick of being the crazy at your holiday dinners
Sick of being the odd one at your Sunday Brunches
Sick of being the sole Black friend to 34 individual white people

Find another connection to the rest of the world
Find something else to make you legitimate
Find some other way to be political and hip

I will not be the bridge to your womanhood
Your manhood
Your human-ness

I'm sick of reminding you not to
Close off too tight for too long

I'm sick of mediating with your worst self
Oh behalf of your better selves

I am sick
Of having to remind you
To breathe
Before you suffocate
Your own fool self

Forget it
Stretch or drown
Evolve or die

The bridge I must be
Is the bridge to my own power
I must translate
My own fears
Mediate
My own weaknesses

I must be the bridge to nowhere
But my true self
And then
I will be useful

La Jornada

Preface, 1981

Cherríe Moraga

Change does not occur in a vacuum. In this preface I have tried to recreate for you my own journey of struggle, growing consciousness, and subsequent politicization and vision as a woman of color. I want to reflect in actual terms how this anthology and the women in it and around it have personally transformed my life, sometimes rather painfully but always with richness and meaning.

I Transfer and Go Underground
(Boston, Massachusetts—July 20, 1980)

It is probably crucial to describe here the way this book is coming together, the journey it is taking me on. The book is still not completed, and I have traveled East to find it a publisher. Such an anthology is in high demand these days. A book by radical women of color. The Left needs it, with its shaky and shabby record of commitment to women, period. Oh, yes, it can claim its attention to "color" issues, embodied in the male. Sexism is acceptable to the white Left publishing house, particularly if spouted through the mouth of a Black man.

The feminist movement needs the book, too. But for different reasons. Do I dare speak of the boredom setting in among the white sector of the feminist movement? What was once a cutting edge, growing dull in the too easy solution to our problems of hunger of soul and stomach. The lesbian separatist utopia? No thank you, sisters. I can't prepare myself a revolutionary packet that makes no sense when I leave the white suburbs of Watertown, Massachusetts, and take the T-line to Black Roxbury.

Take Boston alone, I think to myself and the feminism my so-called sisters have constructed does nothing to help me make the trip from one end of town to another. Leaving Watertown, I board a bus and ride it quietly in my light flesh to Harvard Square, protected by the gold highlights my hair dares to take on, like an insult, in this miserable heat.

I transfer and go underground.

Julie told me the other day how they stopped her for walking through the suburbs. Can't tell if she's a man or a woman, only know that it's Black moving through that part of town. They wouldn't spot her here, moving underground.

The train is abruptly stopped. A white man in jeans and tee shirt breaks into the car I'm in, throws a Black kid up against the door, handcuffs him and carries him away. The train moves on. The day before, a 14-year-old Black boy was shot in the head by a white cop. And, the summer is getting hotter.

I hear there are some women in this town plotting a *lesbian* revolution. What does this mean about the boy shot in the head is what I want to know. I am a lesbian. I want a movement that helps me make some sense of the trip from Watertown to Roxbury, from white to Black. I love women the entire way, beyond a doubt.

Arriving in Roxbury, arriving at Barbara's[1]. . . . By the end of the evening of our first visit together, Barbara comes into the front room where she has made a bed for me. She kisses me. Then grabbing my shoulders she says, very solid-like, "We're sisters." I nod, put myself into bed, and roll around with this word—"sisters"—for two hours before sleep takes on. I earned this with Barbara. It is not a given between us—Chicana and Black—to come to see each other as sisters. I keep wanting to repeat over and over and over again, the pain and shock of difference, the joy of commonness, the exhilaration of meeting through incredible odds against it.

And the passage is *through*, not over, not by, not around, but through. This book, as long as I see it for myself as a passage through, I hope will function for others, colored[2] or white, in the same way. How do we develop a movement that can live with the fact of the loves and lives of these women in this book?

I would grow despairing if I believed, as Rosario Morales refutes, we were unilaterally defined by color and class. Lesbianism is then a hoax, a fraud. I have no business with it. Lesbianism is supposed to be about connection.

What drew me to politics was my love of women, the agony I felt in observing the straightjackets of poverty and repression I saw in my own family. But the deepest political tragedy I have experienced is how with such grace, such blind faith, this commitment to women in the feminist movement grew to be exclusive and reactionary. *I call my white sisters on this.*

I have had enough of this. And I am involved in this book because more than anything else I need to feel enlivened again in a movement that can finally, as my friend Amber Hollibaugh states, "ask the right questions and admit to not having all the answers."

A Bridge Gets Walked Over
(Boston, Massachusetts—July 25, 1980)

I am ready to go home now. I am ready. Very tired. Couldn't sleep all night. Missing home. There is a deep fatigue in my body this morning. I feel used up. Adrienne asks me if I can write of what has happened with me while here in Boston. She asks me if I can, not would. I say, yes, I think so. And now I doubt it. The pain of racism, classism. Such overused and trivialized words. The pain of it all. I do not feel people of color are the only ones hurt by racism.

Another meeting. Again walking into a room filled with white women, a splattering of women of color around the room. The issue on the table, Racism. The dread and terror in the room lay like a thick immovable paste above all our shoulders, white, and colored, alike. We, Third World women in the room, thinking—*back to square one again.*

How can we—this time—not use our bodies to be thrown over a river of tormented history to bridge the gap? Barbara says last night: "A bridge gets walked over." Yes, over and over and over again.

I watch the white women shrink before my eyes, losing their fluidity of argument, of confidence. They pause awkwardly at the word "race," the word "color." The pauses keeping the voices breathless, the bodies taut, erect—unable to breathe deeply, to laugh, to moan in despair, to cry in regret. I cannot continue to use my body to be walked over to make a connection. Feeling every joint in my body tense this morning, used.

What the hell am I getting myself into? Gloria's voice has recurred to me throughout this trip. A year and a half ago, she warned and encouraged: "This book will change your life, Cherríe. It will change both our lives." And it has. *Gloria, I wish you were here.*

A few days ago, an old friend said to me how when she first met me, I seemed so white to her. I said in honesty, I used to feel more white. You know, I really did. But at the meeting last night, dealing with white women here on this trip, I have felt so very dark: dark with anger, with silence, with the feeling of being walked over.

I wrote in my journal: "My growing consciousness as a woman of color is surely seeming to transform my experience. How could it be that the more I feel with other women of color, the more I feel myself Chicana, the more susceptible I am to racist attack!"

A Place of Breakthrough: Coming Home
(San Francisco, California—September 20, 1980)

When Audre Lorde, speaking of racism, states: "I urge each one of us here to reach down into that deep place of knowledge inside herself and touch that terror and loathing of any difference that lives there."[3] I am driven to do so because of the passion for women that lives in my body. I know now that the major obstacle for me, personally, in completing this book has occurred when I stopped writing it for myself, when I looked away from my own source of knowledge.

Audre is right. It is also the source of terror—how deeply separation between women hurts me. How discovering difference, profound differences between myself and women I love has sometimes rendered me helpless and immobilized.

I think of my sister here. How I still haven't gotten over the shock that she would marry a white man, rather than enter onto the journey I knew I was taking. (This is the model we have from my mother, nurturing/waiting on my father and brother all the days of her life. Always how if a man walked into the room, he was paid attention to [indulged] in a particular Latin-woman-to-man way). For years, and to this day, I am still recovering from the disappointment that this girl/ this sister who had been with me every day of my life growing up—who slept, ate, talked, cried, worked, fought with me—was suddenly lost to me through this man and marriage. I still struggle with believing I have a right to my feelings, that it is not "immature" or "queer" to refuse such separations, to still mourn over this early abandonment, "this homesickness for a woman."[4] So few people really understand how deep the bond between sisters can run. I was raised to rely on my sister, to believe sisters could be counted on "to go the long hard way with you."

Sometimes for me "that deep place of knowledge" Audre refers to seems like an endless reservoir of pain, where I must continually unravel the damage done to me. It is a calculated system of damage, intended to ensure our separation from other women, but particularly those we learned to see as most different from ourselves and therefore, most fearful. The women whose pain we do not want to see as our own. Call it racism, class oppression, men, or dyke-baiting, the system thrives.

I mourn the friends and lovers I have lost to this damage. I mourn the women whom I have betrayed with my own ignorance, my own fear.

The year has been one of such deep damage. I have felt between my hands the failure to bring a love I believed in back to life. Yes, the failure between lovers, sisters, mother and daughter—the betrayal. How have we turned our backs on each other—the bridge collapsing—whether it be for public power, personal gain, private validation, or more closely, to save face, to save our children, to save our skins.

"See whose face it wears,"[5] Audre says. And I know I must open my eyes and mouth and hands to name the color and texture of my fear.

I had nearly forgotten why I was so driven to work on this anthology. I had nearly forgotten that I wanted/needed to deal with racism because I couldn't stand being separated from other women. Because I took my lesbianism that seriously. I first felt this the most acutely with Black women—Black dykes—who I felt ignored me, wrote me off because I looked white. And yet, the truth was that I didn't know Black women intimately (Barbara says "it's about who you can sit down to a meal with, who you can cry with, whose face you can touch"). I had such strong "colored hunches" about our potential connection, but was basically removed from the lives of most Black women. The ignorance. The painful, painful ignorance.

I had even ignored my own bloodline connection with Chicanas and other Latinas. Maybe it was too close to look at, too close to home. Months ago in a journal entry I wrote: "I am afraid to get near to how deeply I want the love of other Latin women in my life." In a real visceral way I hadn't felt the absence (only assumed the fibers of alienation I so often felt with anglo women as normative). Then for the first time, speaking on a panel about racism here in San Francisco, I could physically touch what I had been missing. There in the front row, nodding encouragement and identification, sat five Latina sisters. Count them! Five avowed Latina Feminists: Gloria, Jo, Aurora, Chabela y Mirtha. For once in my life every part of me was allowed to be visible and spoken for in one room at one time.

After the forum, the six of us walk down Valencia Street singing songs in Spanish. We buy burritos y cerveza from "La Cumbre" and talk our heads off into the night, crying from the impact of such a reunion.

Sí, son mis comadres. Something my mother had with her women friends and sisters. Coming home. For once, I didn't have to choose between being a lesbian and being Chicana; between being a feminist and having family.

I Have Dreamed of a Bridge
San Francisco, California—September 25, 1980

Literally, for two years now, I have dreamed of a bridge. In writing this conclusion, I fight the myriad voices that live inside me. The voices that stop my pen at every turn of the page. They are the voices that tell me here I should be talking more "materialistically" about the oppression of women of color, that I should be plotting out a "strategy" for Third World Revolution. But what I really want to write about is faith. That without faith, I'd dare not expose myself to the potential betrayal, rejection, and failure that lives throughout the first and last gesture of connection.

And yet, so often I have lost touch with the simple faith I know in my blood. My mother. On some very basic level, the woman cannot be shaken from the ground on which she walks. Once at a very critical point in my work on this book, where everything I loved—the people, the writing, the city—all began to cave in on me, feeling such utter despair and self-doubt, I received in the mail a card from my mother. A holy card of St. Anthony de Padua, her patron saint, her "special" saint, wrapped in a plastic cover. She wrote in it: "Dear Cherríe, I am sending you this prayer of St. Anthony. Pray to God to help you with this book." And a cry came up from inside me that I had been sitting on for months, cleaning me out—a faith healer. Her faith in this saint did actually once save her life. That day, it helped me continue the labor of this book.

I am not talking here about some lazy faith, where we resign ourselves to the tragic splittings in our lives with an upward turn of the hands or a vicious beating of our breasts. I am talking about believing that we have the power to actually transform our experience, change our lives, save our lives. Otherwise, why this book? It is the faith of activists I am talking about.

The materialism in this book lives in the flesh of these women's lives: the exhaustion we feel in our bones at the end of the day, the fire we feel in our hearts when we are insulted, the knife we feel in our backs when we are betrayed, the nausea we feel in our bellies when we are afraid, even the hunger we feel between our hips when we long to be touched.

Our strategy is how we cope—how we measure and weigh what is to be said and when, what is to be done and how, and to whom and to whom and to whom, daily deciding/risking who it is we can call an ally, call a friend (whatever that person's skin, sex, or sexuality). We are women without a line. We are women who contradict each other.

This book is written for all the women in it and all whose lives our lives will touch. We are a family who first only knew each other in our dreams, who have come together on these pages to make faith a reality and to bring all of our selves to bear down hard on that reality.

It is about physical and psychic struggle. It is about intimacy, a desire for life between all of us, not settling for less than freedom even in the most private aspects of our lives. A total vision.

For the women in this book, I will lay my body down for that vision. *This Bridge Called My Back.*

In the dream, I am always met at the river.

Notes

1. I want to acknowledge and thank Barbara Smith for her support as a sister, her insights as a political activist and visionary, and especially for her way with words in helping me pull this together.
2. Throughout the text, the word "colored" will be used by the editors as a way of talking amongst ourselves ("entrenos"), in referring to all Third World people of color unless otherwise specified.
3. From "The Master's Tools Will Never Dismantle the Master's House" (see her essay in this volume).
4. Adrienne Rich, "Trancendental Etude," *The Dream of a Common Language* (New York: Norton, 1978), 75.
5. From "The Master's Tools Will Never Dismantle the Master's House" (see her essay in this volume).

Introduction, 1981

Cherríe Moraga and Gloria Anzaldúa

How It All Began

In February of 1979, Gloria attended a women's retreat in the country just north of San Francisco. At Merlin Stone's insistence, three Third World women were to receive scholarships to her workshop on goddesses and heroines taking place during the retreat. Only one made it—Gloria. The management and some of the staff made her feel an outsider, the poor relative, the token woman of color. And all because she was not white nor had she paid the $150 fee the retreat organizers had set for the workshop. The seed that germinated into this anthology began there in Gloria's talks with Merlin.

What had happened at the women's retreat was not new to our experience. Both of us had first met each other working as the only two Chicanas in a national feminist writers organization. After two years of involvement with the group which repeatedly refused to address itself to its elitist and racist practices, we left the organization and began work on this book.

In April, 1979, we wrote:

> We want to express to all women—especially to white middle-class women—the experiences which divide us as feminists; we want to examine incidents of intolerance, prejudice and denial of differences within the feminist movement. We intend to explore the causes and sources of, and solutions to, these divisions. We want to create a definition that expands what "feminist" means to us.
>
> (From the original soliciting letter)

The Living Entity

What began as a reaction to the racism of white feminists soon became a positive affirmation of the commitment of women of color to our own feminism. Mere words on a page began to transform themselves into a living entity in our guts. Now, over a year later, feeling greater solidarity with other feminists of color across the country through the making of this book, we assert:

This Bridge Called My Back intends to reflect an uncompromised definition of feminism by women of color in the US.

We named this anthology "radical" for we were interested in the writings of women of color who want nothing short of a revolution in the hands of women—who agree that that is the goal, no matter how we might disagree about the getting there or the possibility of seeing it in our own lifetimes. We use the term in its original form—stemming from the word "root"—for our feminist politic emerges from the roots of both of our cultural oppression and heritage.

The Parts of the Whole

The six sections of *This Bridge Called My Back* intend to reflect what we feel to be the major areas of concern for Third World women in the US in forming a broad-based political movement: 1) how visibility/invisibility as women of color forms our radicalism; 2) the ways in which Third World women derive a feminist political theory specifically from our racial/cultural background and experience; 3) the destructive and demoralizing effects of racism in the women's movement; 4) the cultural, class, and sexuality differences that divide women of color; 5) Third World women's writing as a tool for self-preservation and revolution; and 6) the ways and means of a Third World feminist future.

The Writers and Their Work

The women in whose hands *This Bridge Called My Back* was wrought identify as Third World women and/or women of color. Each woman considers herself a feminist, but draws her feminism from the culture in which she grew. Most of the women appearing in this book are first-generation writers. Some of us do not see ourselves as writers, but pull the pen across the page anyway or speak with the power of poets.

The selections in this anthology range from extemporaneous stream of consciousness journal entries to well-thought-out theoretical statements; from intimate letters to friends to full-scale public addresses. In addition, the book includes poems and transcripts, personal conversations and interviews. The works combined reflect a diversity of perspectives, linguistic styles, and cultural tongues.

In editing the anthology, our primary commitment was to retaining this diversity, as well as each writer's especial voice and style. The book is intended to reflect our color loud and clear, not tone it down. As editors we sought out, and believe we found, non-rhetorical, highly personal chronicles that present a political analysis in everyday terms.

In compiling the anthology, Cherríe was primarily responsible for the thematic structure and organization of the book as a whole. She also wrote the introductions to the first four sections of the book which cover 1) The Roots of Our Radicalism; 2) Theory in the Flesh; 3) Racism in the Women's Movement; and 4) On Culture, Class, and Homophobia. Gloria wrote the introductions to the final two sections of the book which explore The Third World Woman Writer and The Vision of the Third World feminist. Together as editors, we both bore the burden of the book (even more than we had anticipated—this being our first attempt at such a project), not only doing the proofreading and making editorial decisions, but also acting as a telephone answering and courier service, PR persons and advertisers, interviewers and transcribers, and even occasionally, muses for some of the contributors during their sometimes rather painful "writing blocks." Most important, we saw our major role as editors being to encourage writers to delve even more deeply into their lives, to make some meaning out of it for themselves and their readers.

Time and Money

Many people have commented on the relative speed in which this book was produced. In barely two years, the anthology grew from a seed of an idea to a published work. True, everyone has worked fast, including the publishers. The anthology was created with a sense of urgency. From the moment of its conception, it was already long overdue. Two years ago when we started, we knew it was a book that should already have been in our hands.

How do you concentrate on a project when you're worried about paying the rent? We have sorely learned why so few women of color attempt this kind of project: no money to fall back on. In compiling this book we both maintained two or more jobs just to keep the book and ourselves alive. No time to write while waiting tables. No time for class preparation, to read students' papers, argue with your boss, have a love life or eat a decent meal when the deadline must be met. No money to buy stamps, to hire a lawyer "to go over the contract," to engage an agent. Both of us became expert jugglers of our energy and the few pennies in our piggybanks: Gloria's "little chicken" and Cherríe's "tecate bucket."

Agradecimientos

But oh there were the people who helped: Leslie, Abigail, Leigh and her IBM selectric, Randy, David, Mirtha's arroz con picadillo and loving encouragement, Merlin and Adrienne's faith in the book, Jane and Sally's letting Cherríe change her mind, our women's studies students at San Francisco State University who put up with their two over-tired grumpy teachers, Debbie's backrubs, Jo who typed the whole damn manuscript, Barbara C. and her camera and crew, Barbara S.'s work in spreading the word in Boston, the friends who lent us money, and all the other folks who supported our readings, our benefit parties, our efforts to get this book to press.

Most especially, of course, we wish to thank all the contributors whose commitment and insight made the nightly marathons we spent pulling out our hair worth it. They inspired the labor.

Putting Our Words into Practice

With the completion of this anthology, a hundred other books and projects are waiting to be developed. Already, we hear tell in the wind from other contributors the possibility of a film about Third World Feminists, an anthology by Latina lesbians, a Third World feminist publishing house. We, women of color, are not without plans. This is exactly the kind of service we wish for the anthology to provide. It is a catalyst, not a definitive statement on "Third World Feminism in the US."

We see the book as a revolutionary tool falling into the hands of people of all colors. Just as we have been radicalized in the process of compiling this book, we hope it will radicalize others into action. We envision the book being used as a *required* text in most women's studies courses. And we don't mean just "special" courses on Third World Women or Racism, but also courses dealing with sexual politics, feminist thought, women's spirituality, etc. Similarly, we want to see this book on the shelf of, and used in the classroom by, every ethnic studies teacher in this country, male and female alike. Off campus, we expect the book to function as a consciousness-raiser for white women meeting together or working alone on the issues of racism. And, we want to see our colored sisters using this book as an educator and agitator around issues specific to our oppression as women.

We want the book in libraries, bookstores, at conferences, and union meetings in every major city and hole-in-the-wall in this country. And, of course, we hope to eventually see this book translated and leave this country, making tangible the link between Third World women in the US and throughout the world.

Finally tenemos la esperanza que *This Bridge Called My Back* will find its way back into our families' lives.

The revolution begins at home.

I

Children Passing in the Streets

The Roots of Our Radicalism

Hulleah Tsinhnahjinnie, *Mattie Looks for Steven Biko*, 1985
Photocollage, 22" × 24"
Collection of the Artist

Children Passing in the Streets

The Roots of Our Radicalism

> *I learned to make my mind large, as the universe is large, so that there is room for paradoxes.*
>
> —Maxine Hong Kingston[1]

We are women from all kinds of childhood streets: the farms of Puerto Rico, the downtown streets of Chinatown, the barrio, city-Bronx streets, quiet suburban sidewalks, the plains, and the reservation.

In this first section, you will find voices from childhoods, our youth. What we learned about survival—trying-to-pass-for-white, easy-to-pass-for-white, "she couldn't pass in a million years." Here, we introduce to you the "color problem" as it was first introduced to us: "not white enuf, not dark enuf," always up against a color chart that first got erected far outside our families and our neighborhoods, but which invaded them both with systematic determination.

In speaking of color and class, Tillie Olsen once said: "There's no such thing as passing."[2] Here are women of every shade of color and grade of class to prove that point. For although some of us traveled more easily from street corner to corner than the sister whose color or poverty made her an especially visible target to the violence on the street, *all* of us have been victims of the invisible violation which happens indoors and inside ourselves: the self-abnegation, the silence, the constant threat of cultural obliteration.

We were born into colored homes. We grew up with the inherent contradictions in the color spectrum right inside those homes: the lighter sister, the mixed-blood cousin, being the darkest one in the family. It doesn't take many years to realize the privileges, or lack thereof, attached to a particular shade of skin or texture of hair. It is this experience that moves light-skinned or "passable" Third World women to put themselves on the line for their darker sisters. We are all family. From those families we were on the one hand encouraged to leave, to climb up white. And with the other hand, the reins were held tight on us, our parents understanding the danger that bordered our homes.

We learned to live with these contradictions. This is the root of our radicalism.

Notes

1. Maxine Hong Kingston, *The Woman Warrior* (New York: Vintage, 1977), 35.
2. From a talk given at The Women's Building sponsored by The Feminist Writers' Guild, San Francisco, November 1979.

When I Was Growing Up

Nellie Wong

I know now that once I longed to be white.
How? you ask.
Let me tell you the ways.

  when I was growing up, people told me
  I was dark and I believed my own darkness
  in the mirror, in my soul, my own narrow vision

      when I was growing up, my sisters
      with fair skin got praised
      for their beauty, and in the dark
      I fell further, crushed between high walls

  when I was growing up, I read magazines
  and saw movies, blonde movie stars, white skin,
  sensuous lips and to be elevated, to become
  a woman, a desirable woman, I began to wear
  imaginary pale skin

      when I was growing up, I was proud
      of my English, my grammar, my spelling
      fitting into the group of smart children
      smart Chinese children, fitting in,
      belonging, getting in line

  when I was growing up and went to high school,
  I discovered the rich white girls, a few yellow girls,
  their imported cotton dresses, their cashmere
  sweaters,
  their curly hair and I thought that I too should have
  what these lucky girls had

      when I was growing up, I hungered
      for American food, American styles,
      coded: white and even to me, a child
      born of Chinese parents, being Chinese

[handwritten annotation: separate things]

5

was feeling foreign, was limiting,
was unAmerican.

when I was growing up and a white man wanted
to take me out, I thought I was special,
an exotic gardenia, anxious to fit
the stereotype of an oriental chick

[handwritten margin note: not wanting to fit to the stereotype]

when I was growing up, I felt ashamed
of some yellow men, their small bones,
their frail bodies, their spitting
on the streets, their coughing,
their lying in sunless rooms,
shooting themselves in the arms

when I was growing up, people would ask
if I were Filipino, Polynesian, Portuguese.
They named all colors except white, the shell
of my soul, but not my dark, rough skin

when I was growing up, I felt
dirty. I thought that god
made white people clean
and no matter how much I bathed,
I could not change, I could not shed
my skin in the gray water

[handwritten margin note: white = good, dark = bad]

when I was growing up, I swore
I would run away to purple mountains,
houses by the sea with nothing over
my head, with space to breathe,
uncongested with yellow people in an area
called Chinatown, in an area I later learned
was a ghetto, one of many hearts
of Asian America

I know now that once I longed to be white.
How many more ways? you ask.
Haven't I told you enough?

on not bein

mary hope whitehead lee

be a smart child trying to be dumb . . .
not blk enuf to lovinly ignore . . .
not bitter enuf to die at a early age . . .

—ntozake shange[1]

she never wanted
no never once
did she wanna
be white/to pass
dreamed only of bein darker
she wanted to be darker
not yellow/not no high brown neither
but brown/warm brown
she dreamed/her body
moist earth brown
she prayed/for chocolate
semi/sweet/bitter/sweet
dark chocolate nipples crownin
her small chested tits
2 hersheys kisses
sittin sweet like top of
2 round scoops of smooth
milk chocolate ice cream

momma took her outta
almost all black lincoln high
cuz she useta catch hell
every day in gym class
the other girls reactin to her like
she was the cause of some
kinda gawdawful allergy they all had
contact could be fatal
survivors would be scarred
   with kindness

cuz she wasn dark enuf
   was smart enuf
   wasn rowdy enuf
   had a white girl friend
cuz none of them would be

beige or buff/ecru or chamois
jus wasn color/ed enuf
to get picked for the softball team
wasn sufficient protection
'gainst gettin' tripped in the shower

she wondered/
would they have treated florence ballard
  so shabbily

❖

but she envied them all
felt every once now and then
they just mighta been
righteously justified
since/after all
they was brown like
the sun loved they skin special
cuz it warmed 'em

      chestnut
      bronze
      copper
      sepia
      cinnamon
      cocoa
      mahogany

her/she was drab faded out
yellow like a scorched july sky
just fore it rains & rinses
away the hint of brown from the smog

she wasn/
no maureen peal
no 'high yellow dream child'
not/dichty
    a hex muttered
not/hinkty
    a curse let fly
not/saditty
like girls was spozed to be
did they went to catholic school or
was they from germantown or
baldwin hills or
valencia park

(the man she married/cuz he was the first one to ask/her bein afraid no body else would/said he thought he was gonna hafta marry hisself white cuz/he couldn find him no colored girl was/in-tel-li-gent e-nuf/but with her bein the next best thing to white . . .

Note

1. *Nappy Edges* (New York: St. Martin's Press, 1978).

For the Color of My Mother

Cherríe Moraga

I am a white girl gone brown to the blood color of my mother
speaking for her through the unnamed part of the mouth
the wide-arched muzzle of brown women

at two
my upper lip split open
clear to the tip of my nose
it spilled forth a cry that would not yield
that traveled down six floors of hospital
where doctors wound me into white bandages
only the screaming mouth exposed

the gash sewn back into a snarl
would last for years

I am a white girl gone brown to the blood color of my mother
speaking for her

at five, her mouth
pressed into a seam
a fine blue child's line drawn across her face
her mouth, pressed into mouthing english
mouthing yes yes yes
mouthing stoop lift carry
(sweating wet sighs into the field
her red bandana comes loose from under the huge brimmed
hat moving across her upper lip)

at fourteen, her mouth
painted, the ends drawn up
the mole in the corner colored in darker larger mouthing yes
she praying no no no
lips pursed and moving

at forty-five, her mouth
bleeding into her stomach
the hole gaping growing redder

deepening with my father's pallor
finally stitched shut from hip to breastbone
    an inverted V
    Vera
    Elvira

I am a white girl gone brown to the blood color of my mother
speaking for her

as it should be
dark women come to me
            sitting in circles
I pass through their hands
the head of my mother
painted in clay colors

touching each carved feature
                swollen eyes and mouth
they understand the explosion the splitting
open   contained within the fixed expression

they cradle her silence
          nodding to me

I Am What I Am

Rosario Morales

I am what I am and I am US American   I haven't wanted to say
it because if I did you'd take away the Puerto Rican but now I say
go to hell   I am what I am and you can't take it away with all the
words and sneers at your command   I am what I am   I am Puerto
Rican   I am US American   I am New York Manhattan and the
Bronx   I am what I am I'm not hiding under no stoop   behind
no curtain   I am what I am   I am Boricua as boricuas come from
the isle of Manhattan and I croon Carlos Gardel tangos in my sleep and
Afro-Cuban beats in my blood and Xavier Cugat's lukewarm latin is so
familiar and dear   sneer dear but he's familiar and dear   but not
Carmen Miranda   who's a joke because I never was a joke   I was
a bit of a sensation   See! here's a true honest-to-god Puerto Rican
girl and she's in college   Hey! Mary   come here and look she's
from right here   a South Bronx girl and she's honest-to-god in college
now   Ain't that something   who would believed it Ain't science
wonderful or some such thing a wonder a wonder
       And someone who did languages for a living stopped me in the
subway because how I spoke was a linguist's treat   I mean there it
was yiddish and Spanish and fine refined college educated english and
irish which I mainly keep in my prayers   It's dusty now   I haven't
said my prayers in decades but try my Hail Marrrry full of grrrace
with the nun's burr with the nun's disdain   it's all true and it's all
me   do you know how I got an English accent from the BBC I
always say   For years in the mountains of Puerto Rico when I was
22 and 24 and 26   all those young years   I listened to the BBC
and Radio Moscow's English   english announcers announce and
denounce and then I read Dickens all the way thru three or four times
at least and then later I read Dickens aloud in voices and when I came
back to the US I spoke mockdickens and mockBritish especially when I
want to be crisp efficient I know what I am doing and you can't scare
me   tough   that's why I am what I am and I'm a bit of a snob
too   Shit! why am I calling myself names   I really really dig the
funny way the British speak   and it's real it's true   and I love
too the singing of yiddish sentences that go with shrugs and hands and
arms doing melancholy or lively dances   I love the sound and look of

yiddish in the air   in the body   in the streets   in the English
language   nooo   so what's new   so go by the grocer and buy
some fruit   oye vey   gevalt gefilte fish   raisele   oh and
those words   hundreds of them dotting the english language like raisins
in the bread   shnook and schlemiel   suftik   tush schmata   all
those soft sweet sounds saying sharp sharp things   I am what I am and
I'm naturalized Jewish-American   wasp is foreign and new but Jewish-
American is old show familiar   schmata familiar and its me dears its
me   bagels blintzes and all   I am what I am   Take it or leave me
alone.

Dreams of Violence

Naomi Littlebear Morena

I was awakened by the sound of school children screaming at each other. I thought I heard them beating someone. Loud solid thumps quivered in my ears, a hoarse voice, horribly chanting in rapid succession, "oh my god, oh my god" . . .

I closed my eyes and sunk into a panic that terrorized my morning. I flew back in time, somewhere in grade school, walking home with my cousin Virginia . . .

I

There was an unmistakable bitter taste in the air around us, forewarning. It was the moment before the actual sight of them coming that froze our hearts with fear. Suddenly like a stampede of wild bulls they plummeted toward us. A half dozen or more boys, a frenzied blur of leather jackets, screaming wild devils, thrashing at us with the harsh stiff leather, metal teeth zippers battering our bewildered bodies. We ran on rubber band legs; I could hear Virginia calling, "Mama, Mama." In my ears was a sound like the beating of wings, barbed wings that stung my skin, that made my lip swell in pain, we ran hard thru the obstacle course of confused bodies, their horrifying shrieks of rage thru the rain of leather.

By some miracle they scattered, the same force that brought them seemed to snatch them up again and they were scattered to other dark corners of the barrio.

My face was hot and swollen, i felt my tears burning rivers down my cheeks. I could still hear Virginia crying for her mother, though now she was just a mass of pain & crying. I could remember my own silence thundering thru my body.

As we neared home, my fear increased. I knew what would await me there. I could close my eyes and see the vision a hundred times over.

I would slowly approach the door and before my entire body entered, she could smell the mischief, sense the energy—my grandmother immediately stopped whatever she was doing and demanded a full story. But always my story would be cut in mid-sentence. Because whatever state i was in, i provoked it.

"Why are you Dirty?" "Have you been fighting?" "Did you tear your dress?"—a volley of quick demands and accusations came threateningly to me, making me feel scared, watching her come towards me, reaching over to the door where the razor strap hung, "her bonito," as she called it. Reaching towards me, strap in hand. My feet turning to lead. Trying to run away, backing into a corner.

II

But where the strap couldn't reach me, a vicious pinch could. I flew thru the door being chased by more leather stings.

I ran far, sometimes two blocks away, my skin boiling, red crisscrosses atop the scratches that the leather jackets had made. I cried alone barely able to make out the shapes of people and cars thru my tears.

I am awake now, my lover still sleeping beside me, wondering how we can blend our two worlds. How to mend the holes in our pasts, walk away bravely from the nightmares.

Her attacks were more subtle, hidden within the false shelter of her home; instead of gangs of boys chasing her, her brother was the nightly intrusion, using her young child body to masturbate with, as she closed her eyes too numb and scared to speak.

We both have no choice but to be survivors though the fears are still there. Whenever i see a crowd of men, my heart sinks to my feet, whenever i hear sudden noises, sudden crashing, anger, male noises, their very laughter is abrasive to my ears. I shrink inside, walk close to the walls of my soul, i look for a place to hide.

He Saw

Chrystos

his roots/went back to the reservation old
pain/old hunger
None of the ghosts were there
He went fishing   caught
one or more every
day   The fishing is what he needed to do
Gathering wild rice, remembered after years of suits, ties, clocks
adjustments
what he began
& left
He writes me about the fish
I grow hungry

He gave me all the whitest advantages
square house, football school, white mother baking white bread in a
                                        white oven
He wanted to spare me his pain
didn't
Silently our misunderstandings shred   rage clouds our blood ties
I stare at his words   wonder who he is
Lonely red daddy cradling ghost of his mama   died when he was nine
pretending he was born without a father   without straightjackets
Daddy you write in a painfully practiced scrawl
you learned   learned learned beaten down a dying fish
You go back & can't stay
Bring me a sack of rice
      I want your wildness, want the boy who left on a freight car
I want a boy who cried because his mother is dead
& his daddy's gone crazy
I want the one who gathered water & wood
I don't want this man who cut off his hair
joined the government
to be safe

We are both in danger
of your ancient fear
I learned to fish on my own
stopped
Now I'm learning to weave nets

II

Entering the Lives of Others

Theory in the Flesh

Yolanda M. López, *Portrait of the Artist as the Virgin of Guadalupe*, 1978
Oil pastel on paper, 32" × 24"
Collection of the Artist

Entering the Lives of Others

Theory in the Flesh

> *I am not interested in pursuing a society that uses analysis, research, and experimentation to concretize their vision of cruel destinies for those bastards of the pilgrims; a society with arrogance rising, moon in oppression, and sun in destruction.*
>
> —Barbara Cameron

A theory in the flesh means one where the physical realities of our lives—our skin color, the land or concrete we grew up on, our sexual longings—all fuse to create a politic born out of necessity. Here, we attempt to bridge the contradictions in our experience:

We are the colored in a white feminist movement.

We are the feminists among the people of our culture.

We are often the lesbians among the straight.

We do this bridging by naming our selves and by telling our stories in our own words.

The theme echoing throughout most of these stories is our refusal of the *easy* explanation to the conditions we live in. There is nothing *easy* about a collective cultural history of what Mitsuye Yamada calls "unnatural disasters": the forced encampment of Indigenous people on government reservations, the forced encampment of Japanese American people during WWII, the forced encampment of our mothers as laborers in factories/in fields/in our own and other people's homes as paid or unpaid slaves.

Closer to home, we are still trying to separate the fibers of experience we have had as daughters of a struggling people. Daily, we feel the pull and tug of having to choose between which parts of our mothers' heritages we want to claim and wear and which parts have served to cloak us from the knowledge of ourselves. "My mother and I work to unravel the knot" (Levins Morales). This is how our theory develops. We are interested in pursuing a society that uses flesh and blood experiences to concretize a vision that can begin to heal our "wounded knee" (Chrystos).

Wonder Woman

Genny Lim

Sometimes I see reflections on bits of glass on sidewalks
I catch the glimmer of empty bottles floating out to sea
Sometimes I stretch my arms way above my head and wonder if
There are women along the Mekong doing the same

Sometimes I stare longingly at women who I will never know
Generous, laughing women with wrinkled cheeks and white teeth
Dragging along chubby, rosy-cheeked babies on fat, wobbly legs
Sometimes I stare at Chinese grandmothers
Getting on the 30 Stockton with shopping bags
Japanese women tourists in European hats
Middle-aged mothers with laundry carts
Young wives holding hands with their husbands
Lesbian women holding hands in coffee-houses
Smiling debutantes with bouquets of yellow daffodils
Silver-haired matrons with silver rhinestoned poodles
Painted prostitutes posing along MacArthur Boulevard
Giddy teenage girls snapping gum in fast cars
Widows clutching bibles, crucifixes

I look at them and wonder if
They are a part of me
I look in their eyes and wonder if
They share my dreams

I wonder if the woman in mink is content
If the stockbroker's wife is afraid of growing old
If the professor's wife is an alcoholic
If the woman in prison is me

There are copper-tanned women in Hyannis Port playing tennis
Women who eat with finger bowls
There are women in factories punching time clocks
Women tired of every waking hour of the day
I wonder why there are women born with silver spoons in their mouths
Women who have never known a day of hunger

Women who have never changed their own bed linen
And I wonder why there are women who must work
Women who must clean other women's houses
Women who must shell shrimps for pennies a day
Women who must sew other women's clothes
Who must cook
Who must die
In childbirth
In dreams

Why must woman stand divided?
Building the walls that tear them down?
Jill-of-all-trades
Lover, mother, housewife, friend, breadwinner
Heart and spade
A woman is a ritual
A house that must accommodate
A house that must endure
Generation after generation
Of wind and torment, of fire and rain
A house with echoing rooms
Closets with hidden cries
Walls with stretchmarks
Windows with eyes

Short, tall, skinny, fat
Pregnant, married, white, yellow, black, brown, red
Professional, working-class, aristocrat
Women cooking over coals in sampans
Women shining tiffany spoons in glass houses
Women stretching their arms way above the clouds
In Samarkand, in San Francisco
Along the Mekong

La Güera

Cherríe Moraga

It requires something more than personal experience to gain a philosophy or point of view from any specific event. It is the quality of our response to the event and our capacity to enter into the lives of others that help us to make their lives and experiences our own.

—Emma Goldman[1]

I am the very well-educated daughter of a woman who, by the standards in this country, would be considered largely illiterate. My mother was born in Santa Paula, Southern California, at a time when much of the central valley there was still farmland. Nearly thirty-five years later, in 1948, she was the only daughter of six to marry an anglo, my father.

I remember all of my mother's stories, probably much better than she realizes. She is a fine storyteller, recalling every event of her life with vividness of the present, noting each detail right down to the cut and color of her dress. I remember stories of her being pulled out of school at the ages of five, seven, nine, and eleven to work in the fields, along with her brothers and sisters; stories of her father drinking away whatever small profit she was able to make for the family; of her going the long way home to avoid meeting him on the street, staggering toward the same destination. I remember stories of my mother lying about her age in order to get a job as a hat-check girl at Agua Caliente Racetrack in Tijuana. At fourteen, she was the main support of the family. I can still see her walking home alone at 3 a.m., only to turn all of her salary and tips over to her mother, who was pregnant again.

The stories continue through the war years and on: walnut-cracking factories, the Voit Rubber factory, and then the computer boom. I remember my mother doing piecework for the electronics plant in our neighborhood. In the late evening, she would sit in front of the TV set, wrapping copper wires into the backs of circuit boards, talking about "keeping up with the younger girls." By that time, she was already in her mid-fifties.

Meanwhile, I was college-prep in school. After classes, I would go with my mother to fill out job applications for her, or write checks for her at the supermarket. We would have the scenario all worked out ahead of time. My mother would sign the check before we'd get to the store. Then, as we'd approach the checkstand, she would say—within earshot of the cashier—"oh honey, you go 'head and make out the check," as if she couldn't be bothered with such an insignificant detail. No one asked any questions.

I was educated, and wore it with a keen sense of pride and satisfaction, my head propped up with the knowledge, from my mother, that my life would be easier than hers. I was educated; but more than this, I was "la güera": fair-skinned. Born with the features of my Chicana mother, but the skin of my Anglo father, I had it made.

No one ever quite told me this (that light was right), but I knew that being light was something valued in my family (who were all Chicano, with the exception of my father). In fact, everything about my upbringing (at least what occurred on a conscious level) attempted to bleach me of what color I did have. Although my mother was fluent in it, I was never taught much Spanish at home. I picked up what I did learn from school and from overheard snatches of conversation among my relatives and mother. She often called other lower-income Mexicans "braceros," or "wetbacks," referring to herself and her family as "a different class of people." And yet, the real story was that my family, too, had been poor (some still are) and farmworkers. My mother can remember this in her blood as if it were yesterday. But this is something she would like to forget (and rightfully), for to her, on a basic economic level, being Chicana meant being "less." It was through my mother's desire to protect her children from poverty and illiteracy that we became "anglocized"; the more effectively we could pass in the white world, the better guaranteed our future.

From all of this, I experience, daily, a huge disparity between what I was born into and what I was to grow up to become. Because, (as Goldman suggests) these stories my mother told me crept under my "güera" skin. I had no choice but to enter into the life of my mother. *I had no choice*. I took her life into my heart, but managed to keep a lid on it as long as I feigned being the happy, upwardly mobile heterosexual.

When I finally lifted the lid to my lesbianism, a profound connection with my mother reawakened in me. It wasn't until I acknowledged and confronted my own lesbianism in the flesh, that my heartfelt identification with and empathy for my mother's oppression—due to being poor, uneducated, and Chicana—was realized. My lesbianism is the avenue through which I have learned the most about silence and oppression, and it continues to be the most tactile reminder to me that we are not free human beings.

You see, one follows the other. I had known for years that I was a lesbian, had felt it in my bones, had ached with the knowledge, gone crazed with the knowledge, wallowed in the silence of it. Silence *is* like starvation. Don't be fooled. It's nothing short of that, and felt most sharply when one has had a full belly most of her life. When we are not physically starving, we have the luxury to realize psychic and emotional starvation. It is from this starvation that other starvations can be recognized—if one is willing to take the risk of making the connection—if one is willing to be responsible to the result of the connection. For me, the connection is an inevitable one.

What I am saying is that the joys of looking like a white girl ain't so great since I realized I could be beaten on the street for being a dyke. If my sister's being beaten because she's Black, it's pretty much the same principle. We're both getting beaten any way you look at it. The connection is blatant; and in the case of my own family, the difference in the privileges attached to looking white instead of brown are merely a generation apart.

In this country, lesbianism is a poverty—as is being brown, as is being a woman, as is being just plain poor. The danger lies in ranking the oppressions. *The danger lies in failing to acknowledge the specificity of the oppression.* The danger lies in attempting to deal with oppression purely from a theoretical base. Without an emotional, heartfelt grappling with the source of our own oppression, without naming the enemy within ourselves and outside of us, no authentic, non-hierarchical connection among oppressed groups can take place.

When the going gets rough, will we abandon our so-called comrades in a flurry of racist/heterosexist/what-have-you panic? To whose camp, then, should the lesbian of color retreat? Her very presence violates the ranking and abstraction of oppression. Do we merely live hand to mouth? Do we merely struggle with the "ism" that's sitting on top of our own heads?

The answer is: yes, I think first we do; and we must do so thoroughly and deeply. But to fail to move out from there will only isolate us in our own oppression—will only insulate, rather than radicalize us.

To illustrate: a gay male friend of mine once confided to me that he continued to feel that, on some level, I didn't trust him because he was male; that he felt, really, if it ever came down to a "battle of the sexes," I might kill him. I admitted that I might very well. He wanted to understand the source of my distrust. I responded, "You're not a woman. Be a woman for a day. Imagine being a woman." He confessed that the thought terrified him because, to him, being a woman meant being raped by men. He *had* felt raped by men; he wanted to forget what that meant. What grew from that discussion was the realization that in order for him to create an authentic alliance with me, he must deal with the primary source of his own sense of oppression. He must, first, emotionally come to terms with what it feels like to be a victim. If he—or anyone—were to truly do this, it would be impossible to discount the oppression of others, except by again forgetting how we have been hurt.

And yet, oppressed groups are forgetting all the time. There are instances of this in the rising Black middle class, and certainly an obvious trend of such "unconsciousness" among white gay men. Because to remember may mean giving up whatever privileges we have managed to squeeze out of this society by virtue of our gender, race, class, or sexuality.

Within the women's movement, the connections among women of different backgrounds and sexual orientations have been fragile, at best. I think this phenomenon is indicative of our failure to seriously address ourselves to some very frightening questions: How have I internalized my own oppression? How have I oppressed? Instead, we have let rhetoric do the job of poetry. Even the word "oppression" has lost its power. We need a new language, better words that can more closely describe women's fear of, and resistance to, one another; words that will not always come out sounding like dogma.

What prompted me in the first place to work on an anthology by radical women of color was a deep sense that I had a valuable insight to contribute, by virtue of my birthright and background. And yet, I don't really understand firsthand what it feels like being shitted on for being brown. I understand much more about the joys of it—being Chicana and having family are synonymous for me. What I know about loving, singing, crying, telling stories, speaking with my heart and hands, even having a sense of my own soul comes from the love of my mother, aunts, cousins . . .

But at the age of twenty-seven, it is frightening to acknowledge that I have internalized a racism and classism, where the object of oppression is not only someone outside of my skin, but the someone inside my skin. In fact, to a large degree, the real battle with such oppression, for all of us, begins under the skin. I have had to confront the fact that much of what I value about being Chicana, about my family, has been subverted by anglo culture and my own cooperation with it. This realization did not occur to me overnight. For example, it wasn't until long after my graduation from the private college I'd attended in Los Angeles that I realized the major reason for my total alienation from and fear of my classmates was rooted in class and culture. CLICK.

Three years after graduation, in an apple-orchard in Sonoma, a friend of mine (who comes from an Italian Irish working-class family) says to me, "Cherríe, no wonder you felt like such a nut in school. Most of the people there were white and rich." It was true. All along I had felt the difference, but not until I had put the words "class" and "color" to the experience, did my feelings make any sense. For years, I had berated myself for not being as "free" as my classmates. I completely bought that they simply had more guts than I did—to rebel against their parents and run around the country hitchhiking, reading books and studying "art." They had enough privilege to be atheists, for chrissake. There was no one around filling in the disparity for me between their parents, who were Hollywood filmmakers, and my parents, who wouldn't know the name of a filmmaker if their lives depended on it (and precisely because their lives didn't depend on it, they couldn't be bothered). But I knew nothing about "privilege" then. White was right. Period. I could pass. If I got educated enough, there would never be any telling.

Three years after that, another CLICK. In a letter to Barbara Smith, I wrote:

> I went to a concert where Ntozake Shange was reading. There, everything exploded for me. She was speaking a language that I knew—in the deepest parts of me—existed, and that I had ignored in my own feminist studies and even in my own writing. What Ntozake caught in me is the realization that in my development as a poet, I have, in many ways, denied the voice of my brown mother—the brown in me. I have acclimated to the sound of a white language which, as my father represents it, does not speak to the emotions in my poems—emotions which stem from the love of my mother.
>
> The reading was agitating. Made me uncomfortable. Threw me into a week-long terror of how deeply I was affected. I felt that I had to start all over again. That I turned only to the perceptions of white middle-class women to speak for me and all women. I am shocked by my own ignorance.

Sitting in that auditorium chair was the first time I had realized to the core of me that for years I had disowned the language I knew best—ignored the words and rhythms that were the closest to me. The sounds of my mother and aunts gossiping—half in English, half in Spanish—while drinking cerveza in the kitchen. And the hands—I had cut off the hands in my poems. But not in conversation; still the hands could not be kept down. Still they insisted on moving.

The reading had forced me to remember that I knew things from my roots. But to remember puts me up against what I don't know. Shange's reading agitated me because she spoke with power about a world that is both alien and common to me: "the capacity to enter into the lives of others." But you can't just take the goods and run. I knew then, sitting in the Oakland auditorium (as I know in my poetry), that the only thing worth writing about is what seems to be unknown and, therefore, fearful.

The "unknown" is often depicted in racist literature as the "darkness" within a person. Similarly, sexist writers will refer to fear in the form of the vagina, calling it "the orifice of death." In contrast, it is a pleasure to read works such as Maxine Hong Kingston's *Woman Warrior*, where fear and alienation are described as "the white ghosts." And yet, the bulk of literature in this country reinforces the myth that what is dark and female is evil. Consequently, each of us—whether dark, female, or both—has in some way *internalized* this oppressive imagery. What the oppressor often succeeds in doing is simply *externalizing* his fears, projecting them into the bodies of women, Asians, gays, disabled folks, whoever seems most "other."

> call me
> roach and presumptuous
> nightmare on your white pillow
> your itch to destroy
> the indestructible
> part of yourself

—Audre Lorde[2]

But it is not really difference the oppressor fears so much as similarity. He fears he will discover in himself the same aches, the same longings as those of the people he has shitted on. He fears the immobilization threatened by his own incipient guilt. He fears he will have to change his life once he has seen himself in the bodies of the people he has called different. He fears the hatred, anger, and vengeance of those he has hurt.

This is the oppressor's nightmare, but it is not exclusive to him. We women have a similar nightmare, for each of us in some way has been both oppressed and the oppressor. We are afraid to look at how we have failed each other. We are afraid to see how we have taken the values of our oppressor into our hearts and turned them against ourselves and one another. We are afraid to admit how deeply "the man's" words have been ingrained in us.

To assess the damage is a dangerous act. I think of how, even as a feminist lesbian, I have so wanted to ignore my own homophobia, my own hatred of myself for being queer. I have not wanted to admit that my deepest personal sense of myself has not quite "caught up" with my "woman-identified" politics. I have been afraid to criticize lesbian writers who choose to "skip over" these issues in the name of feminism. In 1979, we talk of "old gay" and "butch and femme" roles as if they were ancient history. We toss them aside as merely patriarchal notions. And yet, the truth of the matter is that I have sometimes taken society's fear and hatred of lesbians to bed with me. I have sometimes hated my lover for loving me. I have sometimes felt "not woman enough" for her. I have sometimes felt "not man enough." For a lesbian trying to survive in a heterosexist society, there is no easy way around these emotions. Similarly, in a white-dominated world, there is little getting around racism and our own internalization of it. It's always there, embodied in someone we least expect to rub up against.

When we do rub up against this person, *there* then is the challenge. *There* then is the opportunity to look at the nightmare within us. But we usually shrink from such a challenge.

Time and time again, I have observed that the usual response among white women's groups when the "racism issue" comes up is to deny the difference. I have heard comments like, "Well, we're open to *all* women; why don't they (women of color) come? You can only do so much . . ." But there is seldom any analysis of how the very nature and structure of the group itself may be founded on racist or classist assumptions. More important, so often the women seem to feel no loss, no lack, no absence when women of color are not involved; therefore, there is little desire to change the situation. This has hurt me deeply. I have come to believe that the only reason women of a privileged class will dare to look at *how* it is that *they* oppress, is when they've come to know the meaning of their own oppression. And understand that the oppression of others hurts them personally.

The other side of the story is that women of color and working-class women often shrink from challenging white middle-class women. It is much easier to rank oppressions and set up a hierarchy, rather than take responsibility for changing our own lives. We have failed to demand that white women, particularly those who claim to be speaking for all women, be accountable for their racism.

The dialogue has simply not gone deep enough.

I have many times questioned my right to even work on an anthology which is to be written "exclusively by Third World women." I have had to look critically at my claim to color, at a time when, among white feminist ranks, it is a "politically correct" (and sometimes peripherally advantageous) assertion to make. I must acknowledge the fact that, physically, I have had a *choice* about making that claim, in contrast to women who have not had such a choice, and have been abused for their color. I must reckon with the fact that for most of my life, by virtue of the very fact that I am white-looking, I identified with, and aspired toward, white values, and that I rode the wave of that Southern Californian privilege as far as conscience would let me.

Well, now I feel both bleached and beached. I feel angry about this—the years when I refused to recognize privilege, both when it worked against me, and when I worked it, ignorantly, at the expense of others. These are not settled issues. This is why this work feels so risky to me. It continues to be discovery. It has brought me into contact with women who invariably know a hell of a lot more than I do about racism, as experienced in the flesh, as revealed in the flesh of their writing.

I think: what is my responsibility to my roots—both white and brown, Spanish-speaking and English? I am a woman with a foot in both worlds; and I refuse the split. I feel the necessity for dialogue. Sometimes I feel it urgently.

But one voice is not enough, nor two, although this is where dialogue begins. It is essential that radical feminists confront their fear of, and resistance to, each other, because without this, there *will* be no bread on the table. Simply, we will not survive. If we could make this connection in our heart of hearts, that if we are serious about a revolution—better—if we seriously believe there should be joy in our lives (real joy, not just "good times"), then we need one another. We women need each other. Because my/your solitary, self-asserting "go-for the throat-of-fear" power is not enough. The real power, as you and I well know, is collective. I can't afford to be afraid of you, nor you of me. If it takes head-on collisions, let's do it: this polite timidity is killing us.

As Lorde suggests in the passage I cited earlier, it is in looking to the nightmare that the dream is found. There, the survivor emerges to insist on a future, a vision, yes, born out of what is dark and female. The feminist movement must be a movement of such survivors, a movement with a future.

September 1979[3]

Notes

1. Alix Kates Shulman, "Was My Life Worth Living?," *Red Emma Speaks* (New York: Random House, 1972), 388.
2. From "The Brown Menace or Poem to the Survival of Roaches," *The New York Head Shop and Museum* (Detroit: Broadside, 1974), 48.
3. Thanks to Maria Stecenko for her editing help in the original version of this essay.

Invisibility Is an Unnatural Disaster
Reflections of an Asian American Woman

Mitsuye Yamada

Last year for the Asian segment of the Ethnic American Literature course I was teaching, I selected a new anthology entitled *Aiiieeeee!* compiled by a group of outspoken Asian American writers. During the discussion of the long but thought-provoking introduction to this anthology, one of my students blurted out that she was offended by its militant tone and that as a white person she was tired of always being blamed for the oppression of all the minorities. I noticed several of her classmates' eyes nodding in tacit agreement. A discussion of the "militant" voices in some of the other writings we had read in the course ensued. Surely, I pointed out, some of these other writings have been just as, if not more, militant as the words in this introduction? Had they been offended by those also but failed to express their feelings about them? To my surprise, they said they were not offended by any of the Black American, Chicano, or American Indian writings, but were hard-pressed to explain why when I asked for an explanation. A little further discussion revealed that they "understood" the anger expressed by the Black Americans and Chicanos and they "empathized" with the frustrations and sorrow expressed by the American Indian. But the Asian Americans??

Then finally, one student said it for all of them: "It made me angry. *Their* anger made *me* angry, because I didn't even know the Asian Americans felt oppressed. I didn't expect their anger."

At this time I was involved in an academic due process procedure begun as a result of a grievance I had filed the previous semester against the administrators at my college. I had filed a grievance for violation of my rights as a teacher who had worked in the district for almost eleven years. My student's remark "Their anger made me angry . . . I didn't expect their anger," explained for me the reactions of some of my own colleagues as well as the reactions of the administrators during those previous months. The grievance procedure was a time-consuming and emotionally draining process, but the basic principle was too important for me to ignore. That basic principle was that I, an individual teacher, do have certain rights that are given and my superiors cannot, should not, violate them with impunity. When this was pointed out to them, however, they responded with shocked surprise that I, of all people, would take them to task for violation of what was clearly written policy in our college district. They all seemed to exclaim, "We don't understand this; this is so uncharacteristic of her; she seemed such a nice person, so polite, so obedient, so non-trouble-making." What was even more surprising was once they were forced to acknowledge that I was determined to start the due process action, they assumed I was not doing it on my own. One of the administrators suggested someone must have pushed me into this, undoubtedly some of "those feminists" on our campus, he said wryly.

In this age when women are clearly making themselves visible on all fronts, I, an Asian American woman, am still functioning as a "front for those feminists" and therefore invisible. The realization of this sinks in slowly. Asian Americans as a whole are finally coming to claim their own, demanding that they be included in the multicultural history of our country. I like to think, in spite of my administrator's myopia, that the most stereotyped minority of them all, the Asian American woman, is just now emerging to become part of that group. It took forever. Perhaps it is important to ask ourselves why it took so long. We should ask ourselves this question just when we think we are emerging as a viable minority in the fabric of our society. I should add to my student's words, "because I didn't even know they felt oppressed," that it took this long because we Asian American women have not admitted to ourselves that we *were* oppressed. We, the visible minority that is invisible.

I say this because until a few years ago I have been an Asian American woman working among non-Asians in an educational institution where most of the decision makers were men;[1] an Asian American woman thriving under the smug illusion that I was *not* the stereotypic image of the Asian woman because I had a career teaching English in a community college. I did not think anything assertive was necessary to make my point. People who know me, I reasoned, the ones who count, know who I am and what I think. Thus, even when what I considered a veiled racist remark was made in a casual social setting, I would "let it go" because it was pointless to argue with people who didn't even know their remark was racist. I had supposed that I was practicing passive resistance while being stereotyped, but it was so passive no one noticed I was resisting; it was so much my expected role that it ultimately rendered me invisible.

My experience leads me to believe that contrary to what I thought, I had actually been contributing to my own stereotyping. Like the hero in Ralph Ellison's novel *Invisible Man*, I had become invisible to white Americans, and it clung to me like a bad habit. Like most bad habits, this one crept up on me because I took it in minute doses like Mithradates' poison, and my mind and body adapted so well to it I hardly noticed it was there.

For the past eleven years I have busied myself with the usual chores of an English teacher, a wife of a research chemist, and a mother of four rapidly growing children. I hadn't even done much to shatter this particular stereotype: the middle-class woman happy to be bringing home the extra income and quietly fitting into the man's world of work. When the Asian American woman is lulled into believing that people perceive her as being different from other Asian women (the submissive, subservient, ready-to-please, easy-to-get-along-with Asian woman), she is kept comfortably content with the state of things. She becomes ineffectual in the milieu in which she moves. The seemingly apolitical middle-class woman and the apolitical Asian woman constituted a double invisibility.

I had created an underground culture of survival for myself and had become in the eyes of others the person I was trying not to be. Because I was permitted to go to college, permitted to take a stab at a career or two along the way, given "free choice" to marry and have a family, given a "choice" to eventually do both, I had assumed I was more or less free, not realizing that those who are free make and take choices; they do not choose from options proffered by "those out there."

I, personally, had not "emerged" until I was almost fifty years old. Apparently through a long conditioning process, I had learned how *not* to be seen for what I am. A long history of ineffectual activities had been, I realize now, initiation rites toward my eventual invisibility. The training begins in childhood; and for women and minorities, whatever is started in childhood is continued throughout their adult lives. I first recognized just how invisible I was in my first real confrontation with my parents a few years after the outbreak of World War II.

During the early years of the war, my older brother, Mike, and I left the concentration camp in Idaho to work and study at the University of Cincinnati. My parents came to Cincinnati soon after my father's release from Internment Camp (these were POW camps to which many of the Issei[2] men, leaders in their communities, were sent by the FBI), and worked as domestics in the suburbs. I did not see them too often because by this time I had met and was much influenced by a pacifist who was out on a "furlough" from a conscientious objectors' camp in Trenton, North Dakota. When my parents learned about my "boy friend" they were appalled and frightened. After all, this was the period when everyone in the country was expected to be one-hundred percent behind the war effort, and the Nisei[3] boys who had volunteered for the Armed Forces were out there fighting and dying to prove how American we really were. However, during interminable arguments with my father and overheard arguments between my parents, I was devastated to learn they were not so much concerned about my having become a pacifist, but they were more concerned about the possibility of my marrying one. They were understandably frightened (my father's prison years of course were still fresh on his mind) about repercussions on the rest of the family. In an attempt to make my father understand me, I argued that even if I didn't marry him, I'd still be a pacifist; but my father reassured me that it was "all right" for me to be a pacifist because as a Japanese national and a "girl" *it didn't make any difference to anyone.* In frustration I remember shouting, "But can't you see, *I'm* philosophically committed to the pacifist cause," but he dismissed this with "In my college days we used to call philosophy, foolosophy," and that was the end of that. When they were finally convinced I was not going to marry "my pacifist," the subject was dropped and we never discussed it again.

As if to confirm my father's assessment of the harmlessness of my opinions, my brother Mike, an American citizen, was suddenly expelled from the University of Cincinnati while I, "an enemy alien," was permitted to stay. We assumed that his stand as a pacifist, although he was classified a 4-F because of his health, contributed to his expulsion. We were told the Air Force was conducting sensitive wartime research on campus and requested his removal, but they apparently felt my presence on campus was not as threatening.

I left Cincinnati in 1945, hoping to leave behind this and other unpleasant memories gathered there during the war years, and plunged right into the politically active atmosphere at New York University where students, many of them returning veterans, were continuously promoting one cause or other by making speeches in Washington Square, passing out petitions, or staging demonstrations. On one occasion, I tagged along with a group of students who took a train to Albany to demonstrate on the steps of the State Capitol. I think I was the only Asian in this group of predominantly Jewish students from NYU. People who passed us were amused and shouted, "Go home and grow up." I suppose Governor Dewey, who refused to see us, assumed we were a group of adolescents without a cause as most college students were considered to be during those days. It appears they weren't expecting any results from our demonstration. There were no newspersons, no security persons, no police. No one tried to stop us from doing what we were doing. We simply did "our thing" and went back to our studies until next time, and my father's words were again confirmed: it made no difference to anyone, being a young student demonstrator in peacetime, 1947.

Not only the young, but those who feel powerless over their own lives know what it is like not to make a difference on anyone or anything. The poor know it only too well, and we women have known it since we were little girls. The most insidious part of this conditioning process, I realize now, was that we have been trained not to expect a response in ways that matter. We may be listened to and responded to with placating words and gestures, but our psychological mindset has already told us time and again that we were born into a ready-made world into which we must fit ourselves, and that many of us do it very well.

This mindset is the result of not believing that the political and social forces affecting our lives are determined by some person, or a group of persons, probably sitting behind a desk or around a conference table.

Just recently I read an article about "the remarkable track record of success" of the Nisei in the United States. One Nisei was quoted as saying he attributed our stamina and endurance to our ancestors whose characters had been shaped, he said, by their living in a country which has been constantly besieged by all manner of natural disasters, such as earthquakes and hurricanes. He said the Nisei has inherited a steely will, a will to endure and hence, to survive.

This evolutionary explanation disturbs me, because it equates the "act of God" (i.e., natural disasters) to the "act of man" (i.e., the war, the evacuation). The former is not within our power to alter, but the latter, I should think, is. By putting the "acts of God" on par with the acts of man, we shrug off personal responsibilities.

I have, for too long a period of time, accepted the opinion of others (even though they were directly affecting my life) as if they were objective events totally out of my control. Because I separated such opinions from the persons who were making them, I accepted them the way I accepted natural disasters; and I endured them as inevitable. I have tried to cope with people whose points of view alarmed me in the same way that I had adjusted to natural phenomena, such as hurricanes, which plowed into my life from time to time. I would readjust my dismantled feelings in the same way that we repaired the broken shutters after the storm. The Japanese have an all-purpose expression in their language for this attitude of resigned acceptance: "Shikataganai." "It can't be helped." "There's nothing I can do about it." It is said with the shrug of the shoulders and tone of finality, perhaps not unlike the "those-were-my-orders" tone that was used at the Nuremberg trials. With all the sociological studies that have been made about the causes of the evacuations of the Japanese Americans during World War II, we should know by now that "they" knew that the West Coast Japanese Americans would go without too much protest, and of course, "they" were right, for most of us (with the exception of those notable few) resigned to our fate, albeit bewildered and not willingly. We were not perceived by our government as responsive Americans; we were objects that happened to be standing in the path of the storm.

Perhaps this kind of acceptance is a way of coping with the "real" world. One stands against the wind for a time, and then succumbs eventually because there is no point to being stubborn against all odds. The wind will not respond to entreaties anyway, one reasons; one should have sense enough to know that. I'm not ready to accept this evolutionary reasoning. It is too rigid for me; I would like to think that my new awareness is going to make me more visible than ever, and to allow me to make some changes in the "man-made disaster" I live in at the present time. Part of being visible is refusing to separate the actors from their actions, and demanding that they be responsible for them.

By now, riding along with the minorities' and women's movements, I think we are making a wedge into the main body of American life, but people are still looking right through and around us, assuming we are simply tagging along. Asian American women still remain in the background and we are heard but not really listened to. Like Muzak, they think we are piped into the airwaves by someone else. We must remember that one of the most insidious ways of keeping women and minorities powerless is to let them only talk about harmless and inconsequential subjects, or let them speak freely and not listen to them with serious intent.

We need to raise our voices a little more, even as they say to us "This is so uncharacteristic of you." To finally recognize our own invisibility is to finally be on the path toward visibility. Invisibility is not a natural state for anyone.

Notes

1. It is hoped this will change now that a black woman is chancellor of our college district.
2. Issei—Immigrant Japanese, living in the US.
3. Nisei—Second-generation Japanese, born in the US.

It's in My Blood, My Face—
My Mother's Voice, the Way I Sweat

Anita Valerio*

Hey ya hey ya ho—
where the sun does not malign the seasons

I remember the place where the sun does not malign the seasons flutes of penitentes & headdresses for the Okan[1]   we rub our offerings of dried meat into the earth and the holy woman comes out and dances   she is wearing the sacred headdress   she is one of the last qualified to do this   my mother says it is because she has only been with her husband and never any other man it makes her a virgin of sorts   my mother says it's hard to find a woman like that these days   a holy woman and that is why I sometimes don't want to think about being Indian   why sometimes I could really care less these days   it's sad. There was a time three years back when I was so angry so proud I wanted so much to reclaim my language the symbols and sacred gestures   the land   but now?   I went back to the reserve for two months   traditional cultures are conservative and this one is patriarchal.

What does it mean that it is a holy woman who sets up the Okan? and why does it make her holy that only one man has touched her? is it really because she has been a good little piece of property to that one man or is it because she is a pure vessel of female power not permeated with the male? is her setting up the Okan—which is the principal ceremony of the culture—a hearkening back to earlier matriarchal times? it seems as though you can't always trust people's interpretations as their minds have been colored by Catholicism—t.v. etc. Some would like to believe that the values of the Roman Catholic Church and the values of the Native American tribal religions are one and the same. Hah! being totally traditional seems wrong as well as it seems the task is first to find out what was our tradition—feel it through the skin.

My earlier memories are the best   innocence may be an escalation of memory   brings desires   smells of morning—standing on the porch smelling morning   blue sky   rolling hills   unrest

---

*Anita Valerio transitioned from female to male in 1989 and is now Max Wolf Valerio.

ecstasy was in my soul   there seemed to be balance then before I
knew the meaning of the word   later I wanted to go back to it   the
wild spacious morning air   the horses corralled the red barn and the
sticky hot summer nights watching the pickup trucks come in from
town   Being an Indian . . . I didn't even realize that's what I was—an
Indian—in fact I jumped up and down in protest "I'm not an Indian—I'm
not an Indian!" when my relatives would tell me I was. After all, Indians
were the bad guys on T.V. and though we didn't have running water that
year or even telephones—yes—we did have television. Apparently, there
were also times when I'd scream "I'm an Indian, I'm an Indian" when
my relatives would say I wasn't . . . Such has been life.

Just what it is to be an "Indian"—Native American—a Skin . . . &
more importantly how do I—half blood Indian and half Chicana relate to
it all? Well, sometimes I've made quite an occupation of thinking about
it and sometimes, more recently, I'd rather not bother. Why bother? It
seems too conceptual—and worse—too bound up with invectives. Yet—
I cannot forget and I don't want to. It's in my blood, my face   my
mother's voice   it's in my voice   my speech rhythms my dreams
and memories   it's the shape of my legs   and though I am light
skinned it is my features—my eyes and face shape . . . it must even be
the way I sweat! Why it's damn near everything!   and I feel it's my
yearning for wide spaces—for the flat and nude plains. Yes, I've been
denied. What a shame not to speak Blackfoot. It was my mother's first
language—she'd talk it over the phone long distance—she'd speak it
when she went home (the blood reserve in Southern Alberta) she even
spoke it in my dreams but I never learned. All that talking denied me.

Weird, superstitious, unnatural—Imagine in this day and age!

My mother talking: "Edward's wife cries by his bed. His dead wife,
she cries by his bed. He had to go to a medicine man to see what was
happening. She committed suicide a couple years back, she must be
restless." "My, imagine . . . What must it be like?" I say, "My that's
something, weird." Weird? The word foreign to me as soon as I've said
it. Weird? A shadow flits across my mother's eyes. How could that have
come up? I recoil inside, I don't know the part of me that's said it. My
stomach tingles. I feel tight. The word is dry, false—"weird." Of course,
I remember, of course I know. "Weird" only a non-Indian would say that.
Someone who doesn't know, who hasn't been raised to see that life is a
continuous whole from flesh to spirit, that we're not as easily separated
as some think. I knew that.

"Yea—that's good he went to see that medicine man," I say. I've been around too many people who don't see it that way, that easily. Spirits? They need proof, they are skeptical. One time I talked with some white friends for nearly two hours straight about ghosts. "Who knows? Ghosts might be real; sometimes there is proof," they said. They told me there are pictures now. Good, maybe now they will know. And that is where I learned to say "weird." Weird, superstitious, unnatural—Imagine, in this day and age.

The weeping was all of our pain—a collective wound

I remember my great-grandfather Makwyiapi in his tipi. Smelling the sweet grass, mother telling me it was holy and not to touch his things. I never really got to know him. Makwyiapi, "Wolf Old Man" his english was broken and he always spoke Blackfoot. He had a sweat² lodge outside his house. He was a medicine man and once cured a man of face cancer by dreaming of a certain mixture of herbs and roots. This came to him in a dream. I grew up knowing about dreams and remedies, spirits—the still black nights on the plains. I attended my first sweat when I was sixteen, it was high in the mountains. We went to a lodge afterwards. This first sweat was so miraculous, so refreshing and so magical—it was as though God had appeared before me and walked about and danced. It reinstated my sense of the Marvelous and also a sense of sacredness. I cried inside that sweat, it seemed as though I could never stop crying as though my heart was being tugged at and finally torn loose inside my chest. Other people cried too. So much emotion is expressed in the sweat and in the medicine lodge. And the weird thing about it is—you don't really know what it is you're crying about. The emotions seem to come out of some primeval cavity—some lonesome half-remembered place. It seems when I cried it was more than an individual pain. The weeping was all of our pain—a collective wound—it is larger than each individual. In the sweat it seems as though we all remember a past—a collective presence—our past as Native people before being colonized and culturally liquidated.

Barrier between myself and my people

At age seven I had a wild crush on a girl a year younger than myself that lasted a whole year. I would stare at her picture in the second grade yearbook and cry. I drew her pictures of dragons and gave them to her. It seemed a bit odd to me, but I wanted to marry her. I felt as though I was the only girl who'd ever felt these things. Perhaps there had been a mistake. I decided it would be better to be a boy and I stayed awake at night praying to turn into one. If I was a boy it would be easier to be a superhero and to be president. Finally—I decided to remain a girl and make the best of it.

We moved and I left her behind—but the memory of that early, intense feeling stayed on. It seemed so natural and heartfelt and it scared me a little. I was already becoming aware of my emotions as a lesbian—as different.

That is one of the barriers between myself and the reserve. How to explain, who can I tell, should I tell anyone? I grew up with these people, my relatives, my cousins, my aunts and uncles—various friends. I grew up loving that land and always needing to return there. In '77 I lived there for two months. I went out to Babb and drank at the Indian bar, I went to sweats (not right after partying however—as you have to either give up drinking completely or wait four days after last imbibing before entering the sweat lodge). I'd chase horses—go get them to ride, I jogged on the plains (all the while watching for bulls which might chase me) and hung around the house—reading, watching television, and cleaning. I felt the ennui of reserve life, the timelessness, I also sensed conservatism and a limitation. People expected me to be more tied to my parents than I am, to want to live close to them, to feel more homesick at the age of twenty for my mother and father. And yet sometimes I feel almost crippled by a homesickness inside me.

There is something sturdy and healthy about extended families, the way people care for each other, the way they depend upon and take care of one another. I feel lucky to have been touched by such a situation while growing up. But now, I would find that hard to live with. More than anything because it is patriarchal, women have a certain limited role (as do men), and I am gay. Perhaps in the old days, in some way or other I could have fit in there. But today, my lesbianism has become a barrier between myself and my people. What to say when my grandmother or aunt asks if I've met a boyfriend. The perennial lesbian problem—how to tell the folks and what to tell them.

It is hard to be around other people talking about their lives and not be able to talk about your own in the same way. It causes a false and painful separateness—which I'll have to live with and ignore until I know how and what to do otherwise.

You will return to the Indian way

I lived at the North End for about a year. I was five. We had no running water so when we bathed we got water from a nearby river. For a year

I enjoyed the nearby hills where there are supposed to be spirits. Now the river is thick with pollution from a factory upstream, the grass has grown tall around the old house, my grandfather has been dead twelve years. Still, each year my family visits the reserve.

Once an uncle of mine came to me in a dream, he picked me up as though I was a child saying, "Apoyakee, Apoyakee when are you going to come home and take care of the little ones?" Apoyakee is my Blackfoot name given to me by my grandpa, Shade. It means, "Light or fair-haired woman," obviously given to me because of my light hair (I was blonde as a child, the only fair complected person in my family).

Off and on, I think of going back "home" to live for a good six to twelve months. Work, have a good time, learn Blackfoot, learn how to set up a sweat, how to open up a medicine bundle, maybe learn the handgame and some songs.

Five years ago I dreamt myself walking out of my home in Littleton and out to a flat, long desert. There, beneath a shelter of poles and sticks, an old Kainah woman sat, dressed in a kerchief and a long blue dress. Some strange looking pipes were being passed around, none of them were handed to me as none were quite right for me. These pipes were not holy or in any way recognizable to me as anything special. The old lady looked at me a long time, then she said, "You will return to the Indian way."

Notes

1. The Sundance.
2. A sweat is a religious purification ceremony.

"Gee, You Don't Seem Like an Indian from the Reservation"

Barbara Cameron

One of the very first words I learned in my Lakota language was *wasicu* which designates white people. At that early age, my comprehension of wasicu was gained from observing and listening to my family discussing the wasicu. My grandmother always referred to white people as the "wasicu sica" with emphasis on *sica*, our word for terrible or bad. By the age of five I had seen one Indian man gunned down in the back by the police and was a silent witness to a gang of white teenage boys beating up an elderly Indian man. I'd hear stories of Indian ranch hands being "accidentally" shot by white ranchers. I quickly began to understand the wasicu menace my family spoke of.

My hatred for the wasicu was solidly implanted by the time I entered first grade. Unfortunately in first grade I became teacher's pet so my teacher had a fondness for hugging me which always repulsed me. I couldn't stand the idea of a white person touching me. Eventually I realized that it wasn't the white skin that I hated, but it was their culture of deceit, greed, racism, and violence.

During my first memorable visit to a white town, I was appalled that they thought of themselves as superior to my people. Their manner of living appeared devoid of life and bordered on hostility even for one another. They were separated from each other by their perfectly, politely fenced square plots of green lawn. The only lawns on my reservation were the lawns of the BIA[1] officials or white christians. The white people always seemed so loud, obnoxious, and vulgar. And the white parents were either screaming at their kids, threatening them with some form of punishment or hitting them. After spending a day around white people, I was always happy to go back to the reservation where people followed a relaxed yet respectful code of relating with each other. The easy teasing and joking that were inherent with the Lakota were a welcome relief after a day with the plastic faces.

I vividly remember two occasions during my childhood in which I was cognizant of being an Indian. The first time was at about three years of age when my family took me to my first pow-wow. I kept asking my grandmother, "Where are the Indians? Where are the Indians? Are they going to have bows and arrows?" I was very curious and strangely excited about the prospect of seeing real live Indians even though I myself was one. It's a memory that has remained with me through all these years because it's so full of the subtleties of my culture. There was a sweet wonderful aroma in the air from the dancers and from the traditional food booths. There were lots of grandmothers and grandfathers with young children running about. Pow-wows in the Plains usually last for three days, sometimes longer, with Indian people traveling from all parts of our country to dance, to share food and laughter, and to be with each other. I could sense the importance of our gathering times and it was the beginning of my awareness that my people are a great and different nation.

The second time in my childhood when I knew very clearly that I was Indian occurred when I was attending an all white (except for me) elementary school. During Halloween my friends and I went trick or treating. At one of the last stops, the mother knew all of the children except for me. She asked me to remove my mask so she could see who I was. After I removed my mask, she realized I was an Indian and quite cruelly told me so, refusing to give me the treats my friends had received. It was a stingingly painful experience.

I told my mother about it the next evening after I tried to understand it. My mother was outraged and explained the realities of being an Indian in South Dakota. My mother paid a visit to the woman which resulted in their expressing a barrage of equal hatred for one another. I remember sitting in our pickup hearing the intensity of the anger and feeling very sad that my mother had to defend her child to someone who wasn't worthy of her presence.

I spent a part of my childhood feeling great sadness and helplessness about how it seemed that Indians were open game for the white people, to kill, maim, beat up, insult, rape, cheat, or whatever atrocity the white people wanted to play with. There was also a rage and frustration that has not died. When I look back on reservation life it seems that I spent a great deal of time attending the funerals of my relatives or friends of my family. During one year I went to funerals of four murder victims. Most of my non-Indian friends have not seen a dead body or been to a funeral. Death was so common on the reservation that I did not understand the implications of the high death rate until after I moved away and was surprised to learn that I've seen more dead bodies than my friends will probably ever see in their lifetime.

Because of experiencing racial violence, I sometimes panic when I'm the only non-white in a roomful of whites, even if they are my closest friends; I wonder if I'll leave the room alive. The seemingly copacetic gay world of San Francisco becomes a mere dream after the panic leaves. I think to myself that it's truly insane for me to feel the panic. I want to scream out my anger and disgust with myself for feeling distrustful of my white friends and I want to banish the society that has fostered those feelings of alienation. I wonder at the amount of assimilation which has affected me and how long my "Indianness" will allow me to remain in a city that is far removed from the lives of many Native Americans.

"Alienation" and "assimilation" are two common words used to describe contemporary Indian people. I've come to despise those two words because what leads to "alienation" and "assimilation" should not be so concisely defined. And I generally mistrust words that are used to define Native Americans and Brown People. I don't like being put under a magnifying glass and having cute liberal terms describe who I am. The "alienation" or "assimilation" that I manifest is often in how I speak. There isn't necessarily a third world language but there is an Indian way of talking that is an essential part of me. I like it, I love it, yet I deny it. I "save" it for when I'm around other Indians. It is a way of talking that involves "Indian humor" which I know for sure non-Indian people would not necessarily understand.

Articulate. Articulate. I've heard that word used many times to describe third world people. White people seem so surprised to find brown people who can speak fluent english and are even perhaps educated. We then become "articulate." I think I spend a lot of time being articulate with white people. Or as one person said to me a few years ago, "Gee, you don't seem like an Indian from the reservation."

I often read about the dilemmas of contemporary Indians caught between the white and Indian worlds. For most of us, it is an uneasy balance to maintain. Sometimes some of us are not so successful with it. Native Americans have a very high suicide rate.

> *When I was about 20, I dreamt of myself at the age of 25–26, standing at a place on my reservation, looking to the North, watching a glorious, many-colored horse galloping toward me from the sky. My eyes were riveted and attracted to the beauty and overwhelming strength of the horse. The horse's eyes were staring directly into mine, hypnotizing me and holding my attention. Slowly from the East, an eagle was gliding toward the horse. My attention began to be drawn toward the calm of the eagle but I still did not want to lose sight of the horse. Finally the two met with the eagle sailing into the horse causing it to disintegrate. The eagle flew gently on.*

I take this prophetic dream as an analogy of my balance between the white (horse) and Indian (eagle) world. Now that I am 26, I find that I've gone as far into my exploration of the white world as I want. It doesn't mean that I'm going to run off to live in a tipi. It simply means that I'm not interested in pursuing a society that uses analysis, research, and experimentation to concretize their vision of cruel destinies for those who are not bastards of the Pilgrims; a society with arrogance rising, moon in oppression, and sun in destruction.

Racism is not easy for me to write about because of my own racism toward other people of color, and because of a complex set of "racisms" within the Indian community. At times animosity exists between half-breed, full-blood, light-skinned Indians, dark-skinned Indians, and non-Indians who attempt to pass as Indians. The US government has practiced for many years its divisiveness in the Indian community by instilling and perpetuating these Indian vs. Indian tactics. Native Americans are the foremost group of people who continuously fight against premeditated cultural genocide.

I've grown up with misconceptions about Blacks, Chicanos, and Asians. I'm still in the process of trying to eliminate my racist pictures of other people of color. I know most of *my* images of other races come from television, books, movies, newspapers, and magazines. Who can pinpoint exactly where racism comes from? There are certain political dogmas that are excellent in their "analysis" of racism and how it feeds the capitalist system. To intellectually understand that it is wrong or politically incorrect to be racist leaves me cold. A lot of poor or working-class white and brown people are just as racist as the "capitalist pig." We are *all* continually pumped with gross and inaccurate images of everyone else and we *all* pump it out. I don't think there are easy answers or formulas. My personal attempts at eliminating my racism have to start at the base level of those mindsets that inhibit my relationships with people.

Racism among third world people is an area that needs to be discussed and dealt with honestly. We form alliances loosely based on the fact that we have a common oppressor, yet we do not have a commitment to talk about our own fears and misconceptions about each other. I've noticed that liberal, consciousness-raised white people tend to be incredibly polite to third world people at parties or other social situations. It's almost as if they make a point to SHAKE YOUR HAND or to introduce themselves and then run down all the latest right-on third world or Native American books they've just read. On the other hand it's been my experience that if there are several third world gay people at a party, we make a point of avoiding each other, and spend our time talking to the whites to show how sophisticated and intelligent we are. I've always wanted to introduce myself to other third world people but wondered how I would introduce myself or what would I say. There are so many things I would want to say, except sometimes I don't want to remember I'm Third World or Native American. I don't want to remember sometimes because it means recognizing that we're outlaws.

At the Third World Gay Conference in October 1979, the Asian and Native American people in attendance felt the issues affecting us were not adequately included in the workshops. Our representation and leadership had minimal input which resulted in a skimpy educational process about our struggles. The conference glaringly pointed out to us the narrow definition held by some people that third world means black people only. It was a depressing experience to sit in the lobby of Harambee House with other Native Americans and Asians, feeling removed from other third world groups with whom there is supposed to be this automatic solidarity and empathy. The Indian group sat in my motel room discussing and exchanging our experiences within the third world context. We didn't spend much time in workshops conducted by other third world people because of feeling unwelcomed at the conference and demoralized by having an invisible presence. What's worse than being invisible among your own kind?

It is of particular importance to us as third world gay people to begin a serious interchange of sharing and educating ourselves about each other. We not only must struggle with the racism and homophobia of straight white america, but must often struggle with the homophobia that exists within our third world communities. Being third world doesn't always connote a political awareness or activism. I've met a number of third world and Native American lesbians who've said they're just into "being themselves," and that politics has no meaning in their lives. I agree that everyone is entitled to "be themselves" but in a society that denies respect and basic rights to people because of their ethnic background, I feel that individuals cannot idly sit by and allow themselves to be co-opted by the dominant society. I don't know what moves a person to be politically active or to attempt to raise the quality of life in our world. I only know what motivates my political responsibility . . . the death of Anna Mae Aquash—Native American freedom fighter—"mysteriously" murdered by a bullet in the head; Raymond Yellow Thunder—forced to dance naked in front of a white VFW club in Nebraska—murdered; Rita Silk-Nauni—imprisoned for life for defending her child; my dear friend Mani Lucas-Papago—shot in the back of the head outside of a gay bar in Phoenix. The list could go on and on. My Native American History, recent and past, moves me to continue as a political activist.

And in the white gay community there is rampant racism which is never adequately addressed or acknowledged. My friend Chrystos from the Menominee Nation gave a poetry reading in May 1980, at a Bay Area feminist bookstore. Her reading consisted of poems and journal entries in which she wrote honestly from her heart about the many "isms" and contradictions in most of our lives. Chrystos' bluntly revealing observations on her experiences with the white-lesbian-feminist-community are similar to mine and are probably echoed by other lesbians of color.

Her honesty was courageous and should be representative of the kind of forum our community needs to openly discuss mutual racism. A few days following Chrystos' reading, a friend who was in the same bookstore overheard a white lesbian denounce Chrystos' reading as anti-lesbian and racist.

A few years ago, a white lesbian telephoned me requesting an interview, explaining that she was taking Native American courses at a local university, and that she needed data for her paper on gay Native Americans. I agreed to the interview with the idea that I would be helping a "sister" and would also be able to educate her about Native American struggles. After we completed the interview, she began a diatribe on how sexist Native Americans are, followed by a questioning session in which I was to enlighten her mind about why Native Americans are so sexist. I attempted to rationally answer her inanely racist and insulting questions, although my inner response was to tell her to remove herself from my house. Later it became very clear how I had been manipulated as a sounding board for her ugly and distorted views about Native Americans. Her arrogance and disrespect were characteristic of the racist white people in South Dakota. If I tried to point it out, I'm sure she would have vehemently denied her racism.

During the Briggs Initiative[2] scare, I was invited to speak at a rally to represent Native American solidarity against the initiative. The person who spoke prior to me expressed a pro-*Bakke*[3] sentiment which the audience booed and hissed. His comments left the predominantly white audience angry and in disruption. A white lesbian stood up demanding that a third world person address the racist comments he had made. The MC, rather than taking responsibility for restoring order at the rally, realized that I was the next speaker and I was also T-H-I-R-D-W-O-R-L-D!! I refused to address the remarks of the previous speaker because of the attitudes of the MC and the white lesbian that only third world people are responsible for speaking out against racism. *It is inappropriate for progressive or liberal white people to expect warriors in brown armor to eradicate racism.* There must be co-responsibility from people of color and white people to equally work on this issue. It is not just MY responsibility to point out and educate about racist activities and beliefs.

Redman, redskin, savage, heathen, injun, american indian, first americans, Indigenous peoples, natives, amerindian, native american, nigger, negro, black, wetback, greaser, mexican, Spanish, latin, hispanic, chicano, chink, oriental, asian, disadvantaged, special interest group, minority, third world, fourth world, people of color, illegal aliens—oh yes about them, will the US government recognize that the Founding Fathers (you know George Washington and all those guys) are this country's first illegal aliens.

We are named by others and we are named by ourselves.

Epilogue . . .

Following writing most of this, I went to visit my home in South Dakota. It was my first visit in eight years. I kept putting off my visit year after year because I could not tolerate the white people there and the rural-ness and poverty of the reservation. And because in the eight years since I left home, I came out as a lesbian. My visit home was overwhelming. Floods and floods of locked memories broke. I rediscovered myself there in the hills, on the prairies, in the sky, on the road, in the quiet nights, among the stars, listening to the distant yelps of coyotes, walking on Lakota earth, seeing Bear Butte, looking at my grandparents' cragged faces, standing under wakiyan, smelling the Paha Sapa (Black Hills), and being with my precious circle of relatives.

My sense of time changed, my manner of speaking changed, and a certain freedom with myself returned.

I was sad to leave but recognized that a significant part of myself has never left and never will. And that part is what gives me strength—the strength of my people's enduring history and continuing belief in the sovereignty of our lives.

Notes

1. Bureau of Indian Affairs.
2. The 1978 (ultimately defeated) California Proposition 6 would have banned gays and lesbians from working in California public schools. *(Editor, 2015)*
3. *Regents of the University of California v. Bakke* was a landmark decision by the US Supreme Court, which made impermissible the use of quotas on the basis of race, as part of UC's affirmative action admission policy. It also laid the groundwork for the eventual voter-approved elimination of affirmative action in California's university systems through Proposition 209 in 1996. *(Editor, 2015)*

"... And Even Fidel Can't Change That!"

Aurora Levins Morales

1

Cherríe, you asked me to write about internationalism, and at first it made sense . . . I'm a Latin woman in the United States, closely involved with Latin American movements in the rest of the continent. I *should* write about the connection. But when I tried, all I could think was: No, write about the separation.

2

For me the point of terror, the point of denial is the New York Puerto Rican. My mother was born in New York in 1930, raised in Spanish Harlem and the Bronx. I represent the generation of return. I was born deep in the countryside of Puerto Rico and except for four years when I was very young, lived there until I was 13. For my mother, the Barrio is safety, warmth. For me, it's the fear of racist violence that clipped her tongue of all its open vowels, into crisp, imitation British. She once told me her idea of hell was to be a single mother of two children under five in the South Bronx. I'm afraid of ever knowing what she meant.

Where I grew up, I fought battles to prove I was Puerto Rican with the kids who called me "Americanita," but I stayed on the safe side of that line: Caribbean island, not Portah Ricah; exotic tropical blossom, not spic—living halfway in the skin and separating myself from the dark, bad city kids in Nueva York.

3

The point of terror, of denial, the point of hatred is the tight dress stretched across my grandmother's big breasts, the coquettish, well-made-up smile: grandmother, aunt and greataunts all decked out in sex, talking about how I'm pretty, talking about how men are only good for one thing, hating sex and gloating over the hidden filthiness in everything, looking me over, in a hurry to find me a boyfriend, and in the same breath: "You can't travel alone! You don't know what men are like . . . *they only want one thing* . . ." Women teaching women our bodies are disgusting and dirty, our desires are obscene, men are all sick and want only one sickening thing from us. Saying, you've got to learn how to hold out on 'em just enough to get what you want. It's the only item you can put on the market, so better make it go far, and when you have to deliver, lie down and grit your teeth and bear it, because there's no escape.

4

And yet, I tell you, I love those women for facing up to the ugliness there. No romance, no roses and moonlight and pure love. You say pure love to one of these women and they snort and ask you what the man has between his legs and is it pure? I love these women for the bitch sessions that pool common knowledge and tell the young wife: "Oh, yes, the first time he cheated on me I tried that, too, but he just beat me. Listen, don't give him the satisfaction. The next time . . ." These women don't believe in the sanctity of the marriage bond, the inviolable privacy of the husband-wife unit. The cattiness is mixed with the information, tips. The misery is communal.

5

Claustrophobia. A reality I can't make a dent in . . . because it's the misery that's communal. The resistance is individual and frowned upon. It rocks the boat. How many times has a Latin woman stood up for me in private, then stabbed me in the back when the moment comes for the support that counts. How many times has a Latin woman used me to bitch to and then gone running to men for approval, leaving me in the lurch. The anger is real and deep. You have forced me to turn out of my own culture to find allies worthy of the name; you have forced me into a room full of Anglo women who nod sympathetically and say: "Latin men are soooo much worse than Anglo men . . . Why the last time I was in Mexico, you couldn't walk down the streets without some guy . . . It must be so hard for you to be a Latin feminist . . ." And not to betray you in the face of their racism, I betray myself, and in the end, you, by not saying: It's not the men who exile me . . . it's the women. I don't trust the women.

6

Points of terror. Points of denial. Repeat the story that it was my grand-mother who went to look at apartments. Light skinned, fine, black hair: I'm Italian, she would tell them, keeping the dark-skinned husband, keeping the daughters out of sight. I have pretended that pain, that shame, that anger never touched me, does not stain my skin. She could pass for Italian. She kept her family behind her. I can pass for anyone. Behind me stands my grandmother working at the bra and girdle factory, speaking with an accent, lying to get an apartment in Puertoricanless neighborhoods.

7

Piri Thomas' book *Down These Mean Streets* followed me around for years, in the corner of my eye on bus terminal bookracks. Finally, in a gritted teeth desperation I faced the damn thing and said, "OK, tell me." I sweated my way through it in two nights: Gang fights, knifings, robberies, smack, prison. It's the standard Puerto Rican street story, except *he* lived. The junkies could be my younger brothers. The prisoners could be them. I could be the prostitute, the welfare mother, the sister and lover of junkies, the child of alcoholics. There is nothing but circumstance and good English, nothing but my mother marrying into the middle class, between me and that life.

8

The image stays with me of my mother's family fleeing their puertori-canness, the first spies on the block, behind them, the neighborhoods collapsing into slums. There was a war, she told me. The enemy was only a step behind. I borrow the pictures from my other family, the nightmares of my Jewish ancestry, and imagine them fleeing through the streets. My mother never went back to look. This year she saw on television the ruins of the Tiffany Street of her childhood, unrecogniz-able, bombarded by poverty and urban renewal into an image of some European city: 1945. Like the Jews, like many people, the place she could have returned to has been destroyed.

9

I saw a baby once, the same age as my fat, crowing baby brother, then six months old. I was twelve, and under the influence of our Seventh

Day Adventist teacher some of the girls in the seventh grade took up a collection for two poor families in the neighborhood. We bought them each one bag of groceries. This baby was just a little bit of skin stretched over a tiny skeleton. It hardly moved. It didn't even cry. It just lay there. The woman's husband had left her. The oldest boy, he was 13 or 14, worked picking coffee to help out. When we came the younger kids hid in the mother's skirts and she just stood there, crying and crying.

I ran straight home when we left and the first thing I did was to find my brother and hug him very tightly. Then I spent the rest of the afternoon feeding him.

If something had happened to my father, the ghost over my mother's shoulder would have caught up with us. Papi was our middle-class passport. I grew up a professor's daughter, on the road to college, speaking good English. I can pass for anyone. Behind me stands my grandmother. Behind me lie the mean streets. Behind me my little brother is nothing but skin and skeleton.

10

Writing this I am browner than I have ever been. Spanish ripples on my tongue and I *want* the accent. I walk through the Mission drinking in the sounds. I go into La Borinqueña and buy *yautía* and *plátano* for dinner. Facing up to the terror, ending the denial, refusing to obey the rule: "Don't talk bad about your own people in front of anyone else." I have never learned to dance salsa. My body goes rigid when the music plays. Oh yes, I tap my feet, and now and then I do a few steps, swing around the room with someone who doesn't know more than I do . . . but if I'm in a Latin scene I freeze. I can't make my hips fluid or keep my feet from tripping. It's the perversion of sexuality that frightens me. It's the way the women around me exude a sexiness that has nothing to do with the heart. Of course Latin Women love as well as any other women . . . but while the chilliest Anglo-Saxon repression of sex pretends it simply doesn't exist, Latin repression says it's a filthy fact of life, use it for what it's worth . . . shake it in his face, wear it as a decoy. It's all over the floor and it's cold and savage. It's the hatred of the powerless, turned crooked.

11

Sitting in the kitchen in oh-so-white New Hampshire with old friends, mother and daughter, Ceci says, "It takes three generations. If you resolve your relationship with your mother you'll both change, and your daughter will have it easier, but *her* daughter will be raised differently. In the third generation the daughters are free." I'm not thinking then of this essay, but days later when I sit down again to work, the phrase keeps ringing: *In the third generation the daughters are free.*

12

Don't you think I've swallowed my mouthful of blood? It's different for a man. You're too stubborn . . . you've always wanted your own way. It was this way for my grandmother, it was this way for my mother, it was this way for me . . . because this is the way it is. God made men and women different and even Fidel can't change that! Anything is better than being alone.

—Older woman in *Portrait of Teresa*
Cuban film, 1979

My mother and I work to unravel the knot. The task is daily: bloody, terrifying and necessary, and filled with joy.

13

The relationship between mother and daughter stands in the center of what I fear most in our culture. Heal that wound and we change the world.
    A revolution capable of healing our wounds. If we're the ones who can imagine it, if we're the ones who dream about it, if we're the ones who need it most, then no one else can do it.

We're the ones.

I Walk in the History of My People

Chrystos

There are women locked in my joints
for refusing to speak to the police
My red blood full of those
arrested, in flight, shot
My tendons stretched brittle with anger
do not look like white roots of peace
In my marrow are hungry faces who live on land the whites don't want
In my marrow women who walk 5 miles every day for water
In my marrow the swollen faces of my people who are not allowed
to hunt
to move
to be

In the scars on my knee you can see children torn from their families
bludgeoned into government schools
You can see through the pins in my bones that we are prisoners
    of a long war

My knee is so badly wounded no one will look at it
The pus of the past oozes from every pore
The infection has gone on for at least 300 years
My sacred beliefs have been made pencils, names of cities, gas stations
My knee is wounded so badly that I limp constantly
Anger is my crutch
I hold myself upright with it
My knee is wounded
see
How I Am Still Walking

III

And When You Leave, Take Your Pictures with You

Racism in the Women's Movement

Betye Saar, *The Liberation of Aunt Jemima*, 1972
Mixed media assemblage, 11.75" × 8" × 2.75", signed
Collection of the University of California, Berkeley Art Museum;
purchased with the aid of funds from the National Endowment for the Arts
(selected by The Committee for the Acquisition of Afro-American Art)
Courtesy of Michael Rosenfeld Gallery, LLC, New York, NY
Photograph by Joshua Nefsky

And When You Leave,
Take Your Pictures with You

Racism in the Women's Movement

> *The reason racism is a feminist issue is easily explained by the inherent defi-*
> *nition of feminism. Feminism is the political theory and practice to free all*
> *women: women of color, working-class women, poor women, physically chal-*
> *lenged women, lesbians, old women, as well as white economically privileged*
> *heterosexual women. Anything less than this is not feminism, but merely*
> *female self-aggrandizement.*[1]

—Barbara Smith

We women of color are the veterans of a class and color war that is still escalating in the feminist movement. This section attempts to describe in tangible ways how, under the name of feminism, white women of economic and educational privilege have used that privilege at the expense of Third World women. Although the original intent of including a section in this anthology specifically about racism in the movement was to make a *connection* with white women, it *feels* now more like a separation.

Things have gotten worse. In academic and cultural circles, Third World women have become the subject matter of many literary and artistic endeavors by white women, and yet we are refused access to the pen, the publishing house, the galleries, and the classroom. "The lies, pretensions, the snobbery & cliquishness   The racism that bled through . . ." (Chrystos). Our traditional native cultures are ripped off from us and are displayed as the artifacts of "primitive" peoples by white Bohemian liberated women headed for the West Coast. In leftist feminist circles we are dealt with as a political issue, rather than as flesh and blood human beings. We represent the party line, but the truth is, "We're not as happy as we look/on their/wall" (Carrillo). We have had it with the word "*out*reach" referring to our joining racist white women's

57

organizations. The question keeps coming up—where exactly then, is *in*? It smells like "white" to us. We have had it.

Repeatedly acknowledged throughout this section and infusing the entire contents of this anthology is our understanding that theory alone cannot wipe out racism. We do not experience racism, whether directed at ourselves or others, theoretically. Neither do white women.

How does one then emotionally come to terms with racism? None of us in this book can challenge others to confront questions that we ourselves have not confronted. How do we deal with the ways in which this diseased society has infused our very blood systems? How do we take personal responsibility for our own racist actions and assumptions?

As Third World women we clearly have a different relationship to racism than white women, but all of us are born into an environment where racism exists. Racism affects all of our lives, but it is only white women who can "afford" to remain oblivious to these effects. The rest of us have had it breathing or bleeding down our necks. "Mama . . . Mama/ Get off that damn box and come home to me" (Rushin).

But you work with what you have, whatever your skin color. Racism is societal and institutional. It implies the power to implement racist ideology. Women of color do not have such power, but white women are born with it and the greater their economic privilege, the greater their power. This is how white middle-class women emerge among feminist ranks as the greatest propagators of racism in the movement. Rather than using the privilege they have to crumble the institutions that house the source of their own oppression—sexism, along with racism—they oftentimes deny their privilege in the form of "downward mobility," or keep it intact in the form of guilt. Fear is a feeling—fear of losing one's power, fear of being accused, fear of a loss of status, control, knowledge. Guilt is *not* a feeling. It is an intellectual mask to a feeling. Fear is real. Possibly this is the emotional, non-theoretical place from which serious anti-racist work among white feminists can begin.

The women writing here are committed feminists.[2] We are challenging white feminists to be accountable for their racism because at the base we still *want* to believe that they really *want* freedom for *all* of us. The letter from Audre Lorde to Mary Daly appearing in this section is an example to all of us of how we as feminists can criticize each other. It is an act of love to take someone at her word, to expect the most out of a woman who calls herself a feminist—to challenge her as you yourself wish to be challenged.

As women, we all know oppression on some level. We must use this knowledge, as Rosario Morales suggests, to "identify, understand, and feel with the oppressed as a way out of the morass of racism and guilt."

59

. . . . For "We are all in the same boat."
And it is sinking fast.

Notes

1. From a talk given at the closing session at the National Women's Studies Association (NWSA) Conference, May 1979; appeared in *Frontiers* 5, no. 1 (1980).
2. In our commitment to feminism, the specificity of how each of the writers herein experiences racism—its physicality and ill spirit—is given uncensored voice. The late 1970s and early 1980s was one of the most virulent periods of discord between white women and women of color in the movement, due in part to the truly "minority" position women of color—especially lesbians—held in the feminist organizations. By 1980, we were still in the early stages of organizing autonomously as "feminists of color" and had just begun to politically find one another in significant numbers. *Bridge* was part of that discovery. *(Editor, 2015)*

And When You Leave, Take Your Pictures with You

Jo Carrillo

Our white sisters
radical friends
love to own pictures of us
sitting at a factory machine
wielding a machete
in our bright bandanas
holding brown yellow black red children
reading books from literacy campaigns
holding machine guns bayonets bombs knives

Our white sisters
radical friends
should think
again.
Our white sisters
radical friends
love to own pictures of us
walking to the fields in hot sun
with straw hat on head if brown
bandana if black
in bright embroidered shirts
holding brown yellow black red children
reading books from literacy campaigns
smiling.
Our white sisters radical friends
should think again.
No one smiles
at the beginning of a day spent
digging for souvenir chunks of uranium
of cleaning up after
our white sisters
radical friends

And when our white sisters
radical friends see us

in the flesh
not as a picture they own,
they are not quite as sure
if
they like us as much.
We're not as happy as we look
on
their
wall.

Beyond the Cliffs of Abiquiu[1]

Jo Carrillo

She calls you a rock.
He calls you a rock.
They both agree that you
are unworthy
of anything
but a slow death.

Her skin is white;
more parched than
the land she hates.
Silver fades into her arm
turquoise matches
nothing
more than her
eyes
but she wears it.

two cliffs little trees lots of rocks
is this land nothing but a rock? She asks
while gracefully walking back to her
MG

OH, yes I know, I live here
in this desert
and let me tell you. . . !
The whole place is
parched.
Just one great big rock.

Let me see,
do I have time to put on my
my
my
squash blossom.

It's Authentic Navajo Indian Laguna Pueblo
design from

Buen Muir Indian Trading Post
completely
staffed
by
whites
except of course
for the janitor.

How can it be
that the mines
the uranium cancer causing dangerous radon gas emitting mines
are worked by Navajos and other assorted
types
and the trading posts
are all
all
worked over
by whites?

The mines belong to them
too;
don't enjoy the work as much?
Rather sell Authentic Navajo Hopi Zuni Indian made
real
live
Laguna Santa Ana Santo Domingos?

It's
less
of a mess.

Oh, those Indians.
They are
all
just
drunks.
Can't even go through Gallup
without seeing at least
at least
at least
ten of them.
Oh, let's step into this Navajo rug shop
while we're here.

Bet you don't have *that*
in San Francisco Los Angeles New York
Albuquerque.
They are really lovely rugs
my whole house is done
in
Navajo rugs
it's adobe
in Corrales
by the river
lots of
rich
whites
with Authentic Navajo Hopi Zuni Indian made real live
Laguna Santa Ana Santo Domingo
artifacts.

There is a village
over
that
hill.

Note

1. My poem to the land that, along with South Dakota, is a "proposed National
    Sacrifice" area for energy (uranium, coal, coal gasification, etc.).

I Don't Understand Those Who Have Turned Away from Me

Chrystos

5:23 a.m.—May 1980

   I am afraid of white people   Never admitted that before
deep secret
   I think about all the white women I knew in San Francisco
Women with Master's degrees from Stanford University & cars that daddy
bought, women with straight white teeth & clear skins from thousands
of years of proper nutrition   They chose to be poor   They were
quite convincing in the role of oppressed victim   I want to tell them
to go down to Fillmore & Haight & tell somebody about it   Tell
Jim my old landlord who picked cotton since he was 6   moved here
for a better life lost his hearing & his teeth & his hair from working in
the shipyards for 35 years   The constant vibration of his drill on the
metal literally shook his teeth out   He went bald from always wearing
a safety helmet   He can't hear after years of that racket   He worked
so hard for 35 years & he is still poor   They live on Webster Street,
across from the projects   The house is an old Victorian which will
not be paid off unless he lives to be 89 which is unlikely.
   I read the funniest line in a health book yesterday   It said, that
for some "unknown" reason, more black people had hypertension than
white people   Not funny   No mystery   Most Indian people don't
usually live long enough to even GET hypertension   All the deaths I
carry so heavily   Faces I knew   Mani murdered in Phoenix by whites
outside a bar   whites who still have not gone to trial   Ron dying
of pneumonia   I still mourn him   death   None of my relatives
have a degree from Stanford   Neither did Jim   So those poor white
girls are still suffering mightily in my old home town of San Francisco
   It did not help that it occurred to me that no amount of education
was going to improve my lot in life if I didn't also change my attitude
about the society   I still think that 98% of what happens—liberal,
conservative or radical lesbian separatist is: bullshit   My attitude is
all I own   so I quit school
   All the schools & crazy houses I was in were simply brainwashing &
most of the feminist movement that I worked so hard to be a part of was
propaganda   This is heresy but it held no solution for me   Surely
Jane suffers oppression on her job because she is a woman   All the

65

problems and issues which feminism raises are valid & important   It simply does not give me any answers for correct behavior in my own life   Certainly I won't obey that lesbian mafia nonsense that one must dress in a certain way or cut off one's hair to be real   Those are all the most superficial rules   silly   I no longer believe that feminism is a tool which can eliminate racism—or even promote better understanding between different races & kinds of women   I have felt less understanding between different races & from many lesbian women than I do from some straight people   At least their heterosexual indifference allows me more freedom to be myself   I felt so much stricture & censorship from lesbians   I was supposed to be a carpenter to prove I was a real dyke   My differences were sloughed over   None of them came to a pow wow or an AIM[1] fundraiser to see about *me*   Above all I could not enjoy & love being a woman   Jane commented when I first met her that she didn't care for most lesbians because they didn't like women   didn't like themselves   Of course it is extremely difficult to like oneself in a culture which thinks you are a disease

Many of the lesbians I knew seemed to throw off the outer trappings of their culture & were very vocal in criticizing it   Yet, they had no joy, no new roads   Night after night in endless picky meetings discussing everyone's inadequacies & faults & the harm which men do or night after night in dreary body shop bars drinking themselves into a stupor I worked so hard as part of a local women's coffeeshop & bookstore, harder than I've ever worked   I ordered for the kitchen, & the art shows, did shifts, brought flowers, cleaned, met the pest man & phone man, did entertainment, washed a million coffee cups   Recently someone told me that a young lesbian whose parents have given her a law practice, commented that she remembered me   I didn't work she said   all I did was talk to people   I remember her too   she was one of the thousands of women whose names & faces I memorized & tried to understand only to have them disappear after 3 months or whenever they found a lover   After 3 1/2 years I had so little left of myself   so many bitter memories of women who disrespected me & others   A woman who called herself a communist but supported capitalist enterprises of women, rather than our brave collective worker-owned effort The lies, pretensions, the snobbery & cliquishness The racism which bled through every moment at every level   The terrifying & useless struggle to be accepted   The awful gossip, bitchiness, backbiting & jealousy   The gross lack of love

I left the women's movement utterly drained   I have no interest in returning   My dreams of crossing barriers to true understanding were false   Most of the white women I thought I was close to want nothing to do with me now   Perhaps white women are so rarely loyal because they do not have to be   There are thousands of them to pick up & discard   No responsibility to others   The bathing beauties They want the status of reality & respect without labor   Respect us simply because we exist   Give us what we want now   My bitterness distorts my words

I don't understand those who turned away from me

Note

1. American Indian Movement.

Asian Pacific American Women and Feminism

Mitsuye Yamada

Most of the Asian Pacific American women I know agree that we need to make ourselves more visible by speaking out on the condition of our sex and race on certain political issues that concern us. Some of us feel that visibility through the feminist perspective is the only logical step for us. However, this path is fraught with problems that we are unable to solve among us, because in order to do so, we need the help and cooperation of the white feminist leaders, the women who coordinate programs, direct women's buildings, and edit women's publications throughout the county. Women's organizations tell us they would like to have us "join" them and give them "input." These are the better ones; at least they know we exist and feel we might possibly have something to say of interest to them, but every time I read or speak to a group of people about the condition of my life as an Asian Pacific woman, it is as if I had never spoken before, as if I were speaking to a brand new audience of people who had never known an Asian Pacific woman who is other than the passive, sweet etc. stereotype of the "Oriental" woman.

When Third World women are asked to speak representing our racial or ethnic group, we are expected to move, charm or entertain, but not to educate in ways that are threatening to our audiences. We speak to audiences that sift out those parts of our speech (if what we say does not fit the image they have of us), come up to shake our hands with "That was lovely my dear, just lovely," and go home with the same mindset they come in with. No matter what we say or do, the stereotype still hangs on. I am weary of starting from scratch each time I speak or write, as if there were no history behind us, of hearing that among the women of color, Asian women are the least political, or the least oppressed, or the most polite. It is too bad not many people remember that one of the two persons in Seattle who stood up to contest the constitutionality of the Evacuation Order in 1942 was a young Japanese American woman. As individuals and in groups, we Asian Pacific women have been (more intensively than ever in the past few years) active in community affairs and speaking and writing about our activities. From the highly political writings published in *Asian Women* in 1971 (incisive and trenchant articles, poems, and other pieces), to more recent voices from the Basement Workshop in New York City to Unbound Feet in San Francisco, as well as those Asian Pacific women showcased at the Asian Pacific Women's Conferences in New York, Hawaii and California this year, these all tell us we *have* been active and vocal. And yet, we continue to hear, "Asian women are of course traditionally not attuned to being political," as if most other women are; or that Asian women are too happily bound to their traditional roles as mothers and wives, as if the same cannot be said of a great number of white American women among us.

When I read in *Plexus* recently that at a Workshop for Third World women in San Francisco, Cherríe Moraga exploded with "What each of us needs to do about what we don't know is to go look for it," I felt like standing up and cheering her. She was speaking at the Women's Building to a group of white sisters who were saying, in essence, "It is *your* responsibility as Third World women to teach *us*." If the majority culture knows so little about us, it must be *our* problem, they seem to be telling us; the burden of teaching is on us. I do not want to be unfair; I know individual women and some women's groups that have taken on the responsibility of teaching themselves through reaching out to women of color, but such gestures by the majority of women's groups are still tentatively made because of the sometimes touchy reaction of women who are always being asked to be "tokens" at readings and workshops.

Earlier this year, when a group of Asian Pacific American women gathered together in San Francisco poet Nellie Wong's home to talk about feminism, I was struck by our general agreement on the subject of feminism *as an ideal*. We all believed in equality for women. We agreed that it is important for each of us to know what it means to be a woman in our society, to know the historical and psychological forces that have shaped and are shaping our thoughts, which in turn determine the directions of our lives. We agreed that feminism means a commitment to making changes in our own lives and a conviction that as women we have the equipment to do so. One by one, as we sat around the table and talked (we women of all ages ranging from our early twenties to the mid-fifties, single and married, mothers and lovers, straight women and lesbians), we knew what it was we wanted out of feminism, and what it was supposed to mean to us. For women to achieve equality in our society, we agreed, we must continue to work for a common goal.

But there was a feeling of disappointment in that living room toward the women's movement as it stands today. One young woman said she had made an effort to join some women's groups with high expectations but came away disillusioned because these groups were not receptive to the issues that were important to her as an Asian woman. Women in these groups were, she said, "into pushing their own issues" and were no different from the other organizations that imposed opinions and goals on their members rather than having them shaped by the needs of the members in the organizations. Some of the other women present said that they felt the women's organizations with feminist goals are still "a middle-class women's thing." This pervasive feeling of mistrust toward the women in the movement is fairly representative of a large group of women who live in the psychological place we now call Asian Pacific America. A movement that fights sexism in the social structure must deal with racism, and we had hoped the leaders in the women's movement would be able to see the parallels in the lives of the women of color and themselves, and would "join" *us* in our struggle and give *us* "input."

It should not be difficult to see that Asian Pacific women need to affirm our own culture while working within it to change it. Many of the leaders in the women's organizations today had moved naturally from civil rights politics of the '60s to sexual politics, while very few of the Asian Pacific women who were involved in radical politics during the same period have emerged as leaders in these same women's organizations. Instead they have become active in groups promoting ethnic identity, most notably ethnic studies in universities, ethnic theater groups or ethnic community agencies. This doesn't mean that we have placed our loyalties on the side of ethnicity over womanhood. The two are not at war with one another; we shouldn't have to sign a "loyalty oath" favoring one over the other. However, women of color are often made to feel that we must make a choice between the two.

If I have more recently put my energies into the Pacific Asian American Center (a job center for Asians established in 1975, the only one of its kind in Orange County, California) and the Asian Pacific Women's Conferences (the first of its kind in our history), it is because the needs in these areas are so great. I have thought of myself as a feminist first, but my ethnicity cannot be separated from my feminism.

Through the women's movement, I have come to truly appreciate the meaning of my mother's life and the lives of immigrant women like her. My mother, at nineteen years of age, uprooted from her large extended family, was brought to this country to bear and raise four children alone. Once here, she found that her new husband who had been here as a student for several years prior to their marriage was a bachelor at heart and had no intention of changing his lifestyle. Stripped of the protection and support of her family, she found the responsibilities of raising us alone in a strange country almost intolerable during those early years. I thought for many years that my mother did not love us because she often spoke of suicide as an easy way out of her miseries. I know now that for her to have survived "just for the sake" of her children took great strength and determination.

If I digress it is because I, a second-generation Asian American woman who grew up believing in the American Dream, have come to know who I am through understanding the nature of my mother's experience; I have come to see connections in our lives as well as the lives of many women like us, and through her I have become more sensitive to the needs of Third World women throughout the world. We need not repeat our past histories; my daughters and I need not merely survive with strength and determination. We can, through collective struggle, live fuller and richer lives. My politics as a woman are deeply rooted in my immigrant parents' and my own past.

Not long ago at one of my readings a woman in the audience said she was deeply moved by my "beautifully tragic but not bitter camp poems which were apparently written long ago,"[1] but she was distressed to hear my poem "To a Lady." "Why are you, at this late date, so angry, and why are you taking it so personally?" she said. "We need to look to the future and stop wallowing in the past so much." I responded that this poem *is not* all about the past. I am talking about what is happening to us right now, about our nonsupport of each other, about our noncaring about each other, about not seeing connections between racism and sexism in our lives. As a child of immigrant parents, as a woman of color in a white society and as a woman in a patriarchal society, what is personal to me *is* political.

These are the connections we expected our white sisters to see. It should not be too difficult, we feel, for them to see why being a feminist activist is more dangerous for women of color. They should be able to see that political views held by women of color are often misconstrued as being personal rather than ideological. Views critical of the system held by a person in an "out group" are often seen as expressions of personal angers against the dominant society. (If they hate it so much here, why don't they go back?) Many lesbians I know have felt the same kind of frustration when they supported unpopular causes regarded by their critics as vindictive expressions to "get back" at the patriarchal system. They, too, know the disappointments of having their intentions misinterpreted.

In the 1960s when my family and I belonged to a neighborhood church, I became active in promoting the Fair Housing Bill, and one of my church friends said to me, "Why are you doing this to us? Haven't you and your family been happy with us in our church? Haven't we treated you well?" I knew then that I was not really part of the church at all in the eyes of this person, but only a guest who was being told I should have the good manners to behave like one.

Remembering the blatant acts of selective racism in the past three decades in our country, our white sisters should be able to see how tenuous our position in this country is. Many of us are now third- and fourth-generation Americans, but this makes no difference; periodic conflicts involving Third World peoples can abruptly change white Americans' attitudes toward us. This was clearly demonstrated in 1941 to the Japanese Americans who were in hot pursuit of the great American Dream, who went around saying, "Of course I don't eat Japanese food, I'm an American." We found our status as true-blooded Americans was only an illusion in 1942 when we were singled out to be imprisoned for the duration of the war by our own government.

The recent outcry against the Iranians because of the holding of American hostages tells me that the situation has not changed since 1941.[2] When I hear my students say "We're not against the Iranians here who are minding their own business. We're just against those ungrateful ones who overstep our hospitality by demonstrating and badmouthing our government," I know they speak about me.

Asian Pacific American women will not speak out to say what we have on our minds until we feel secure within ourselves that this is our home too; and until our white sisters indicate by their actions that they want to join us in our struggle because it is theirs also. This means a commitment to a truly communal education where we learn from each other because we want to learn from each other, the kind of commitment we do not seem to have at the present time. I am still hopeful that the women of color in our country will be the link to Third World women throughout the world, and that we can help each other broaden our visions.

Notes

1. Mitsuye Yamada. *Camp Notes and Other Poems* (San Francisco: Shameless Hussy Press, 1976).
2. The "Iran Hostage Crisis" began on November 4, 1979, with the siege of the US Embassy in Tehran. Captors demanded the extradition of the Shah from the United States in order to stand trail for his crimes against the Iranian people. Fifty-two US citizens were held for 444 days. *(Editor, 2015)*

"—But I Know You, American Woman"

Judit Moschkovich

I am Latina, Jewish, and an immigrant (all at once). When I tell people who I am, I usually see a puzzled look on their face. I am likely to tell them, "I realize that you are a little confused by me—how I can be both Jewish and Latin American at the same time—but just take my word for it. It is possible!

The preceding words were originally written in response to a letter which appeared in a women's newspaper with national distribution. This letter reflected the blatant ignorance most Anglo-American women have of Latin cultures. My response was directed to all women of the dominant American culture.[1] The Anglo woman's letter represented spoken and unspoken views and feelings that I have repeatedly encountered in many Anglo-American women.

My immediate reaction to reading the letter was: *don't speak about someone/something unless you can admit your ignorance on the subject.* Or, "you don't know me, but I know you, American women."

I believe that lack of knowledge about other cultures is one of the basis for cultural oppression. I do not hold any individual American woman responsible for the roots of this ignorance about other cultures; it is encouraged and supported by the American educational and political system, and by the American media. I do hold every woman responsible for the *transformation* of this ignorance.

In her letter, the Anglo woman seemed to ask for information about Latin culture.[2] She wanted to know what we want as Latin people, what we are struggling for, etc. First of all, it is hard for me to respond to even a simple request for more information about Latin cultures without experiencing strong and conflicting feelings. We've all heard it before: *it is not the duty of the oppressed to educate the oppressor.* And yet, I often do feel pressured to become an instructor, not merely a "resource person." I don't usually hear, "Hey, what do you think of the work of such and such Latin American feminist author," but rather, "Teach me everything you know." Latin American women write books, music, etc. A great deal of information about Latin America is readily available in most libraries and bookstores. I say: read and listen. We may, then, have something to share.

Second, it is very hard to respond to a request for information when it follows paragraph after paragraph that belittle and insult Latin culture. Anyone who was raised and educated in this country has a very good chance of being ignorant about other cultures, whether they be minority cultures in this country or those of other countries. It's a sort of cultural isolationism, a way of life enforced on the people in this country so as to let them have a free conscience with respect to how they deal with the rest of the world or with subcultures in America. Notice the lack of emphasis on learning other languages, and the lack of knowledge even about where other countries are located. Often, I am asked questions like, "Is Argentina in Europe or Africa?" or "Don't you speak Portuguese down there?" How can one feel guilt about screwing over someone/some country she knows nothing about?

Think of it in terms of men's and women's cultures: women live in male systems, know male rules, speak male language when around men, etc. But what do men really know about women? Only screwed up myths concocted to perpetuate the power imbalance. It is the same situation when it comes to dominant and non-dominant or colonizing and colonized cultures/countries/people. As a bilingual/bicultural woman whose native culture is not American, I live in an American system, abide by American rules of conduct, speak English when around English speakers, etc., only to be confronted with utter ignorance or concocted myths and stereotypes about my own culture.

My Latin culture means many things to me: the food I like to eat, the music I love, the books I read, the language I speak, the land and trees I remember in another country, the jokes I tell, how I am used to kissing and hugging people when I greet them, etc., etc., etc. . . . I could go on forever. It also means the things I'd like to change in Latin culture and I'm not speaking of changing men, but of changing *systems* of oppression. As a result of these changes, I do not foresee a culture-less vacuum because "all cultures are bad so I don't want any of them." That culture-less vacuum proposed would actually be the American culture of French Fries and Hamburgers (or soyburgers), American music on the radio (even if it's American women's music on a feminist radio show), not kissing and hugging every time you greet someone, etc. And it would ultimately still be the culture of exploitation of other countries/cultures combined with ignorance about them.

I want to illustrate more specifically some of the uninformed statements made in the Anglo woman's letter. The fascist government of Spain which she referred to (and suggests as Latin people's sole nation of heritage) was made possible by ample economic and political support from the US, as are multiple other fascist governments in the world right now, particularly in the Third World. When people are not democratically represented by their government, there is a real difference between the policies of that government and the country's people/culture. If one knows about the bitter struggle of the Spanish people against fascism during the Spanish Civil War, and during Franco's regime, one would never equate Spanish with fascist. I do not equate "American" with imperialist/racist, but I *do* equate American people who do *not* transform their ignorance about "non-dominant" cultures and their relationship to these cultures with imperialism and racism.

As to the "historical" accident that both North and South America are not dominated by Latin (i.e., non-Anglo) culture, I don't call the appropriation of Mexican land an accident, but an imperialist/expansionist move by the United States. Latin America is a mixture of Native, Black, Spanish and sometimes other European cultures, but it is *dominated* by American *mass* culture as Latin American economic systems are dominated by American interests (this applies to most Latin American countries, not all). In Latin America, in addition to our own cultural expressions, we watch American TV shows, listen to American music on the radio, wear American jeans (if we can afford them); in other words, we do anything that is economically profitable to America. In comparison, how often do you hear songs in Spanish on the radio in the US or see a Spanish show on TV? I'm not talking about radio or TV shows by and for the Latin community; I'm talking about *mainstream American* media.

No one will deny that the Spanish conquistadores did in fact conquer the native people of Latin America, and that the latter are still being oppressed there. It is important, however, to know that the Latin American people residing in the US are not some vague "Spanish" conqueror race, but are a multi-racial/cultural people of Native, Black and European background. Latin American culture is quite different from Anglo culture in that each country has retained and integrated the Indigenous cultures in food, music, literature, etc. For example the folk music of Argentina is largely Native Indian folk music, played on traditional and European instruments, speaking about traditional themes, using lyrics in Spanish and/or Indigenous languages. In the US, you don't often think of Native American music as "American folk music."

I'm sick and tired of continually hearing about the destructive aspects of Latin American culture, especially from women who don't know the culture and can only repeat well-known and worn out myths. Let Latina women tell you what's going on, the good and the bad. I've lived there and I damn well know what it's like. Listen to what I have to say about my culture, rather than believe hearsay, myths or racist stereotypes. No one ever talks about "terminally depressed Scandinavians," or the cut-throat competition instilled by American culture, or the lack of warmth and physical contact in Anglo culture. These are all destructive aspects of Anglo culture, and they cannot be ignored.

The unspoken question always seems to be: "Aren't Latin (or Black, etc.) men *more* macho and women *more* oppressed in that culture?" My answers to that are: 1) It is absurd to compare sexist oppression. Oppression is oppression in whatever form or intensity. 2) Sexist and heterosexist oppression is more or less visible depending on how communicative people in a culture are. That Anglo culture is more Puritan and less visibly expressive does not mean it is less sexist. 3) Most of Latin America is a land economically colonized by the US, and as such can't be compared with a colonizing culture (US). Women's condition in Latin America would be much better were they not living in colonized countries. 4) Most important, are we as feminists concerned with men or with women? There is always a women's culture within every culture. Why is everyone so willing to accept the very male view of Latin American culture as consisting simply of macho males and Catholic priests? There are scores of strong women living in Latin America today and our history is full of famous and lesser known strong women. Are they to be ignored as women have always been ignored?

Culture is not really something I have a choice in keeping or discarding. It is in me and of me. Without it I would be an empty shell and so would anyone else. There was a psychology experiment carried out once in which someone was hypnotized and first told they had no future; the subject became happy and as carefree as a child. When they were told they had no past they became catatonic.

Anglo people should realize when you say we should discard all cultures and start anew that you are speaking English with all its emotional and conceptual advantages and disadvantages.[3] You're not really about to change your taste in food, your basic style of relating to people, nor the way you talk.

I've heard many people say, "Immigrants to this country should learn English, act American, and stop trying to keep their own culture. That's what I would do if I went to another country!"   I say Bullshit!   Being an immigrant or a bicultural/bilingual person is something that can sometimes be understood only when experienced.[4] Would an American woman move to another country and not hold dear her memories of childhood places and people? Would she not remember with longing some special song or food that she has no access to in her new country? And would she not feel her communication limited, no matter how well she learned her second language, because some very deep, emotional things can only be expressed in one's native tongue? Or would she speak to her parents in her newly adopted language? From my personal experience I can say the American woman would experience all of these things. It is very hard to deny who you are, where you come from, and how you feel and express yourself (in the deepest possible sense) without ending up hating yourself.

In conclusion, I hope these words express my frustration. When Anglo-American women speak of developing a new feminist or women's culture, they are still working and thinking within an Anglo-American cultural framework. This new culture would still be just as racist and ethnocentric as patriarchal American culture. I have often confronted the attitude that anything that is "different" is male. Therefore if I hold on to my Latin culture I am holding on to hateful patriarchal constructs. Meanwhile, the Anglo woman who deals with the world in her Anglo way, with her Anglo culture, is being "perfectly feminist."

I would like us some day to get past the point of having to explain and defend our different cultures (as I am doing here). For that to happen the process of learning about other cultures must be a sharing experience. An experience where American women learn on their own without wanting to be spoon-fed by Latinas, but don't become experts after one book, one conversation, or one stereotype. It is a delicate balance which can only be achieved with caring and respect for each other.

Everything I have written about here has been from my personal experience as an immigrant to this country as a teenager. I'm by no means an expert, but these are issues I constantly deal with in myself and with others. I do not speak for all Latinas, or for all non-Anglo-American women. I would like to acknowledge the support and feedback I received from my friends throughout the writing of the original letter. They were all Anglo-American women (at the time there were no Latinas around me); and they cared enough to get beyond their guilt and/or ignorance.

Notes

1. When I say "American culture" I obviously do not include Afro-American, Native American, Asian American, Chicana, etc. I am speaking of the Anglo culture which dominates American society.
2. When I say "Latin culture" I mean Latin American cultures, which have a history of expression different from the European Latin cultures (French, Italian, etc.).
3. Let me illustrate some differences in language. English expository writing goes in a straight line (sound familiar?) from introductory paragraph, to thesis sentence, to conclusion. Spanish composition follows a form more like a zig-zag, sometimes deviating from straight, linear thinking. I am fighting against this when I write in English so I can be understood by English readers.
4. As a Latina and an immigrant, I cannot ignore the fact that many Hispanics have been in this country for more generations than Anglos. The Hispanic cultures in the West and Southwest were established long before their land was colonized by Anglos. The Hispanic people have as much right to their cultural heritage as any Anglo (if not more so, since they were here first).

The Black Back-Ups

Kate Rushin

This is dedicated to Merry Clayton, Fontella Bass,
Vonetta Washington, Carolyn Franklin, Yolanda McCullough,
Carolyn Willis, Gwen Guthrie, Helaine Harris and Darlene Love.
This is for all of the Black women who sang back-up for
Elvis Presley, John Denver, James Taylor, Lou Reed.
Etc. Etc. Etc.

I said Hey Babe
Take a Walk on The Wild Side
I said Hey Babe
Take a Walk on The Wild Side

And the colored girls say
Do dodo do do dodododo
Do dodo do do dodododo
Do dodo do do dodododo ooooo

This is for my Great-Grandmother Esther, my Grandmother
Addie, my Grandmother called Sister, my Great-Aunt Rachael
my Aunt Gladys, my Aunt Helen, my Aunt Ellie, my Cousin
Barbara, my Cousin Dottie and my Great-Great-Aunt Vene.

This is dedicated to all of the Black women riding on buses
and subways back and forth to The Main Line, Haddonfield,
Cherry Hill and Chevy Chase. This is for the women who
spend their summers in Rockport, Newport, Cape Cod and
Camden, Maine. This is for the women who open bundles of
dirty laundry sent home from ivy-covered campuses.

My Great-Aunt Rachel worked for The Carters
ever since I can remember.
There was *The Boy* whose name I never knew,
and there was *The Girl* whose name was Jane.

Great-Aunt Rachael brought Jane's dresses for me to wear.
    Perfectly Good Clothes.

And I should've been glad to get them.
    Perfectly Good Clothes.
No matter they didn't fit quite right.
    Perfectly Good Clothes
brought home in a brown paper bag
with an air of accomplishment and excitement.
    Perfectly Good Clothes
which I hated.

At school in Ohio,
I swear there was always somebody
telling me that the only person
in their whole house who listened and understood them,
despite the money and the lessons
was the housekeeper.
And I knew it was true,
but what was I supposed to say?

I know it's true. I watch her getting off the train,
moving slowly toward the Country Squire
station wagon with her uniform in her
shopping bag. And the closer she gets to the car,
the more the two little kids jump and laugh
and even the dog is about to turn inside out
because they just can't wait until she gets there.
Edna. Edna. Wonderful Edna.

But Aunt Edna to me, or Gram, or Miz Johnson,
or, Sister Johnson on Sundays.

And the colored girls say
Do dodo do do dodododo
Do dodo do do dodododo
Do dodo do do dodododo ooooo

This is for Hattie McDaniel, Butterfly McQueen and Ethel Waters.
This is for Sapphire, Saphronia, Ruby Begonia and Aunt Jemima.

Aunt Jemima on the pancake box.
Aunt Jemima on the pancake box?
AuntJemimaonthepancakebox?
Ainchamamaonthepancakebox?
Ain't chure Mama on the pancake box?

Mama . . . Mama . . .
Get off that damn box and come home to me.
And my Mama leaps off that box and
she swoops down in her nurses' cape
which she wears on Sundays and for
Wednesday Night Prayer Meeting
and she wipes my forehead and she
fans my face and she makes me a cup o' tea.
And it don't do a thing for my real pain except
she is my mama.

Mama Mommy   Mammy
Maa-mee   Maa-mee
I'd Walk a Mill-Yon Miles
For One o' Your Smiles . . .
This is for The Black Back-Ups.
This is for my mama and your mama,
my grandma and your grandma.
This is for the thousand thousand Black Back-Ups.

And the colored girls say
Do dodo do do dodododo
do   dodo
  dodo
        do
            do

The Pathology of Racism

A Conversation with Third World Wimmin

doris davenport

A few years ago in New Haven, I tried to relate to feminism through a local womon's[1] center (located in a Yale basement). I was politely informed that I should "organize" with Black wimmin. In other words, get out. I wanted to start several projects that would include more third world wimmin,[2] but I was told to talk to black wimmin about that. In short, white only. Then, the socialist study group I was interested in was suddenly closed just at the time I wanted to join. And once, in a wimmin's group when a discussion of men came up, it was revealed that half the white wimmin there feared black men, which included me (from the way they glared at me). In other words: *nigger, go home.*

Last year in Los Angeles, after volunteering to work for a local white feminist magazine, repeatedly offering my services and having my ideas and poems rejected, I was finally called to be one of the few token black wimmin at a reception for Ntozake Shange. And the beat, like the song says, goes on. From coast to coast, the feminist movement is racist, but that news is old and stale by now. It is increasingly apparent that the problem is white wimmin.

We, third world wimmin, always discuss this fact. (Frankly, I'm a little tired of it.) However, we usually discuss the varied, yet similar manifestations of racism, without going into *why* white wimmin are racist.

In this article, which I conceive of as a conversation with third world wimmin, I want to explore the whys. I don't see the point of further cataloguing my personal grievances against white racist feminists. You know. Whatever you have experienced, I have too. Extrapolate a little. I think that one of our limitations in dealing with this issue is that we stay on the surface. We challenge symptoms of the disease while neglecting the causes. I intend to examine the causes.

If I were a white feminist and somebody called me a racist, I'd probably feel insulted (especially if I knew it was at least partially true). It's like saying someone has a slimey and incurable disease. Naturally, I would be reactionary and take out my health department/liberal credentials, to prove I was clean. But the fact is, the word "racism" is too simplistic, too general, and too easy. You can use the word and not say that much, unless the term is explained or clarified. Once that happens, racism looks more like a psychological problem (or pathological aberration) than an issue of skin color.

By way of brief clarification, we experience white feminists and their organizations as elitist, crudely insensitive, and condescending. Most of the feminist groups in this country are examples of this elitism. (This anthology came to be as a result of that.) It is also apparent that white feminists still perceive us as the "Other," based on a menial or sexual image: as more sensual, but less cerebral; more interesting, perhaps, but less intellectual; and more oppressed, but less political than they are. (If you need specific examples of this, think about your *own* experiences with them.)

When we attend a meeting or gathering of theirs, we're seen in only one of two limited or oppressive ways: as being whitewashed and therefore sharing all their values, priorities, and goals, etc.; or, if we (even accidentally) mention something particular to the experience of black wimmin, we are seen as threatening, hostile, and subversive to their inter- ests. So when I say racist, these are some of the things I mean. I know this, and so do many white feminists. Because of their one-dimensional and bigoted ideas, we are not respected as feminists or wimmin. Their perverse perceptions of black wimmin mean that they continue to see us as "inferior" to them, and therefore, treat us accordingly. Instead of alleviating the problems of black wimmin, they add to them.

Although black and white feminists can sometimes work together for a common goal with warmth and support, and even love and respect each other occasionally, underneath there is still another message. That is that white feminists, like white boys and black boys, are threatened by us. Moreover, white feminists have a serious problem with truth and "accountability" about how/why they perceive black wimmin as they do.

For example, in a long, and long-winded article, "Disloyal to Civi- lization: Feminism, Racism, and Gynephobia,"[3] Adrienne Rich attempted to address an issue similar to this one. Instead she did what she accused other feminists of doing, she "intellectualized the issues." She evaded it, after apologetically (or proudly, it's hard to tell) saying that "the most unconditional, tender . . . intelligent love I received was given me by a black woman." (Translated, she had a black mammy as a child.[4]) Then, she hid behind a quasi-historical approach that defused the subject. After about fifteen pages, she got close, but apparently also got scared, and backed off. It seems she found it hard, after all, to tell the truth and be "accountable."

On the other hand, and as a brief but necessary digression, black wimmin don't always tell the whole truth about and to white wimmin. We know, for example, that we have at least three distinct areas of aversion to white wimmin which affect how we perceive and deal with them: aesthetic, cultural, and social/political. Aesthetically (& physically) we frequently find white wimmin repulsive. That is, their skin colors are unaesthetic (ugly, to some people). Their hair, stringy and straight, is unattractive. Their bodies: rather like misshapen lumps of whitish clay or dough, that somebody forgot to mold in-certain-areas. Furthermore, they have a strange body odor.

Culturally, we see them as limited and bigoted. They can't dance. Their music is essentially undanceable too, and unpleasant. Plus, they are totally saturated in western or white American culture with little knowledge or respect for the cultures of third world people. (That is, unless they intend to exploit it.) The bland food of white folks is legendary. What they call partying is too low keyed to even be a wake. (A wake is when you sit up all night around the casket of a dead person.) And it goes on and on.

Socially, white people seem rather juvenile and tasteless. Politically, they are, especially the feminists, naïve and myopic. Then too, it has always been hard for us (black folk) to believe that whites will transcend color to make political alliances with us, for any reason. (The women's movement illustrates this point.)

We have these aversions for one thing, because we saw through the "myth" of the white woman. The myth was that white wimmin were the most envied, most desired (and beautiful), most powerful (controlling white boys) wimmin in existence. The truth is that black people saw white wimmin as some of the least enviable, ugliest, most despised and least respected people, period. From our "close encounters" (i.e., slavery, "domestic" workers, etc.) with them, white people increasingly did seem like beasts or subnormal people. In short, I grew up with a certain kind of knowledge that all black folk, especially wimmim, had access to.

This knowledge led to a mixture of contempt and repulsion. I honestly think that most black feminists have some of these feelings. Yet, we constantly keep them hidden (at least from white wimmin), try to transcend them, and work towards a common goal. A few of us even see beyond the so-called privilege of being white, and perceive white wimmin as very oppressed, and ironically, invisible. This perception has sometimes been enough for us to relate to white feminists as sisters.

If *some* of us can do this, it would seem that some white feminists could too. Instead, they cling to their myth of being privileged, powerful, and less oppressed (or equally oppressed, whichever it is fashionable or convenient to be at the time) than black wimmin. Why? Because that is all they have. That is, they have defined, or re-defined, themselves and they don't intend to let anything or anybody interfere. Somewhere deep down (denied and almost killed) in the psyche of racist white feminists there is some perception of their real position: powerless, spineless, and invisible. Rather than examine it, they run from it. Rather than seek solidarity with wimmin of color, they pull rank within themselves. Rather than attempt to understand our cultural and spiritual differences, they insist on their own limited and narrow views. In other words, they act out as both "white supremacists" and as a reactionary oppressed group.

As white supremacists, they still try to maintain the belief that white is right, and "godly" (*sic*). No matter how desperately they try to overcome it, sooner or later it comes out. They really have a hard time admitting that white skin does not insure a monopoly on the best in life, period.

Such a "superiority complex" is obviously a result of compensation. I mean, if whites really knew themselves to be superior, racism could not exist. They couldn't be threatened, concerned, or bothered. I am saying that the "white supremacist" syndrome, especially in white feminists, is the result of a real inferiority complex, or lack of self-identity. Just as a macho male uses wimmin to define himself or to be sure he exists, white feminists use wimmin of color to prove their (dubious) existence in the world.

Anyone familiar with the literature and psychology of an oppressed or *colonized* group knows that as they initially attempt to redefine themselves, they react. Their immediate mental, spiritual, and physical environment is chaotic and confused. The fact is, white wimmin are oppressed; they have been "colonized" by white boys, just as third world people have. Even when white wimmin "belonged" to white boys they had no reality. They belonged as objects, and were treated as such. (As someone else has noted, the original model for colonization was the treatment of white wimmin.) Nobody has yet sufficiently researched or documented the collective psychology of oppressed white wimmin. So consider this as a thesis: they know. And so do I. The reality of their situation is the real pits. Lately, having worked free of the nominal and/or personal control of white boys, white wimmin are desperately reactionary. As a result, they identify with and encourage certain short-sighted goals and beliefs. Their infatuation with the word "power" in the abstract is an example of this: power to them mainly means external established power or control. They have minimal, if any, knowledge of personal power. But most important, as a reactionary oppressed group, they exhibit a strange kind of political bonding or elitism, where white wimmin are the only safe or valid people to be with; all others are threatening. Clearly, this state of mind is a political dead-end, and the reasons for it stem from their great confusion.

So this is my contribution to the conversation. The cause of racism in white feminists is their bizarre oppression (and suppression). This, I contend, is what lies beneath the surface. This pathological condition is what *they* have to admit and deal with, and what we should start to consider and act on. Too often, we discuss their economic freedom while ignoring other aspects of life. We sometimes dwell at length on their color, forgetting that they are still wimmin in a misogynist culture. They have been seriously mutated as a result.

In other words, their elitism and narrow-minded rigidity are defense mechanisms and that, in part, is why they create "alternatives" for themselves and put up psychological signs saying **white women only**. Part of the reason is fear, as a result of centuries of living with dogs and having no identities. Now, they are threatened by anyone different from them in race, politics, mannerisms, or clothing. It's partly a means of self-protection but that does not excuse it. Feminism either addresses itself to all wimmin, or it becomes even more so just another elitist, prurient white organization, defeating its own purposes.

As a partial solution to some of the above, and to begin to end some of the colossal ignorance that white feminists have about us, we (black and white feminists) could engage in "c.r."[5] conversations about and with each other. If done with a sense of honesty, and a sense of *humor*, we might accomplish something. If overcoming our differences were made a priority, instead of the back-burner issue that it usually is, we might resolve some of our problems.

On one hand, my experiences with white feminists prevent me from seeing dialogue as anything but a naïve beginning. I honestly see our trying to "break into" the white feminist movement as almost equivalent to the old, outdated philosophy of integration and assimilation. It is time we stopped this approach. We **know** we have no desire to be white. On the other hand, we know we have some valid concerns and goals that white feminists overlook. By now, in fact, a few of their organizations are as rigid and stagnant as any other "established" institution, with racism included in the by-laws.

So, sisters, we might as well give up on them, except in rare and individual cases where the person or group is deliberately and obviously more evolved mentally and spiritually. This is, un-racist. We should stop wasting our time and energy, until these wimmin evolve. Meanwhile, we can re-channel our energies toward ourselves.

We can start to develop a feminist movement based on the realities and priorities of third world wimmin. Racism would have to be a priority. Misogyny is another major problem of third world wimmin. Not only that, many of our communities are more homophobic (or "lesbophobic") than white ones. Also, a lot of our sisters are straight, and have no intention of changing. We cannot afford to ignore them and their needs, nor the needs of many third world wimmin who are both feminists and nationalists; that is, concerned with our sex and also our race. Finally, a lot of third world wimmin are ignorant about each other. We have yet to make our own realities known to ourselves, or anyone else. So we really do have a lot more to concentrate on beside the pathology of white wimmin. What we need to do is deal with us, first, then maybe we can develop a wimmin's movement that is more international in scope and universal in application.

It is time we stopped letting the rest of this oppressive society dictate our behavior, devour our energies, and control us, body and soul. It is time we dealt with our own energies, and our own revolutionary potential, like the constructive and powerful forces that they are. When we *do* act on our power and potential, there will be a *real* feminist movement in this country, one that will finally include all wimmin.

Notes

1. The spelling of "womon" was popular among some lesbian feminists in the 1970s and early '80s. It was used to symbolically "liberate" the nomenclature of the female sex from the word "man." *(Editor, 2015)*
2. As above: "wimmin" instead of "wo(men)." *(Editor, 2015)*
3. Adrienne Rich, *On Lies, Secrets, and Silence* (New York: Norton, 1979), 280.
4. Adrienne Rich writes "As a child raised in what was essentially the South, Baltimore in the segregated 1930s, I had from birth not only a white, but a black mother." (*Of Woman Born: Motherhood as Experience and Institution*: New York: Norton, 1976), 253. *(Editor, 2015)*
5. "Consciousness Raising." *(Editor, 2015)*

We're All in the Same Boat

Rosario Morales

November 1979
I am not white. I am not middle class.
I am white skinned and puertorican. I was born into the working class
and married into the middle class. I object to the label white and middle
class both because they don't include my working class life and my puertoricanness, but also because "white & middle class" stands for a kind of
politics. *Color and class don't define people or politics.* I get angry with those
in the women's movement and out of it who deal with class & color as
if they defined politics and people.

My experience in the Puerto Rican communist & independence
movements has made me suspicious of and angry at Puerto Rican (& other
Latin American) activist women. They have been sexist and supported
the macho line that we *needed to fight against imperialism first—only later
could we think about women as women.* I desperately want Latina women in
the feminist movement while I fear the entry of hispanic & often black
women because I fear they will play an anti-feminist role.

Racism is an ideology. Everyone is capable of being racist whatever
their color and condition. Only some of us are liable to racist attack.
Understanding the racist ideology—where and how it penetrates—is
what is important for the feminist movement, not "including" women of
color or talking about "including" men. *Guilt* is a fact for us all, white
& colored: an identification with the oppressor and oppressive ideology.
Let us, instead, identify, understand, and feel with the oppressed as a
way out of the morass of racism and guilt.

I want to be whole. I want to claim my self to be puertorican, and
US american, working class & middle class, housewife and intellectual,
feminist, marxist, and anti-imperialist. I want to claim my racism, especially that directed at myself, so I can struggle with it, so I can use my
energy to be a woman, creative and revolutionary.

April, 1980
This society this incredible way of living divides us by class by
color   It says   we are individual and alone and don't you forget
it   It says the only way out of our doom   of our sex our class our
race is some individual gift and character and hard work and then all
we get   all we ever get is to change class or color or sex   to rise

to bleach   to masculinize an enormous game of musical chairs and that's only at its fairy tale Horatio Alger best   that's only at its best

From all directions we get all the beliefs to go with these divisions we believe all kinds of things about: what real men really are   what women must want   what black people feel and smell like   what white people do and deserve   how rich people earn their comforts and cadillacs   how poor people get what's coming to them

O we are all racist   we are all sexist   some of us only some of us are the targets of racism of sexism of homophobia of class denigration but we all   all breathe in racism with the dust in the streets with the words we read and we struggle those of us who struggle we struggle endlessly endlessly to think and be and act differently from all that

Listen you and listen hard   I carry within me a vicious antisemite voice that says   jew him down   that says dirty jew that says things that stop me dead in the street and make the blood leave my face   I have fought that voice for 45 years   all the years that I lived with and among jews who are almost me   whose rhythms of speech and ways of laughing are close beside me   are dear to me   whose sorrows reach deep inside me   that voice that has tried to tell me that that love and identification are unreal   fake   cannot be   and I refuse it I refuse its message

I carry a shell   a white and crisp voiced shell to hide my brown golden soft spanish voiced inner self   to pass   to hide my puertoricanness

I carry a pole 18 inches long to hold me at the correct distance from black-skinned people

I carry hard metal armor with spikes   with shooting weapons in every joint   with fire breathing from every hole   to protect me   to prepare me to assault any man from 13 to 89

I am a whole circus by myself   a whole dance company with stance and posture for being in middle class homes   in upper class buildings   for talking to men   for speaking with blacks   for carefully angling and directing   for choreographing my way thru the maze of classes of people and places thru the little boxes of sex   race   class nationality   sexual orientation   intellectual standing   political preference   the automatic contortions   the exhausting camouflage with which I go thru this social space called

CAPITALIST PATRIARCHY

a daunting but oh so nicely covering name   this is no way to live Listen   listen with care   class and color and sex do not define people do not define politics   a class society defines people by class   a

racist society defines people by color   We   feminists   socialists   radicals   define people by their struggles against the racism
sexism   classism   that they harbor   that surrounds them

So stop saying that she acts that way because she's middle class
that that's all you can expect from that group because it's white   that
they're just men, quit it!

We know different things   some very much more unpleasant
things if we've been women poor black or lesbian or all of those   we
know different things depending on what sex what color   what lives
we live   where we grew up   What schooling   what beatings
with or without shoes   steak or beans   but what politics each of
us is going to be and do is anybody's guess

Being female doesn't stop us from being sexist   we've had to
choose early or late at 7 14 27 56 to think different   dress different   act different   to struggle   to organize   to picket   to
argue   to change other women's minds   to change our own
minds   to change our feelings   ours   yours and mine constantly
to change and change and change   to fight the onslaught   on our
minds and bodies and feelings

I'm saying that the basis of our unity is that in the most important
way we are all in the same boat   all subjected to the violent perni-
cious ideas we have learned to hate   that we must all struggle against
them and exchange ways and means   hints and how tos   that
only some of us are victims of sexism   only some of us are victims
of racism   of the directed arrows of oppression   but all of us are
sexist   racist   all of us.

An Open Letter to Mary Daly

Audre Lorde

Dear Mary,

Thank you for having *Gyn/Ecology* sent to me. So much of it is full of import, useful, generative, and provoking. As in *Beyond God the Father*, many of your analyses are strengthening and helpful to me. Therefore, it is because of what you have given to me in the past work that I write this letter to you now, hoping to share with you the benefits of my insights as you have shared the benefits of yours with me.

This letter has been delayed because of my grave reluctance to reach out to you, for what I want us to chew upon here is neither easy nor simple. The history of white women who are unable to hear black women's words, or to maintain dialogue with us, is long and discouraging. But for me to assume that you will not hear me represents not only history, but an old pattern of relating, sometimes protective and sometimes dysfunctional, which we, as women shaping our future, are in the process of shattering, I hope.

I believe in your good faith toward all women, in your vision of a future within which we can all flourish, and in your commitment to the hard and often painful work necessary to effect change. In this spirit I invite you to a joint clarification of some of the differences which lie between us as a black and a white woman.

When I started reading *Gyn/Ecology*, I was truly excited by the vision behind your words, and nodded my head as you spoke in your first passage of myth and mystification. Your words on the nature and function of the Goddess, as well as the ways in which her face has been obscured, agreed with what I myself have discovered in my searches through African myth/legend/religion for the true nature of old female power.

So I wondered, why doesn't Mary deal with Afrekete as an example? Why are her goddess-images only white, western-european, judeo-christian? Where was Afrekete, Yemanje, Oyo and Mawulisa? Where are the warrior-goddesses of the Vodun, the Dahomey Amazons and the warrior-women of Dan? Well, I thought, Mary has made a conscious decision to narrow her scope and to deal only with the ecology of western-european women.

Then I came to the first three chapters of your second passage, and it was obvious that you were dealing with non-european women, but only as victims and preyers-upon each other. I began to feel my history and my mythic background distorted by the absence of any images of my foremothers in power. Your inclusion of African genital mutilation was an important and necessary piece in any consideration of female ecology, and too little has been written about it. But to imply, however, that all women suffer the same oppression simply because we are women, is to lose sight of the many varied tools of patriarchy. It is to ignore how those tools are used by women without awareness against each other.

To dismiss our black foremothers may well be to dismiss where european women learned to love. As an African-American woman in white patriarchy, I am used to having my archetypal experience distorted and trivialized but it is terribly painful to feel it being done by a woman whose knowledge so much matches my own. As women-identified women, we cannot afford to repeat these same old destructive, wasteful errors of recognition.

When I speak of knowledge, as you know, I am speaking of that dark and true depth which understanding serves, waits upon, and makes accessible through language to ourselves and others. It is this depth within each of us that nurtures vision.

What you excluded from *Gyn/Ecology* dismissed my heritage and the heritage of all other non-european women, and denied the real connections that exist between all of us.

It is obvious that you have done a tremendous amount of work for this book. But simply because little material on non-white female power and symbol exists in white women's words from a radical feminist perspective, to exclude this aspect of connection from even comment in your work is to deny the fountain of non-european female strength and power that nurtures each of our visions. It is to make a point by choice.

Then to realize that the only quotations from black women's words were the ones you used to introduce your chapter on African genital mutilation, made me question why you needed to use them at all. For my part, I felt that you had in fact misused my words, utilized them only to testify against myself as a woman of color. For my words which you used were no more, nor less, illustrative of this chapter, than "Poetry Is Not a Luxury" or any number of my other poems might have been of many other parts of *Gyn/Ecology*.

So the question arises in my mind, Mary, do you ever really read the work of black women? Did you ever read my words, or did you merely finger through them for quotations which you thought might valuably support an already-conceived idea concerning some old and distorted connection between us? This is not a rhetorical question. To me this feels like another instance of the knowledge, crone-logy and work of women of color being ghettoized by a white woman dealing only out of a patriarchal western-european frame of reference. Even your words on page 49 of *Gyn/Ecology*: "The strength which Self-centering women find, in finding our Background, is our *own* strength, which we give back to our Selves" has a different ring as we remember the old traditions of power and strength and nurturance found in the female bonding of African women. It is there to be tapped by all women who do not fear the revelation of connection to themselves.

Have you read my work, and the work of other black women, for what it could give you? Or did you hunt through only to find words that would legitimize your chapter on African genital mutilation in the eyes of other black women? And if so, then why not use our words to legitimize or illustrate the other places where we connect in our being and becoming? If, on the other hand, it was not black women you were attempting to reach, in what way did our words illustrate your point for white women?

Mary, I ask that you be aware of how this serves the destructive forces of racism and separation between women—the assumption that the herstory and myth of white women is the legitimate and sole herstory and myth of all women to call upon for power and background, and that non-white women and our herstories are noteworthy only as decorations, or examples of female victimization. I ask that you be aware of the effect that this dismissal has upon the community of black women, and how it devalues your own words. This dismissal does not essentially differ from the specialized devaluations that make black women prey, for instance, to the murders even now happening in your own city.[1] When patriarchy dismisses us, it encourages our murderers. When radical lesbian feminist theory dismisses us, it encourages its own demise.

This dismissal stands as a real block to communication between us. This block makes it far easier to turn away from you completely than to attempt to understand the thinking behind your choices. Should the next step be war between us, or separation? Assimilation within a solely western-european herstory is not acceptable.

Mary, I ask that you re-member what is dark and ancient and divine within your self that aids your speaking. As outsiders, we need each other for support and connection and all the other necessities of living on the borders. But in order to come together we must recognize each other. Yet I feel that since you have so completely un-recognized me, perhaps I have been in error concerning you and no longer recognize you.

I feel you do celebrate differences between white women as a creative force towards change, rather than a reason for misunderstanding and separation. But you fail to recognize that, as women, those differences expose all women to various forms and degrees of patriarchal oppression, some of which we share, and some of which we do not. For instance, surely you know that for non-white women in this country, there is an 80 percent fatality rate from breast cancer; three times the number of unnecessary eventrations, hysterectomies and sterilizations as for white women; three times as many chances of being raped, murdered, or assaulted as exist for white women. These are statistical facts, not coincidences nor paranoid fantasies. I had hoped the lesbian consciousness of having been "other" would make it easier to recognize the differences that exist in the history and struggle of black women and white women.

Within the community of women, racism is a reality force within my life as it is not within yours. The white women with hoods on in Ohio handing out KKK literature on the street may not like what you have to say, but they will shoot me on sight. (If you and I were to walk into a classroom of women in Dismal Gulch, Alabama, where the only thing they knew about each of us was that we were both Lesbian/Radical/Feminist, you would see exactly what I mean.)

The oppression of women knows no ethnic nor racial boundaries, true, but that does not mean it is identical within those boundaries. Nor do the reservoirs of our ancient power know these boundaries, either. To deal with one without even alluding to the other is to distort our commonality as well as our difference.

For then beyond sisterhood, is still racism.

We first met at the MLA[2] panel, "The Transformation of Silence into Language and Action." Shortly before that date, I had decided never again to speak to white women about racism. I felt it was wasted energy, because of their destructive guilt and defensiveness, and because whatever I had to say might better be said by white women to one another, at far less emotional cost to the speaker, and probably with a better hearing. This letter attempts to break this silence.

I would like not to have to destroy you in my consciousness. So as a sister Hag, I ask you to speak to my perceptions.

Whether or not you do, I thank you for what I have learned from you. This letter is in repayment.

In the hands of Afrekete,
Audre Lorde
May 6, 1979

Notes

1. In the spring of 1979, twelve black women were murdered in the Boston area.
2. Modern Language Association.

The Master's Tools Will Never Dismantle the Master's House

Comments at "The Personal and the Political" Panel
(Second Sex Conference October 29, 1979)

Audre Lorde

I agreed to take part in a New York University Institute for the Humanities conference a year ago, with the understanding that I would be commenting upon papers dealing with the role of difference within the lives of American women; difference of race, sexuality, class, and age. For the absence of these considerations weakens any feminist discussion of the personal and the political.

It is a particular academic arrogance to assume any discussion of feminist theory in this time and in this place without examining our many differences, and without a significant input from poor women, black and third-world women, and lesbians. And yet, I stand here as a black lesbian feminist, having been invited to comment within the only panel at this conference where the input of black feminists and lesbians is represented. What this says about the vision of this conference is sad, in a country where racism, sexism and homophobia are inseparable. To read this program is to assume that lesbian and black women have nothing to say of existentialism, the erotic, women's culture and silence, developing feminist theory, or heterosexuality and power. And what does it mean in personal and political terms when even the two black women who did present here were literally found at the last hour? What does it mean when the tools of a racist patriarchy are used to examine the fruits of that same patriarchy? It means that only the most narrow perimeters of change are possible and allowable.

The absence of any consideration of lesbian consciousness or the consciousness of third world women leaves a serious gap within this conference and within the papers presented here. For example, in a paper on material relationships between women, I was conscious of an either/or model of nurturing which totally dismissed my knowledge as a black lesbian. In this paper there was no examination of mutuality between women, no systems of shared support, no interdependence as exists between lesbians and women-identified-women. Yet it is only in the patriarchal model of nurturance that women "who attempt to emancipate themselves pay perhaps too high a price for the results," as this paper states.

94

For women, the need and desire to nurture each other is not pathological but redemptive, and it is within that knowledge that our real power is rediscovered. It is this real connection, which is so feared by a patriarchal world. For it is only under a patriarchal structure that maternity is the only social power open to women.

Interdependency between women is the only way to the freedom which allows the "I" to "be," not in order to be used, but in order to be creative. This is a difference between the passive "be" and the active "being."

Advocating the mere tolerance of difference between women is the grossest reformism. It is a total denial of the creative function of difference in our lives. For difference must be not merely tolerated, but seen as a fund of necessary polarities between which our creativity can spark like a dialectic. Only then does the necessity for interdependency become unthreatening. Only within that interdependency of different strengths, acknowledged and equal, can the power to seek new ways to actively "be" in the world generate, as well as the courage and sustenance to act where there are no charters.

Within the interdependence of mutual (non-dominant) differences lies that security which enables us to descend into the chaos of knowledge and return with true visions of our future, along with the concomitant power to effect those changes which can bring that future into being. Difference is that raw and powerful connection from which our personal power is forged.

As women, we have been taught to either ignore our differences or to view them as causes for separation and suspicion rather than as forces for change. Without community, there is no liberation, only the most vulnerable and temporary armistice between an individual and her oppression. But community must not mean a shedding of our differences, nor the pathetic pretense that these differences do not exist.

Those of us who stand outside the circle of this society's definition of acceptable women; those of us who have been forged in the crucibles of difference; those of us who are poor, who are lesbians, who are black, who are older, know that *survival is not an academic skill*. It is learning how to stand alone, unpopular and sometimes reviled, and how to make common cause with those others identified as outside the structures, in order to define and seek a world in which we can all flourish. It is learning how to take our differences and make them strengths. *For the master's tools will never dismantle the master's house.* They may allow us temporarily to beat him at his own game, but they will never enable us to bring about genuine change. And this fact is only threatening to those women who still define the master's house as their only source of support.

Poor and third world women know there is a difference between the daily manifestations and dehumanizations of marital slavery and prostitution, because it is our daughters who line 42nd Street. The Black panelists' observation about the effects of relative powerlessness and the differences of relationship between black women and men from white women and men illustrate some of our unique problems as black feminists. If white american feminist theory need not deal with the differences between us, and the resulting difference in aspects of our oppressions, then what do you do with the fact that the women who clean your houses and tend your children while you attend conferences on feminist theory are, for the most part, poor and third world women? What is the theory behind racist feminism?

In a world of possibility for us all, our personal visions help lay the groundwork for political action. The failure of the academic feminists to recognize difference as a crucial strength is a failure to reach beyond the first patriarchal lesson. Divide and conquer, in our world, must become define and empower.

Why weren't other black women and third world women found to participate in this conference? Why were two phone calls to me considered a consultation? Am I the only possible source of names of black feminists? And although the black panelist's paper ends on an important and powerful connection of love between women, what about interracial co-operation between feminists who don't love each other?

In academic feminist circles, the answer to these questions is often "We did not know who to ask." But that is the same evasion of responsibility, the same cop-out, that keeps black women's art out of women's exhibitions, black women's work out of most feminists publications except for the occasional "Special Third World Women's Issue,"[1] and black women's texts off of your reading lists. But as Adrienne Rich pointed out in a recent talk, white feminists have educated themselves about such an enormous amount over the past ten years, how come you haven't also educated yourselves about Black women and the differences between us—white and black—when it is key to our survival as a movement?

Women of today are still being called upon to stretch across the gap of male ignorance, and to educate men as to our existence and our needs. This is an old and primary tool of all oppressors to keep the oppressed occupied with the master's concerns. Now we hear that it is the task of black and third world women to educate white women, in the face of tremendous resistance, as to our existence, our differences, our relative roles in our joint survival. This is a diversion of energies and a tragic repetition of racist patriarchal thought.

Simone de Beauvoir once said:

It is in the knowledge of the genuine conditions of our lives that we must draw strength to live and our reasons for acting.

Racism and homophobia are real conditions of all our lives in this place and this time. I urge each one of us here to reach down into that deep place of knowledge inside herself and touch that terror and loathing of any difference that lives there. See whose face it wears. Then the personal as the political can begin to illuminate all of our choices.

Note

1. *Conditions* of Brooklyn, NY, is a major exception. It has fairly consistently published the work of women of color before it was "fashionable" to do so. (*Editor, 1981*)

IV

Between the Lines

On Culture, Class, and Homophobia

Happy/L.A. Hyder, *New Country Daughter/Lebanese American*, 1981
Black and white photograph, originally printed from two negatives, 11" x 14"
Collection of the artist

Between the Lines

On Culture, Class, and Homophobia

I do not believe/our wants have made all our lies/holy.

—Audre Lorde[1]

What lies between the lines are the things that women of color do not tell each other. There are reasons for our silences: the change in generation between mother and daughter, the language barriers between us, our sexual identity, the educational opportunities we had or missed, the specific cultural history of our race, the physical conditions of our bodies and our labor.

As Audre Lorde states in the preceding section, "Difference is that raw and powerful connection from which our personal power is forged." It is critical now that Third World feminists begin to speak directly to the specific issues that separate us. We cannot afford to throw ourselves haphazardly under the rubric of "Third World Feminism" only to discover later that there are serious differences between us which could collapse our dreams, rather than fuse alliances.

As Third World women, we understand the importance, yet limitations of race ideology to describe our total experience. Culture differences get subsumed when we speak of "race" as an isolated issue: where does the Black Puerto Rican sister stake out her alliance in this country, with the Black community or the Latina? And color alone cannot define her status in society. How do we compare the struggle of the middle-class Black woman with those of the light-skinned Latina welfare mother? Further, how each of us perceives our ability to be radical against this oppressive state is largely affected by our economic privilege and our specific history of colonization in the US. Some of us were brought here centuries ago as slaves, others had our land of birthright taken away from us, some of us are the daughters and granddaughters of immigrants, others of us are still newly immigrated to the US.

Repeated throughout this section is each woman's desire to have all of her sisters of color actively identified and involved as feminists. One of the biggest sources of separation among women of color in terms of feminism has been homophobia. This fear that we (whatever our sexuality) breathe in every day in our communities never fully allows us to feel invulnerable to attack on our own streets, and sometimes even in the homes we grew up in (let alone in the white man's world). So often it is the fear of lesbianism which causes many of us to feel our politics and passion are being ignored or discounted by other Third World people. "There's nothing to be compared with how you feel when you're cut cold by your own . . ." (Barbara Smith). But we refuse to make a choice between our cultural identity and sexual identity, between our race and our femaleness. We even claim lesbianism as an "act of resistance" (Clarke) against the same forces that silence us as people of color.

We write letters home to Ma.

Surfacing from these pages again and again is the genuine sense of loss and pain we feel when we are denied our home because of our desire to free ourselves as specifically female persons. So, we turn to each other for strength and sustenance. We write letters to each other incessantly. Across a kitchen table, Third World feminist strategy is plotted. We talk long hours into the night. It is when this midnight oil is burning, in those *after* hours, that we secretly reclaim our goddesses and our female-identified cultural tradition. "I got myself home, lit me some candles . . . put on some Dinah and Aretha . . ." (Rushin).

The difference that we have feared to mention because of our urgent need for solidarity with each other begins to be spoken to on these pages, but also the similarities that so often go unrecognized—that a light-skinned Latina could feel "at home" and "safe" (Morales) among her Afro-American sisters—that among many of us there is a deep-rooted identification and affinity which we were not, logically, supposed to feel toward each other living in segregated white-america.

We turn to each other to make family and even there, after the exhilaration of our first discovery of each other subsides, we are forced to confront our own lack of resources as Third World women living in the US. Without money, without institutions, without one community center to call our own we so often never get as far as dreamed while plotting in our kitchens. We disappoint each other. Sometimes we even die on each other. How to reconcile with the death of a friend, the death of a spirit?

We begin by speaking directly to the deaths and disappointments. Here we begin to fill in the spaces of silence between us. For between these seemingly irreconcilable lines—the class lines, the politically correct lines, the daily lines we run down to each other to keep difference and desire at a distance—the truth of our connection lies.

"Just keep saying it, Girl, you'll get whole" (Rushin).

Note

1. "Between Ourselves," *The Black Unicorn* (New York: Norton, 1978), 112.

The Other Heritage

Rosario Morales

For June Jordan and Teish and all other Black women at the San Francisco Poetry Workshop; January 1980.

I forgot   I forgot the other heritage   the other strain refrain   the silver thread thru my sound   the ebony sheen to my life   to the look of things to the sound of how I grew up which was in Harlem right down in Spanish Harlem El Barrio and bounded I always say to foreigners from Minnesota   Ohio and Illinois bounded on the North by Italians and on the South by Black Harlem   A library in each of these almost forbidden places so no wonder I didn't take off with books till I hit the South Bronx   What I didn't forget was the look of Ithaca Rochester Minneapolis and Salt Lake   bleached bleeded and bleached the street full of white ghosts like Chinese visions   And the first time Dick and I drove back thru New York past Amsterdam Avenue right thru the heart of Harlem I breathed again   safe brown and black walking the streets   safe   My mami taught me   my teacher taught me   everybody taught me   watch out   black   smelly   savage   keep out of the way   I did too so how come I come to feel   safe! when I hit Harlem   when I hit a city with enough color   when a city gets moved in on   when Main Street Vermont looks mottled   agouti   black and brown and white   when the sounds of the english Black folk speak and the sounds of Spanish wiggle thru the clean lit air   I still shy and start from black men from about thirteen on but then I shy and start from all men starting from when they think to be men and so do the things men do   my mami taught me that and that stuck but   then I learnt that on my own too   I got myself a clean clear sense of danger   that's what smells   not black skin   but danger stalking the streets for me   I can smell it a mile away wafting to me in the breeze   I keep downwind   raise my head to sniff the air   I only muse and rest my neck when in the herd and in the day and loping thru people traffic on the streets surrounded by the sounds of wheeled traffic in the streets   I think and plan and forget and forget to look but not alone and not at nite   I lift my head   I sniff   I smell the danger and the wheel and run long before he thinks   maybe   she looks about right a morsel for my appetite   I bound away and pant   safe   for this time   safe   but

all I feel when I sit down with you black woman   the only danger
in my air is from some whirring voice inside that always says   you
don't belong   and if you don't utter just just right they will know
you don't belong   and toss you out   and I feel that every time
with every group of any color no matter what they speak but what I
feel inside nowhere near that grating prating voice is well OK!   this
sounds just right   this here music is music to my ears here   I
hear   something that feels like   oh like Carlos Gardel moaning
his tangoes   like the special beat caribbean drums do   I forgot
this heritage   african Black up here in this cold place   the sound
of african in english   of drums in these musics   I forgot I breathed
you with my air and declared   fine   and when you're not there I
look and ask for where you've gone   but I know   I know why I
forgot   I'm not supposed to remember   what I do remember is
to walk in straight and white into the store and say good morning in
my see how white how upper class how refined and kind voice all crisp
with consonants bristling with syllables   protective coloring in racist
fields looks white and crisp like cabbage   looks tidy like laid out gardens   like white aprons on black dresses   like please and thank you
and you're welcome   like neat and clean and see I swept and scrubbed
and polished   ain't I nice   que hay de criticar   will I do   will
I pass   will you let me thru   will they let me be   not see me
here beneath my skin   behind my voice   crouched and quiet and
so so still   not see not hear me there where I crouch   hiding my
eyes   my indian bones   my spanish sounds   muttering   mier-
da   que gente fría y fea   se creen gran cosa   aí   escupe chica
en su carifresca   en su carifea   méate ahí en el piso feo y frío   yo
valgo más que un piso limpio   yo valgo más   yo valgo   cágate
en   l'alfombra   chica   arráncale el pelo   yo quiero salir de
aquí   yo quiero salir de tí   yo quiero salir   you see   she's
me   she's the me says   safe   sarita   safe when I see you many
and black around the table   behind me in the big room and up in
front   June Jordan   how you belt it out and how I take it in right
to where she sits brown and golden   and when she and I laughed big
last nite I was not "too loud"   I was not "too much"   I was just
right   just me   just brown and pink and full of drums inside beating rhythm for my feet   my tongue   my eyes   my hands   my
arms swinging and smacking   I was just right   just right   just
right   sépanlo   niñas m'hijas   trigueñas bellas   sépalo June
Jordan   mujer feroz   aquí me quedo y aquí estoy   right!

The Tired Poem: Last Letter from a Typical (Unemployed) Black Professional Woman

Kate Rushin

So it's a gorgeous afternoon in the park.
It's so nice you forget your *Attitude*
(the one your mama taught you)
the one that says: *Don't mess with me.*
You forget until you hear all this whistling and
lip-smacking. You whip around and say,
"I ain't no damn dog." It's a young guy.
His mouth drops open. "Excuse me, Sister.
How you doin'?" You lie and smile and say,
"I'm doing good, everything's cool, Brother."

Then, five minutes later: "Hey you Sweet Devil.
Hey Girl, come here." You tense, sigh, calculate.
You know the lean boys and bearded men are
cousins and lovers and friends.
You've listened to your uncle, after he's had a drink,
talking about how he has to scuffle to get by and
how he'd wanted to be an engineer.
You talk to Jocko who wants to be a singer
buy some clothes, get a house for his mother.

The Soc. and Psych. books say you're domineering and
you've been to enough Sisters-Are-Not-Taking-Care-Of-Business
discussions to know where you went wrong. It's decided
it had to be the day you decided to go to school.
Still, you remember the last time you said "Hey,"
so you keep on walking. "What? You too good to speak?
Don't nobody want you no way."

So, you go home, sit on the front steps and listen to your
neighbor's son brag about girls. He has pictures of them all.
"This real cute one was supposed to go to college.
She knew she could get pregnant. I'll just say it's not mine."

On the back of a picture of a girl in a cap and gown,
written in a child's round print are the words,
"I love you in my own strange way. Thank you."

So, you go into the house,
flip through a magazine and there is
An-Ode-To-My-Black-Queen poem.
It's the kind where The Brother thanks
all of The Sisters who endured.
This thank-you poem is really
no consolation at all, unless, you believe
what the man you met on the train told you
(the Black man who worked for the State
Department and had lived in five countries).
He said, "Dear, you were born to suffer.
Why don't you give me your address and
I'll come visit?"

So you try to talk to your friend about the train and
the park and everything and how it all seems connected,
and he says, "You're just a Typical Black
Professional Woman; some Sisters know how to deal."
He goes on to say how you have always had the advantage.
You have to stop to think about that one.
Maybe you are supposed to be grateful for the sweaty,
beefy-faced white businessmen who try to pick you up at lunchtime.
You wonder how many times your friend has had pennies thrown at him,

how many times he's been felt up in the subway,
how many times he's been cussed out on the street,
how many times he's been offered $10 for a piece of himself.
$10 for a piece . . .

So, you're waiting for the bus and you look up from your book.
A young man is asking if you want to make some money, and
you think how you only get $15 for spending all day with 30 kids.
You remember he could be your brother or cousin.
You begin to explain how $10 wouldn't pay for
what you'd have to give up. He pushes a handful of sticky,
crumpled dollars in your face. "Why not? You think I can't pay?
Look at that roll. Don't tell me you don't need the money,
'cause I know you do . . . I'll give you 15."

You remember a joke you heard . . . but it isn't funny.
You wonder if he would at least give you the money and
not beat you up. Still, you're very cool and say, "No thanks.
You should look for somebody you care about
who cares about you." He waves you off.
"Get outta my face. I don't have time for that.
And remember, you blew it."

Then your voice gets loud and fills the night street.
Your bus comes, the second shift people file on.
The night watchmen and nurse's aides look at you like
you're crazy. "Get on the damn bus." He turns away.
Your bus pulls off. There is no one on the street but you.
And then, it is very quiet.

To Be Continued . . .

Kate Rushin

You didn't think I was going to stand on that corner by myself,
(arms and legs like boards, mouth full of cement) forever, now did you?
Got myself together and grabbed the first cab I saw.
(Blew my budget for the week.)

I got myself home, lit me some candles and some sandalwood,
put on some Dinah and Aretha, took myself a bath,
made myself some grits and eggs,
got on the phone and called up my Girlfriend.

I told her everything that had been going on and you know what she said?
She said, Girl, I know what you mean. I said, for real, don't you think
    I'm crazy?
Listen, she said, only crazy you are is thinking you owe something to
    some fool
come walking up in your face, intruding on your life, talking trash.

Think about it. How it sound you feeling ashamed 'cause somebody
come treating you like you was somebody's pork chop?
Don't worry about it. When you got something to say, say it.
Just make sure you're talking to somebody who shows some interest.

Well, I started thinking about what my Girlfriend said,
and then something clicked. Then it all dawned on me.
Me and my Girlfriend you understand,
we been friends for years.

Now, whenever I get uptight, I remember what she told me:
Keep moving. Keep breathing. Stop apologizing and keep on talking.
When you get scared, keep talking anyway. Tell the truth like Sojourner
    Truth.
Spill all the beans. Let all the cats out of all the bags.

If you are what you eat, you become what you speak.
If you free your tongue, your spirit will follow.
Just keep saying it, Girl, you'll get whole.
Say it again and again, Girl, you'll get free.

If you are what you eat,
you become what you speak.
Free your tongue and your spirit will follow.
Free your spirit, no telling what could happen.

Across the Kitchen Table

A Sister-to-Sister Dialogue

Barbara Smith and Beverly Smith

In June 1980, we sent Beverly and Barbara a number of questions regarding their experiences as Black feminists in the women's movement. The following is a transcript of their responses.

—The Editors

Feminism: More than a "Click" and a Clique

The Editors: *What do you see as the effects of the pervasiveness of white middle-class women in the feminist movement? In your experience how do class and race issues intersect in the movement?*

Beverly: . . . on Saturday night, what happened is that she was flossing her teeth after the meal. I was just so impressed with the fact that she would take such good care of her teeth. And so she said that the reason was that when she was a child her mother had saved up money for her to go and visit her grandmother or something down South. And she had been looking forward to it all year. I think that she usually went. But what happened is that this particular year she went to the dentist right before, and she had 7 cavities. And that wiped out her vacation. Because it was a matter of either/or. But of course, that's not the poorest you can get either. "My God," I said, "I bet there's hardly a white woman that we come into contact with that would have any perception of what that meant." And yet it sounded so familiar to me.

Barbara: Exactly. What we want to describe in this dialogue are the class differences we experience on this kind of basic level which "high-level" analysis and rhetoric don't get to.

An example I can think of and which drives me crazy is the arrogance some white women display about "choosing" not to finish school, you know, "downward mobility." But the thing is they don't have to worry about being asked "Do you have a degree," and then being completely cut out of a whole range of jobs and opportunity if they don't. Race is a concept of having to be twice as qualified, twice as good to go half as far. And I feel like at this point, in these economic times, it's like being three times as good to go half as far. No way in hell would I give up getting a degree or some piece of paper that would give me more economic leverage in this "boys' system." That's not necessarily a perception that white women have. In fact, I know a lot of white women who never finished college, yet are functioning in ways that if they had been Black women would be completely unavailable to them.

This ties in with another thing we had talked about in the past, which is the difference between women's politics, who come to a realization that oppression exists say at 22, 25 or even 18, versus Black women's and other women of color's perspective, which is that your oppression is a lifelong thing. There is a political savviness, I don't know what words to use, canniness—some difference in attitude I think between Black and white feminists. I think what it is, is like the surprise factor. There is virtually no Black person in this country who is surprised about oppression. Virtually not one. Because the thing is we have had it meted out to us from infancy on. And I think that when we are dealing with white women in coalitions, or whatever, that often we're at very different places about how you deal with a problem, how you think about a problem, how you react to a problem. Because they are coming from a perspective like, "Oh! I didn't know. I didn't know. I never knew until . . . I never knew until . . ." There is a difference when you come into your politics because you're Black and oppressed on that level.

Bev: What I would really want to talk about is why the women's movement is basically a middle-class movement. What does it mean? At least middle class in tone. I am not saying everyone in the women's movement is middle class but the thing is that I think that it is middle-class women who dominate in terms of numbers and in terms of what actually gets done, and just how things get done. What gets made the priorities and what have you.

What really are the similarities and differences between women's oppression and class and racial oppression? My perception about racial oppression and class oppression is that it's something that starts from Day One.

Bar: You're born into it and it's grinding.

Bev: It's grinding. And it continues. My sense about the oppression of women is that it's something that people come to oftentimes, but not always, in a more intellectual manner. It's something that's pointed out to them. It's something that they read about and say, "Oh, yeah!" I mean even the concept of the "click," you know, that you can read about in *Ms.* magazine.

Bar: They still have "clicks"!

Bev: Right. They still talk about when you have an experience that makes you realize your oppression as a woman, makes you realize other women's oppression, you know, some revealing incident in your life as a woman. That is a "click." Well I mean, I guess there are "clicks" among racial lines, but the thing is they're so far back in terms of class that they're almost imperceptible. It just feels to me like it's a different kind of thing.

Bar: Another thing when you talk about experiencing racial oppression and class oppression (if indeed you are a recipient of those oppressions) from the very beginning, what is happening to you is from moderately bad to horrible. In other words, being Black in this country there is very little about it that is mild. The oppression is extreme. Probably the only Black people where oppression is somewhat mitigated are those who have class privileges and that is certainly not the majority of Black people here. Likewise if you are a recipient of class oppression, that means that you are poor, you are working class and therefore day to day survival is almost the only thing you can focus on. The thing that's different about women's oppression is that you can be white and middle class and female and live a so-called "nice" life up until a certain point, then you begin to notice these "clicks," but I think the quality of life for the upper- or middle-class white woman is so far ahead of the quality of life for the Black person, the Black child, the working-class child or the poor child.

Bev: I want to attempt to make comparison between different types of oppression. When I think of poverty, I think of constant physical and material oppression. You know, you aren't poor one day and well-to-do the next. If you're poor it's a constant thing, every day, every day. In some ways it's almost more constant than race because, say you're middle class and you're a Black person who is of course subject to racism, you don't necessarily experience it every single day in the same intensity, or to the same degree. Whereas poverty is just something you experience constantly. So what I was trying to come up with is—Is there any oppression that women experience that is that total, in other words literally affects their physical well-being on a day to day basis?

Bar: Can I make a joke, Bev?

Bev: What?

Bar: Heterosexuality. *(Laughing)* Well, moving right along . . .

Bev: Yes, they *are* suffering . . . Well, battering is maybe something, but not necessarily, only in some extreme incidences.

Bar: Well, I think in a way we're almost comparing apples and pears. We don't have a language yet or a framework as to what is the true nature of women's oppression, given where it takes place and who it comes from and how. Maybe the battered woman is not beaten every day, but she has to wait on her husband every day and her children. She's either bored out of her mind or worrying and scraping, trying to make ends meet, both in the context of the nuclear family. Women's oppression is so organic or circular or something. One place on the circle is battering, one place is cat calls, another is rape, another place is the fact that no one takes you seriously even while you worked to put your husband through college. There's a whole range of stuff, that's why it's so hard to pin something down.

Bev: I think for purposes of analysis what we try to do is to break things down and try to separate and compare but in reality, the way women live their lives, those separations just don't work. Women don't live their lives like, "Well this part is race, and this is class, and this part has to do with women's identities," so it's confusing.

Bar: And Black women and women of color in particular don't do that. I think maybe what we have defined as an important component of Black feminism is that maybe, for the short run at least, that's all right. We don't have to rank or separate out. What we have to do is define the nature of the whole, of all the systems impinging on us.

Bev: Given these differences between us, that women are of different races and classes, how can a white middle-class movement actually deal with *all* women's oppression, as it purports to do, particularly if most women are not present to represent their own interests? I think this is one of the most essential questions the movement has to face.

Bar: What we've got to look at is what is the nature of those issues that get multi-oppressed women involved in movement work. What are those issues and how might those issues be incorporated into the women's movements? I am thinking here of all the Black women who were involved in the Civil Rights movement. Fannie Lou Hamer is a name we know, but there were countless thousands of other women whose names we don't know whose material conditions would not indicate that they would have the wherewithal to struggle politically but then they did. Even more recently, poor women have been involved in issues like tenants rights or welfare organizing, etc.

Bev: Sometimes I think maybe twenty-five to fifty years from now we might really understand what the origins of the women's movement were, much more than we know today. We may lose some of the proximity, but we'll gain some of the hindsight and the perspective. One of the things we might discover is that the origins of the feminist movement were basically middle class, but there are reasons for that. Already there is analysis about that from people who are somewhat anti-feminist; Marxists and leftists that have the perception that the women's movement is just an indication that we're in an advanced stage of capitalism. They say that the fact that the women's movement developed in this country at the time it did had to do with how capitalism had developed, in other words, a high enough rate of profit or surplus. I don't know what the terminology is, exactly, but this material surplus made it possible for women to have the "leisure" to demand certain rights.

So, as I see it, in the same way that the welfare rights movement comes out of the needs expressed and experienced by the women receiving welfare, there is a path that the women's movement has followed that originated out of their own middle-class needs.

Bar: Yes, I think that is quite verifiable . . . There is just so much class conflict in this society that it is hard for people who are economically and/or racially oppressed to believe that there are some people who may experience their oppression differently. I think that this is where the laughability of the women's movement comes in. The woman I teach a class with told me how she has a friend who was teaching John Steinbeck's *The Grapes of Wrath*, to a class who had a decent number of Black students in it and the Black students refused to believe that it was about white people. *Refused* to believe, you know? John Steinbeck, Great White Novelist! That's just incredible! What it shows is the class conflict, the class division, that is totally enforced in this society to keep people unaware of each other's situations, commonalities, etc.

The Whitewash of Cultural Identity

Eds: *By virtue of your education, what class assumptions are made about you by white feminists? How do you experience white women trying to "whitewash" you?*

Bar: This is very complicated. There is a sociologist, a Black woman who's here in Boston, she said something very astute about this whole issue of class. She was talking about how sociologists often confuse class with lifestyle. They will throw out all their knowledge about income level, and assume people are of a different class. So they'll see a Black family who makes $6,000 a year, but the thing is they have books and they are stable and blah blah blah and all this crap, you know, they're trying to send their kids to college and they do and the sociologists say, "Well, then, they must be middle class." As she said so succinctly, "$6,000 dollars worth of money buys $6,000 worth of goods." (That would make them poor today. Twenty years ago, working class). It just depends on what you decide to spend it on. There is a difference between economic class and the narrow set of values usually associated with it, you know? Because I think we come from that kind of home . . .

Bev: Sure. Sure.

Bar: Where there were priorities put on things that poor working-class Black people weren't supposed to be thinking about.

Bev: Yeah, it's very confusing. The fact that education was something that was always valued in our family, not just in our generation, but for generations back. I think that's where a lot of white feminists get confused about us. Because of the fact of the education we had and the emphasis on cultural development and on intellectual development that has been in our family at least for three generations, makes people think, well, we must have come from a middle-class background.

Bar: Oh yeah! Sure!

Bev: It's true, we never starved. But I just get so frustrated because I feel people don't understand where we came from. When I look at the photographs in our scrapbook I just think if they looked at the house, would they understand what our class background actually was? Because of where we were living, the size of the rooms . . .

Bar: The fact that there was no automatic washing machine.

Bev: The fact that when you got a chest of drawers, a dresser, and a bed in one of the bedrooms, literally there was no floor space. I think that a lot of where we came from had to do with, as you said, values and managing. One of the values is that you handled money in such a way that you made it stretch as far as you possibly could.

Bar: Don't I remember! *(Laughing)* It was a real value that you live as decently as possible on the money you do make.

Bev: Exactly.

Bar: There was a lot of emphasis on trying.

Bev: Sometimes I do wish people could just see us in the context we grew up in, who our people are.

Bar: In order for people to understand what our background was, in order to place us, they need to have a lot of comprehension about what Black life is all about in this country, period. There is a cookbook, called *Spoonbread and Strawberry Wine* by these two Darden sisters. The reason why I mention it is because they have family history in there. This was a successful Black family, and yet these people worked like hell! They were people who were ex-slaves. Almost anybody in their family who wanted to go to a Black college could have, but that's not nearly the same thing as a family who sent all of their sons to Harvard, all of their daughters to Smith, or whatever. There's just a different social context. Even though this is a successful Black family, there is poverty, struggle, oppression, violence in the history of that family that is totally unrecognizable to outsiders . . .

Bev: Just like within ours. You know one of the things that I've felt for a long time being involved in the women's movement, is that there is so much about Black identity that doesn't get called into practice.

Bar: Indeed! Indeed!

Bev: And that's very upsetting to me. It really makes me think about the choices I have made, either implicitly and less consciously or very consciously. It makes me think about how I live my life because there are so many parts of our Black identity that we no longer get a chance to exercise. And that's just something that is very appalling to me.

Bar: It's just too true. It's too true. Too appalling!

I would just like to mention July 4th which happened a few days ago and watching the Black family who lives in the house behind mine as I have for the last four years and just having this feeling of longing like, you know, I'll never be in that situation. A few days later, I was talking to this white woman I know about that and she said, "Well do you really want to be sitting out there with those men?" and I said, "No." But the thing is that it's the whole thing. The whole damn thing! I realized, too, it was my regret for the past, for those July 4ths that were essentially just like the one I was watching right outside my window and for the fact that it will never be that way again. Well . . .

I don't think we can ever give it to each other as peers because there is a kind of family bonding across generations that is very Black that doesn't happen.[1]

Bev: One of the things I was getting at is that there are ways we act when Black people are together that white women will never see in a largely white context. So I think that's one of the reasons that again, to use to phrase that was asked to us, they are able to "whitewash" us. Now, I don't think this is about acting white in a white context. It's about one, a lack of inspiration. Because the way you act with Black people is because they inspire the behavior. And I *do* mean inspire. And the other thing is that when you are in a white context, you think, "Well why bother? Why waste your time?" If what you're trying to do is get things across and communicate and what-have-you, *you talk in your second language.*

Bar: This is so different from being in a Black context. For example, it just occurred to me this experience I had visiting an old friend of mine that I have known for a number of years. She was staying in this house with this regular old Black nuclear family. And the woman of the house was clearly the person who kept the whole thing together. They had food laid back! *(Laughing)* And the thing is it was really a lot of fun for me to see that, "pervert" that I am—that's in quotes—dyke that I am, I could sit down at a table with these middle-aged Black women who were playing pokeeno and be able to hang, you know? And it was very nice. I had a good time.

Bev: Only one question, Barbara, did you play? *(Laughing)*

Bar: Yeah, I played for a little while. Throughout the day, there must've been twenty people in and out of the house. And it was no particular occasion, just twenty people in and out of the house. At one point, we were talking about television and the woman said, "Oh Barbara doesn't watch TV. She's an intellectual." It was a joke and I felt good enough in that context with people I hardly knew to understand that they said that with a great deal of affection. I realized they were complimenting me and being supportive for something I had accomplished. I'm sure they felt proud of the fact that Alice, the doctor, and Barbara, who teaches at U Mass, were sitting around on a Sunday evening. And the thing is that it was not the kind of hostility that I have sometimes experienced from my so-called peers of Black women about those very same struggles and accomplishments. And it certainly is not the misunderstanding that I have gotten from white women about the meaning of that. Because of course, these people are trying to send their children to school too.

Bev: I wonder is this the trade-off? Is this what everyone who has our identity has to sacrifice? One of my constant questions is how do other lesbians of color live their lives? The other question I have is—"Is this 'fly in the buttermilk' existence a function of our feminism more than our lesbianism?" To ask the question more explicitly—Do black lesbians, who do not identify as feminists and base their lives in the Black community, feel this struggle? I think the answer is that they don't all the time. It's hard to figure out.

Bar: I think the isolation is probably a result much more of being a feminist. I think this has some class factors in it. This almost takes us back to where we began because in order to be involved in this women's movement, as it stands today, you have to be able to deal with "middle-classness." And the Black women who can take it are often the ones with educational privilege.

Lesbian Separatism

Eds.: *Is a lesbian separatist position inherently racist? Is this position a viable political position to take?*

Bar: As we said in our collective statement (Combahee) I think we have real questions because separatism seems like such a narrow kind of politics and also because it seems to be only viably practiced by women who have certain kinds of privilege: white-skinned privilege, class privilege. Women who don't have those kinds of privilege have to deal with this society and with the institutions of this society. They can't go to a harbor of many acres of land, and farm, and "invite the goddess." Women of color are very aware that racism is not gender specific and that it affects all people of color. We have experiences that have nothing to do with being female, but are nonetheless experiences of deep oppression . . . and even violence.

Bev: Maybe the reason that white women got into lesbian separatism was because in being separatist they were separating themselves from white

men, given how there is so much oppression in this world currently that white men have visited on people. In some ways they felt that they had to separate themselves from white men to even have a fighting chance.
Bar: So seldom is separatism involved in making real political change, affecting the institutions in the society in any direct way. If you define certain movement issues as straight women's issues, for example reproductive rights and sterilization abuse, then these identifiable sexual/political issues are ones you are not going to bother with as a separatist.

We have noticed how separatists in our area, instead of doing political organizing often do zap acts. For example they might come to a meeting or series of meetings then move on their way. It is not clear what they're actually trying to change. We sometimes think of separatism as politics without a practice.

Bev: One of the problems of separatism is that I can't see it as a philosophy that explains and analyzes the roots of all oppression and is going to go towards solving it. I think it has some validity in a more limited sphere. To begin to talk about being separate from men is viable. It has some worthwhile aspects.

Bar: Many lesbians are separatist in that sense. You are very aware of the choice—that in being a lesbian you understand that you really don't need men to define your identity, your sexuality, to make your life meaningful or simply to have a good time. That doesn't necessarily mean that you have no comprehension of the oppressions that you share with men. And, you see, white women with class privilege don't share oppression with white men. They're in a critical and antagonistic position whereas Black women and other women of color definitely share oppressed situations with men of their race.

What white lesbians have against lesbians of color is that they accuse us of being "male identified" because we are concerned with issues that affect our whole race. They express anger at us for not "seeing the light." That is another aspect of how they carry on their racism. They are so narrow and adamant about that that they dismiss lesbians of color and women of color who aren't lesbians because we have some concern about what happens to the men of our race.[2] And it's not like we like their sexism or even want to sleep with them. You can certainly be concerned, as we are living here this summer in Boston, when one Black man after another ends up dead.

Bev: It's not only being concerned, it is observing what happens—who does racist acts and who are the targets for racism. It would be incredibly dishonest to say that racism is a thing just experienced by Black women.

Bar: And also politically inexpedient. I think that people who define themselves as Black feminists certainly have decided that the bulk of their political work is in concert with other Black women. That doesn't mean that you're totally oblivious to the reality of racism. I feel that the one thing about racism is that it doesn't play favorites. Look at the history of lynching in this country. And also look at how Black women have experienced violence that is definitely racial. When you read about Black women being lynched, they aren't thinking of us as females. The horrors that we have experienced have absolutely everything to do with them *not even viewing us as women.*

Because if we *are* women some false chivalry *might* enter in and maybe certain things wouldn't happen. I've never read an account of a lynching of a white woman, or one who was pregnant. I think there's a difference between the rape-murder that happens to all women and the lynching that happens specifically to Black women. A contemporary example of that is how Black women who are battered and who physically defend themselves are treated differently than white women by the courts. It's seen differently by the courts when a white middle-class woman murders her husband. Then it's so-called self-defense. I was just reading a case involving a Black woman in Michigan where the Black woman was sold down the river obviously because she was Black. A negative image of Black men and women got her fate delivered.

Bev: One of the most dangerous and erroneous concepts that separatists have put forward is that other oppressions, in addition to sexism, are attributed to men only. Some separatists believe that although women are racist, when men disappear and no longer rule, racism will not be a problem. It's very analogous to people who are Marxists who say, "Well, when class oppression and racism end, definitely the oppression of women and lesbians will end." What lesbian separatists are saying is that when we get rid of men, sexism and racism will end, too. I think that this is one of the most racist aspects of [their ideology] because it does not recognize the racism that women, including lesbians, have.

There is also a dishonesty that I have come across in some lesbians who although they do not regard themselves as separatists, they also do not acknowledge the separatism in their own lifestyles. Many lesbians who don't consider themselves separatists would never live with a man and would not go very far to befriend a man (although they may have a few token men in their lives), but they don't go any further than to disavow their separatism.

Bar: I disagree with that. The so-called disavowal is, from my perspective, the lack of need to deify or glorify those very kinds of choices. Separatists get angry at the fact that I don't make much of the fact that I don't see a man socially from one end of the week to the other. I feel they are trying to collapse political positions that I do not consider in any way trivial. Who you have parties with, as far as I am concerned, is not the bottom line of defining your political commitment.

I also want to say that I don't think that white lesbian separatists are more racist than any other white women in the women's movement. I just think it takes different forms. White lesbian separatism has almost a studied obliviousness to instances of oppression whereas another group of feminists, for example socialists, are even sectarian [about race]. The way their racism would manifest itself is: they would know that racism was an important issue, but they wouldn't be dealing with it in any way except as a theoretical radical issue. Their discomfort in dealing around women of color would be just as palpable; that attitude would be just as apparent. All white people in this country are victims of the disease of racism.

There is no such thing as a non-racist. Sometimes it's as simple as who you can laugh with, who you can cry with and who you can share meals with and whose face you can touch. There are bunches of white women for whom these things that I've mentioned are unknown experiences with women of color.

Bar: *(Aside)* Beverly is fixing this little teddybear. She's been doing surgery on it for the last couple of hours. The bear shows remarkable stamina, like no human being. You could say that we are having a series of operations in our lives.

Bev: If it weren't for Barbara and her relationship with this person who is not myself, I wouldn't be dealing with it. *(Laughing)*

Bar: I don't see that as being relevant to this conversation.

Bev: It is relevant. I'm talking about how I got involved in this surgery.

Homophobia in the Black Community

Eds.: *Describe your experience in dealing with homophobic Black sisters.*

Bar: There's nothing to compare with how you feel when you're cut cold by your own . . . I think the reason that Black women are so homophobic is that attraction-repulsion thing. They have to speak out vociferously against lesbianism because if they don't they may have to deal with their own deep feelings for women. They make great cases for how fucked up it all is, and therefore cover their asses admirably. *Is* homophobia more entrenched in the Black community than in the white community?

Bev: You can argue about that until Jesus comes, really.

Bar: I really must say, historically and politically, there are more reasons for the Black community to be homophobic; one of them being that the women's movement and gay rights have made fewer inroads into the Black community. We can assume that a community that has been subjected to the ideas of the movement is going to have more consciousness. And given how up until the last couple of years the feminist movement has not touched Third World communities, we can expect their attitudes to be much as they have been in the past.

One of the reasons for homophobic attitudes among Black women may be the whole sexual stereotyping used against all Black people anyway, but especially women in relation to homosexuality. You know, the "Black bulldagger" image. Lesbianism is definitely about something sexual, a so-called deviant sexuality. So the way most Black women deal with it is to be just as rigid and closed about it as possible. White people don't have a sexual image that another oppressor community has put on them.

Bev: This country is so racist that it is possible to take many, many things and concepts that have nothing to do with race and talk about them in racial terms. Because people are so dichotomized into either black or white, it defines a continuum. This is so strict and so overwhelming in this country, you can take things that have nothing to do with race and refer to them racially. Therefore, Black people have the option of taking things—sexuality behavior, conflicts, whatever they don't like—and saying, "That's white." Lesbianism is not the only thing seen as a white thing. A real good example is suicide. Black people say, "Yeah, suicide is a white thing."

Bar: Oh yeah, we used to believe that. And of course one felt all the worse for having considered it. I'm thinking of Ntozake Shange's play *for colored girls who have considered suicide*.[3] It's very brave. I mean, she's dealing with a lot of myths, by saying that we have even considered it, if it's supposed to be a white thing.

Bev: Any behavior Black people say is despicable, they can disregard by saying this doesn't belong to the Black community. There's hardly a thing in this world in our experience that is not referred to being either Black or white, from animals on—people talking about "white dogs." They weren't talking about dogs that were white in color, they were talking about dogs that belonged to white people.

Bar: So often lesbianism and male homosexuality are talked about as a white disease within the Black community. It is just so negating of our lives. Very upsetting.

Eds.: *Are Black women more vulnerable to homophobic attack?*

Bar: Yes, Black women are more vulnerable to homophobic attack because we don't have white skin privilege, or class privilege to fall back on if somebody wants to start a smear campaign against us. As I said in my essay, "Towards a Black Feminist Criticism,"[4] heterosexual privilege is always the last to go. [Black lesbians] don't have any of the other privileges;

it really is jumping off the edge in a very fundamental way. Somebody who is already dealing with multiple oppressions is more vulnerable to another kind of attack upon her identity.

Bev: I also feel that Black women are more vulnerable to physical attack as lesbians because they're Black. The stories you hear over the years of Black lesbians being attacked for being lesbian, usually by white men!

Eds.: *What is the relationship between Black women's view of lesbianism and their resistance to identifying as feminists?*

Bar: It's real connected. Feminists have been portrayed as nothing but "lesbians" to the Black community as well. There was a considerable effort in the early seventies to turn the Black community off to feminism. You can look at publications, particularly Black publications making pronouncements about what the feminist movement was and who it reached that would trivialize it, that would say no Black women were involved, that did everything possible to prevent those coalitions between Black and white women from happening because there was a great deal of fear. Black men did not want to lose Black women as allies. And the white power structure did not want to see all women bond across racial lines because they knew that would be an unbeatable unstoppable combination. They did a very good job. You can just document those happenings during that period.

So, yes, most Black women think that to be a feminist you have to be a lesbian. And if not that, then at least you have to deal with being around lesbians. And you see, that is true. It's very hard to be in the women's movement and not be around lesbians. And if you're so homophobic that you can't deal with the thought of lesbianism then you probably won't be involved. I think these things are changing. More and more Black women are becoming sensitive or sympathetic to the women's movement.

Third World Women: Tokenism or Leadership

Eds.: *How, as women of color, can we prevent ourselves from being tokenized by white feminists? How do you see Third World women forming the leadership in the feminist movement?*

Bev: One looks at the question about tokenism and just throws up her hands. There are so many possibilities of tokenization. One of the most tokenized situations that Barbara and I find ourselves in is when we are asked to speak at a certain place. You can be certain to be the only Black person there. You're going to be put in the position of speaking for the

race, for all Black feminists. One of the things that helps is to get paid
and to put it on that level so you don't feel so exploited.

Bar: I think that the service Gloria thought of having and calling it "Dial
a Token"—I mean that's a good thing *(laughs)*. For one thing it puts it
out there. It's saying, "Hey, I know what you're doing and I want to get
paid for it." Another thing, try not to be the only Third World person
there. I was thinking of the meeting that Cherríe went to when she was
here with us [ref. xlvi]. And even though there were several Third World
women present, we were still tokenized. I guess that I am really talking
about support as opposed to defusing tokenization.

Bev: Given the state of things between Black and white women, we're
going to be tokenized quite a bit. It's so hard to get around that.

Bar: But, a solution to tokenism is *not* racial separatism. There are definitely separatist aspects emerging among Black and Third World feminist
communities and that is fine. But, ultimately, any kind of separatism is a
dead end. It's good for forging identity and gathering strength, but I do
feel that the strongest politics are coalition politics that cover a broad
base of issues. There is no way that one oppressed group is going to
topple a system by itself. Forming principled coalitions around specific
issues is very important. You don't necessarily have to like or love the
people you're in coalition with.

This brings me back to the issue of lesbian separatism. I read in
a women's newspaper an article by a woman speaking on behalf of lesbian separatists. She claimed that separatists are more radical than other
feminists. What *I* really feel is radical is trying to make coalitions with
people who are different from you. I feel it is radical to be dealing with
race and sex and class and sexual identity all at one time. I think *that* is
really radical because it has never been done before. And it really pisses
me off that they think of themselves as radical. *I think there is a difference
between being extreme and being radical.*

This is why Third World women are forming the leadership in the
feminist movement because we are not one-dimensional, one-issued in
our political understanding. Just by virtue of our identities we certainly
define race and usually define class as being fundamental issues that we
have to address. The more wide-ranged your politics, the more potentially
profound and transformative they are.

Bev: The way I see it, the function that Third World women play in
the movement is that we're the people who throw the ball a certain
distance and then the white women run to that point to pick it up. I
feel we are constantly challenging white women, usually on the issues
of racism but not always. We are always challenging women to go further, to be more realistic. I so often think of the speech that Sojourner

Truth made not because of the contents so much but more because of the function. She says, "Now children, let's get this together. Let me explain what's going on here. Let me lay it out for you." I must admit that the reason I think of it so often is that I have thought of myself in that situation. "Let me explain this to you one more time, let me take you by the hand, etc." I find myself playing that role. But there's a way though that I feel that Third World women are not in actual leadership *positions* in the women's movement in terms of policy making, etc. But we certainly have the vision.

We are in the position to challenge the feminist movement as it stands to date and, not out of any theoretical commitment. Our analysis of race and class oppression and our commitment to really dealing with those issues, including homophobia, is something we know we have to struggle with to insure our survival. It is organic to our very existence. **Bar**: Thank you, sweetheart. Teddybear just gave me a kiss. *(To the editors)* Bye Girls.

Notes

1. The twin sisters, Barbara and Beverly, were raised in a household headed by women in Cleveland, Ohio. At the time of this conversation, they had already lost those women: their mother (when they were nine years old); and, later, their aunt and maternal grandmother who had raised them. *(Editor, 2015)*
2. An even more striking example of the connection between a Lesbian separatist stance and the disavowal of racism as a central feminist concern can be seen in the incredibly negative responses, coming primarily from separatists, to Elly Bulkin's fine article "Racism and Writing: Some Implications for White Lesbian Critics," *Sinister Wisdom* 13 (Spring 1980).
3. *For Colored Girls Who Have Considered Suicide When the Rainbow Is Enuf* was first published by Shameless Hussy Press in 1976. *(Editor, 2015)*
4. Barbara Smith's avant-garde essay was first published in *Conditions Two*, 1977. *(Editor, 2015)*

Lesbianism
An Act of Resistance

Cheryl Clarke

For a woman to be a lesbian in a male-supremacist, capitalist, misogynist, racist, homophobic, imperialist culture, such as that of North America, is an act of resistance. (A resistance that should be championed throughout the world by all the forces struggling for liberation from the same slave master.) No matter how a woman lives out her lesbianism—in the closet, in the state legislature, in the bedroom—she has rebelled against becoming the slave master's concubine, viz., the male-dependent female, the female heterosexual. This rebellion is dangerous business in patriarchy. Men at all levels of privilege, of all classes and colors have the potential to act out legalistically, moralistically, and violently when they cannot colonize women, when they cannot circumscribe our sexual, productive, reproductive, creative prerogatives and energies. And the lesbian—that woman who, as Judy Grahn says, "has taken a woman lover"[1]—has succeeded in resisting the slave master's imperialism in that one sphere of her life. The lesbian has decolonized her body. She has rejected a life of servitude implicit in Western, heterosexual relationships and has accepted the potential of mutuality in a lesbian relationship—roles notwithstanding.

Historically, this culture has come to identify lesbians as women, who over time, engage in a range and variety of sexual-emotional relationships with women. I, for one, identify a woman as a lesbian who says she is. Lesbianism is a recognition, an awakening, a reawakening of our passion for each (woman) other (woman) and for same (woman). This passion will ultimately reverse the heterosexual imperialism of male culture. Women, through the ages, have fought and died rather than deny that passion. In her essay "The Meaning of Our Love for Women Is What We Have Constantly to Expand" Adrienne Rich states:

> . . . Before any kind of feminist movement existed, or could exist, lesbians existed: women who loved women, who refused to comply with behavior demanded of women, who refused to define themselves in relation to men. Those women, our foresisters, millions whose names we do not know, were tortured and burned as witches, slandered in religious and later in "scientific" tracts, portrayed in art and literature as bizarre,

amoral, destructive, decadent women. For a long time, the lesbian has been a personification of feminine evil.

. . . Lesbians have been forced to live between two cultures, both male-dominated, each of which has denied and endangered our existence. . . . Heterosexual, patriarchal culture has driven lesbians into secrecy and guilt, often to self-hatred and suicide.[2]

The evolving synthesis of lesbianism and feminism—two women-centered and powered ideologies—is breaking that silence and secrecy. The following analysis is offered as one small cut against that stone of silence and secrecy. It is not intended to be original or all-inclusive. I dedicate this work to all the women hidden from history whose suffering and triumph have made it possible for me to call my name out loud.[3]

The woman who embraces lesbianism as an ideological, political, and philosophical means of liberation of all women from heterosexual tyranny must also identify with the world-wide struggle of all women to end male-supremacist tyranny at all levels. As far as I am concerned, any woman who calls herself a feminist must commit herself to the liberation of *all* women from *coerced* heterosexuality as it manifests itself in the family, the state, and on Madison Avenue. The lesbian-feminist struggles for the liberation of all people from patriarchal domination through heterosexism and for the transformation of all socio-political structures, systems, and relationships that have been degraded and corrupted under centuries of male domination.

However, there is no one kind of lesbian, no one kind of lesbian behavior, and no one kind of lesbian relationship. Also there is no one kind of response to the pressures that lesbians labor under to survive as lesbians. Not all women who are involved in sexual-emotional relationships with women call themselves lesbians or identify with any particular lesbian community. Many women are only lesbians to a particular community and *pass* as heterosexuals as they traffic among enemies. (This is analogous to being black and passing for white with only one's immediate family knowing one's true origins.) Yet, those who hide in the closet of heterosexual presumption are sooner or later discovered. The "nigger in-the-woodpile" story retells itself. Many women are politically active as lesbians, but may fear holding hands with their lovers as they traverse heterosexual turf. (This response to heterosexual predominance can be likened to the reaction of the black student who integrates a predominantly white dormitory and who fears leaving the door of her room open when she plays gospel music.) There is the woman who engages in sexual-emotional relationships with women and labels herself *bisexual*. (This is comparable to the Afro-American whose skin-color indicates her mixed ancestry yet who calls herself "mulatto" rather than black.) Bisexual is a safer label than lesbian, for it posits the possibility of a relationship with a man, regardless of how infrequent or non-existent the female bisexual's relationships with men might be. And then there is the lesbian who is a lesbian anywhere and everywhere and who is in direct and constant confrontation with heterosexual presumption, privilege, and oppression. (Her struggle can be compared to that of the Civil Rights activist of the 1960s who was out there on the streets for freedom, while so many of us viewed the action on the television.)

Wherever we, as lesbians, fall along this very generalized political continuum, we must know that the institution of heterosexuality is a die-hard custom through which male-supremacist institutions insure their own perpetuity and control over us. Women are kept, maintained, and contained through terror, violence, and spray of semen. It is as profitable for our colonizers to confine our bodies and alienate us from our own life processes as it was profitable for the European to enslave the African and destroy all memory of a prior freedom and self-determination—Alex Haley notwithstanding. And just as the foundation of Western capitalism depended upon the North Atlantic slave trade, the system of patriarchal domination is buttressed by the subjugation of women through heterosexuality. So, patriarchs must extol the boy-girl dyad as "natural" to keep us straight and compliant in the same way the European had to extol Caucasian superiority to justify the African slave trade. Against that historic backdrop, *the woman who chooses to be a lesbian lives dangerously.*

As a member of the largest and second most oppressed group of people of color, as a woman whose slave and ex-slave foresisters suffered some of the most brutal racist, male-supremacist imperialism in Western history, the black lesbian has had to survive also the psychic mutilation of heterosexual superiority. The black lesbian is coerced into the experience of institutional racism—like every other nigger in America—and must suffer as well the homophobic sexism of the black political community, some of whom seem to have forgotten so soon the pain of rejection, denial, and repression sanctioned by racist America. While most political black lesbians do not give a damn if white America is negrophobic, it becomes deeply problematic when the contemporary black political community (another male-dominated and male identified institution) rejects us because of our commitment to women and women's liberation. Many black male members of that community seem still not to understand the historic connection between the oppression of African peoples in North America and the universal oppression of women. As the women's rights activist and abolitionist Elizabeth Cady Stanton pointed out during the 1850's, racism and sexism have been produced by the same animal, viz., "the white Saxon man."

Gender oppression (i.e., the male exploitation and control of women's productive and reproductive energies on the specious basis of a biological difference) originated from the first division of labor, viz., that between women and men, and resulted in the accumulation of private property, patriarchal usurpation of "mother right" or matrilineage, and the duplicitous, male-supremacist institution of heterosexual monogamy (for women only). Sexual politics, therefore, mirror the exploitative, class-bound relationship between the white slave master and the African slave—and the impact of both relationships (between black and white and woman and man) has been residual beyond emancipation and suffrage. The ruling-class white man had a centuries-old model for his day-to-day treatment of the African slave. Before he learned to justify the African's continued enslavement and the ex-slave's continued disenfranchisement with arguments of the African's divinely ordained mental and moral inferiority to himself (a smokescreen for his capitalist greed) the white man learned, within the structure of heterosexual monogamy and under the system of patriarchy, to relate to black people—slave or free—as a man *relates* to a woman, viz., as property, as a sexual commodity, as a servant, as a source of free or cheap labor, and as an innately inferior being.

Although counterrevolutionary, Western heterosexuality, which advances male supremacy, continues to be upheld by many black people, especially black men, as the most desired state of affairs between men and women. This observation is borne out on the pages of our most scholarly black publications to our most commercial black publications, which view the issue of black male and female relationships through the lens of heterosexual bias. But this is to be expected, as historically heterosexuality was one of our only means of power over our condition as slaves and one of two means we had at our disposal to appease the white man.

Now, as ex-slaves, black men have more latitude to oppress black women, because the brothers no longer have to compete directly with the white man for control of black women's bodies. Now, the black man can assume the "master" role, and he can attempt to tyrannize black women. The black man may view the lesbian—who cannot be manipulated or seduced sexually by him—in much the same way the white slave master once viewed the black male slave, viz., as some perverse caricature of manhood threatening his position of dominance over the female body. This view, of course, is a "neurotic illusion" imposed on black men by the dictates of male supremacy, which the black man can never fulfill because he lacks the capital means and racial privilege.

Historically, the myth in the Black world is that there are only two free people in the United States, the white man and the black woman. The myth was established by the Black man in the long period of his frustration when he longed to be free to have the material and social advantages of his oppressor, the white man. On examination of the myth, this so called freedom was based on the sexual prerogatives taken by the white man on the Black female. It was fantasied by the Black man that she enjoyed it.[4]

While lesbian-feminism does threaten the black man's predatory control of black women, its goal as a political ideology and philosophy is not to take the black man's or any man's position on top.

Black lesbians who do work within "by-for-about-black-people" groups or organizations either pass as "straight" or relegate our lesbianism to the so-called "private" sphere. The more male-dominated or black nationalist bourgeois the organization or group, the more resistant to change, and thus, the more homophobic and anti-feminist. In these sectors, we learn to keep a low profile.

In 1979, at the annual conference of a regional chapter of the National Black Social Workers, the national director of that body was given a standing ovation for the following remarks:

> Homosexuals are even accorded minority status now. . . . And white women, too. And some of you black women who call yourselves feminists will be sitting up in meetings with the same white women who will be stealing your men on the sly.

This type of indictment of women's revolution and implicitly of lesbian liberation is voiced throughout the bourgeois black (male) movement. But this is the insidious nature of male supremacy. While the black man may consider racism his primary oppression, he is hard-put to recognize that sexism is inextricably bound up with the racism the black woman must suffer, nor can he see that no women (or men for that matter) will be liberated from the original "master-slave" relationship, viz., that between men and women, until we are all liberated from the false premise of heterosexual superiority. This corrupted, predatory relationship between men and women is the foundation of the master-slave relationship between white and black people in the United States.

The tactic many black men use to intimidate black women from embracing feminism is to reduce the conflicts between white women and black women to a "tug-o'-war" for the black penis. And since the black lesbian, as stated previously, is not interested in his penis, she undermines the black man's only source of power over her, viz., his heterosexuality. Black lesbians and all black women involved in the struggle for liberation must resist this manipulation and seduction.

The black dyke, like every dyke in America, is everywhere—in the home, in the street, on the welfare, unemployment and social security rolls, raising children, working in factories, in the armed forces, on television, in the public school system, in all the professions, going to college or graduate school, in middle-management, among others. The black dyke, like every other non-white and working-class and poor woman in America, has not suffered the luxury, privilege or oppression of being dependent on men, even though our male counterparts have been present, have shared our lives, work and struggle, and, in addition have undermined our "human dignity" along the way like most men in patriarchy, the imperialist family of man. But we could never depend on them "to take care of us" on their resources alone—and, of course, it is another "neurotic illusion" imposed on our fathers, brothers, lovers, husbands that they are supposed to "take care of us" because we are women. Translate: "to take care of us" equals "to control us." Our brothers', fathers', lovers', husbands' only power is their manhood. And unless manhood is somehow embellished by white skin and generations of private wealth, it has little currency in racist, capitalist patriarchy. The black man, for example, is accorded native elite or colonial guard or vigilante status over black women in imperialist patriarchy. He is an overseer for the slave master. Because of his maleness he is given access to certain privileges, e.g., employment, education, a car, life insurance, a house, some nice vines. He is usually a rabid heterosexual. He is, since emancipation, allowed to raise a "legitimate" family, allowed to have his piece of turf, viz., his wife and children. That is as far as his dictatorship extends, for if his wife decides that she wants to leave that home for whatever reason, he does not have the power or resources to seduce her otherwise if she is determined to throw off the benign or malicious yoke of dependency. The ruling class white man, on the other hand, has always had the power to count women among his pool of low-wage labor, his means of production. Most recently, he has "allowed" women the right to sue for divorce, to apply for AFDC, and to be neocolonialized.

Traditionally, poor black men and women who banded together and stayed together and raised children together did not have the luxury to cultivate dependence among the members of their families. So, the black dyke, like most black women, has been conditioned to be self-sufficient, i.e., not dependent on men. For me personally, the conditioning to be self-sufficient and the predominance of female role models in my life are the roots of my lesbianism. Before I became a lesbian, I often wondered why I was expected to give up, avoid, and trivialize the recognition and encouragement I felt from women in order to pursue the tenuous business of heterosexuality. And I am not unique.

As political lesbians, i.e., lesbians who are resisting the prevailing culture's attempts to keep us invisible and powerless, we must become more visible (particularly black and other lesbians of color) to our sisters hidden in their various closets, locked in prisons of self-hate and ambiguity, afraid to take the ancient act of woman-bonding beyond the sexual, the private, the personal. I am not trying to reify lesbianism or feminism. I am trying to point out that lesbian-feminism has the potential of reversing and transforming a major component in the system of women's oppression, viz., predatory heterosexuality. If radical lesbian-feminism purports an anti-racist, anti-classist, anti-woman-hating vision of bonding as mutual, reciprocal, as infinitely negotiable, as freedom from antiquated gender prescriptions and proscriptions, *then all people struggling to transform the character of relationships in this culture have something to learn from lesbians.*

The woman who takes a woman lover lives dangerously in patriarchy. And woe betide her even more if she chooses as her lover a woman who is not of her race. The silence among lesbian-feminists regarding the issue of lesbian relationships between black and white women in America is caused by none other than the centuries-old taboo and laws in the United States against relationships between people of color and those of the Caucasian race. Speaking heterosexually, the laws and taboos were a reflection of the patriarchal slave master's attempts to control his property via controlling his lineage through the institution of monogamy (for women only) and justified the taboos and laws with the argument that purity of the Caucasian race must be preserved (as well as its supremacy). However, we know that his racist and racialist laws and taboos did not apply to him in terms of the black slave woman just as his classist laws and taboos regarding the relationship between the ruling class and the indentured servants did not apply to him in terms of the white woman servant he chose to rape. The offspring of any unions between the white ruling class slave master and the black slave woman or white woman indentured servant could not legally inherit their white or ruling class sire's property or name, just their mothers' condition of servitude.

The taboo against black and white people relating at any other level than master-slave, superior-inferior has been propounded in America to keep black women and men and white women and men, who share a common oppression at the hands of the ruling class white man, from organizing against that common oppression. We, as black lesbians, must vehemently resist being bound by the white man's racist, sexist laws, which have endangered potential intimacy of any kind between whites and blacks.

It cannot be presumed that black lesbians involved in love, work, and social relationships with white lesbians do so out of self-hate and denial of our racial-cultural heritage, identities, and oppression. Why should a woman's commitment to the struggle be questioned or accepted on the basis of her lover's or comrade's skin color? White lesbians engaged likewise with black lesbians or any lesbians of color cannot be assumed to be acting out of some perverse, guilt-ridden racialist desire.

I personally am tired of going to events, conferences, workshops, planning sessions that involve a coming together of black and other lesbians of color for political or even social reasons and listening to black lesbians relegate feminism to white women, castigate black women who propose forming coalitions with predominantly white feminist groups, minimize the white woman's oppression and exaggerate her power, and then finally judge that a black lesbian's commitment to the liberation of black women is dubious because she does not sleep with a black woman. All of us have to accept or reject allies on the basis of politics not on the specious basis of skin color. *Have not black people suffered betrayal from our own people?*

Yes, black women's experiences of misogyny are different from white women's. However, they all add up to how the patriarchal slave master decided to oppress us. We both fought each other for his favor, approval, and protection. Such is the effect of imperialist, heterosexist patriarchy. Shulamith Firestone, in the essay "Racism: The Sexism of the Family of Man," purports this analysis of the relationship between white and black women:

> How do the women of this racial Triangle feel about each other? Divide and conquer: Both women have grown hostile to each other, white women feeling contempt for the "sluts" with no morals, black women feeling envy for the pampered "powder puffs." The black woman is jealous of the white woman's legitimacy, privilege, and comfort, but she also feels deep contempt. . . . Similarly the white woman's contempt for the black woman is mixed with envy: for the black woman's greater sexual license, for her gutsiness, for her freedom from the marriage bind. For after all, the black woman is not under the thumb of a man, but is pretty much her own boss to come and go, to leave the house, to work (much as it is degrading work) or to be "shiftless." What the white woman doesn't know is that the black woman, not under the

thumb of one man, can now be squashed by all. There is no alternative for either of them than the choice between being public or private property, but because each still believes that the other is getting away with something both can be fooled into mischanneling their frustration onto each other rather than onto the real enemy, "The Man."[5]

Though her statement of the choices black and white women have under patriarchy in America has merit, Firestone analyzes only a specific relationship, i.e., between the ruling class white woman and slave or ex-slave black woman.

Because of her whiteness, the white woman of all classes has been accorded, as the black man has because of his maleness, certain privileges in racist patriarchy, e.g., indentured servitude as opposed to enslavement, exclusive right to public assistance until the 1960s, "legitimate" offspring and (if married into the middle/upper class) the luxury to live on her husband's income, etc.

The black woman, having neither maleness nor whiteness, has always had her heterosexuality, which white men and black men have manipulated by force and at will. Further, she, like all poor people, has had her labor, which the white capitalist man has also taken and exploited at will. These capabilities have allowed black women minimal access to the crumbs thrown at black men and white women. So, when the black woman and the white woman become lovers, we bring that history and all those questions to the relationship as well as other people's problems with the relationships. The taboo against intimacy between white and black people has been internalized by us and simultaneously defied by us. If we, as lesbian-feminists, defy the taboo, then we begin to transform the history of relationships between black women and white women.[6]

In her essay "Disloyal to Civilization: Feminism, Racism, Gynephobia," Rich calls for feminists to attend to the complexities of the relationship between black and white women in the United States. Rich queries:

What caricatures of bloodless fragility and broiling sensuality still imprint our psyches, and where did we receive these imprintings? What happened between the several thousand northern white women and southern black women who together taught in the schools founded under Reconstruction by the Freedmen's Bureau, side by side braving the Ku Klux Klan harrassment, terrorism, and the hostility of white communities?[7]

So, all of us would do well to stop fighting each other for our space at the bottom, because there ain't no more room. We have spent so much time hating ourselves. Time to love ourselves. And that, for all lesbians, as lovers, as comrades, as freedom fighters, is the final resistance.

Notes

1. Judy Grahn, "The Common Woman," *The Work of a Common Woman* (Oakland: Diana Press, 1978), 67.
2. Adrienne Rich, *On Lies, Secrets, and Silence: Selected Prose 1966–1978* (New York: WW Norton, 1979), 225.
3. I would like to give particular acknowledgement to the Combahee River Collective's "A Black Feminist Statement." Because this document espouses "struggling against racial, sexual, heterosexual, and class oppression," it has become a manifesto of radical feminist thought, action and practice.
4. Pat Robinson et al., "Poor Black Women's Study Papers by Poor Black Women of Mount Vernon, New York," in *The Black Woman: An Anthology*, edited by Toni Cade (New York: New American Library, 1970), 194.
5. Shulamith Firestone, *The Dialectic of Sex: The Case for Feminist Revolution* (New York: Bantam Books, 1972), 113.
6. One such example is the Port Royal Experiment (1862), the precursor of the Freedmen's Bureau. Port Royal was a program of relief for "freed men and women" in the South Carolina Sea Islands, organized under the auspices of the Boston Education Commision and the Freedmen's Relief Association, in New York and the Port Royal Relief Association, in Philadelphia, and sanctioned by the Union Army and the Federal Government. See *The Journal of Charlotte Forten on the "Port Royal Experiment"* (Boston: Beacon Press, 1969). Through her Northern bourgeois myopia, Forten recounts her experiences as a black teacher among the black freed men and women and her Northern white women peers.
7. Rich, On Lies, Secrets, and Silence, 298.

Lowriding through the Women's Movement

Barbara Noda

One road winds down the mountains, past apple orchards, and into the half-awake town of Watsonville, California. Not quite disturbed by the university students of Santa Cruz or the tourists of Monterey, an eye-distance from the blue roar of the Pacific, Watsonville is still a sleepy town where lowriders drag Main in search of non-existent action. The lowriders are left to their own destiny, to cruise against a backdrop of fog-shrouded artichokes when the sun has gone down. Thorny spears thrust into a star-studded night, and the lowriders bail out at deserted beaches, drink six-packs of beer, and stare at the foam.

Sharon's kitchen in Watsonville was the center of a different kind of activity. We assembled in the evening: Sharon; Sharon's zealous sister who would soon be led to Christianity; a black lesbian who lived in a cottage behind Sharon's house who was an unforgivable romantic and who probably led a past life as an opera singer; a Chicana, self-named after a revolutionary, struggling to earn a doctorate in the University of California's ethereal mountaintop program called "History of Consciousness"; and myself.

We were probably among the first of our kind back in the early seventies: a third world women's group. There, in the quiet of residential Watsonville, we discussed the "colonized" and the "colonizer." Sharon distributed green tea, Chinese pastries, and Aime Cesaire's *Discourse on Colonialism*. As the evening wound down we stormed out together—third world sisters—and dragged Main with the masses, drank beer and howled at the empty, innocent face of the sky who oppressed us.

Whether *Race* was our answer or our question, certainly it held us together if even for a few brief months in our lives during a time when *nothing else* in the world that we saw around us had any solid identity or meaning. It was a vaporous season, like a lost summer, and desperately we needed to hold on to each other and croon a few songs from the underworld.

Now, so many years later, it is still difficult to believe that Sharon is dead. I keep thinking that one day I'll see her in the midst of a demonstration, shouting through a megaphone and glaring into the pale eye who dares to tell her to "go back to where you came from." She is *not* from China. But perhaps shouting into a megaphone was not her way. I remember the last time I saw her in newly established living quarters in the Outer Mission. We shared a sweet piece of watermelon that floated like a bright red iceberg in the middle of our plate, unmistakably a bite of paradise. Old differences over "correct" politics slithered harmlessly from our mouths with the black seeds we spit out. We talked about Asian American poetry and Tule Lake,[1] co-existed for a moment then parted ways.

As one who was so sincerely dedicated to the "cause," for her to be broadsided while driving past the pine and sand that border Highway One and killed instantly is a mystery beyond all comprehension. There is no understanding of such things. Maybe we knew something then that we needed to forget in order to live more meaningful lives, when we joined the lowriders in the flagrant pursuit of their destiny.

I rode the elevator down from the 21st floor, marched to the bakery where Sharon used to buy pastries on her visits to the city, and ate my lunch in Portsmouth Square. I had been plugged into a dictaphone all morning and Chinatown squirmed with life.

Pigeons softly gurgling. Game tables obscured and surrounded by the beating hearts of groups of men. Women carrying bags of groceries nearly flying above sedate heads, like kites trailed by small children. Old people deciphering the ancient language of their worn out books. The red benches. My red sweater. The color RED sang out at me, and I was a glorious part of it.

Across the street was the leveled site of the I-Hotel.[2] A fortress barricaded with the strategy of ardent organizers, it was now a parking lot. The damp cold of the building, the loneliness of the tenants and of us (I was not sure whether we had been the youthful guardians of the building or stray cats who had wandered in) had been demolished into a flattened expanse of less than nothing. Even nothing speaks. This was merely city grime, fumes, noise, pollution. The humanity that had kept us warm and huddled together through makeshift Christmas dinners, internal crises and external warfare had been strained from the air. Not even a mirage existed, only the city life around me.

Notes

1. Tule Lake was a Japanese American internment camp during WWII, located Siskiyou County, California. *(Editor, 2015)*
2. The International Hotel, the last remnant of "Manilatown" in San Francisco, was the site of a 1970s decade-long anti-eviction struggle led by young Asian American radicals, in concert with the elder Filipino residents. *(Editor, 2015)*

Letter to Ma

Merle Woo

January, 1980

Dear Ma,

I was depressed over Christmas, and when New Year's rolled around, do you know what one of my resolves was? Not to come by and see you as much anymore. I had to ask myself why I get so down when I'm with you, my mother, who has focused so much of her life on me, who has endured so much; one who I am proud of and respect so deeply for simply surviving.

I suppose that one of the main reasons is that when I leave your house, your pretty little round white table in the dinette where we sit while you drink tea (with only three specks of Jasmine) and I smoke and drink coffee, I am down because I believe there are chasms between us. When you say, "I support you, honey, in everything you do except . . . except . . ." I know you mean except my speaking out and writing of my anger at all those things that have caused those chasms. When you say I shouldn't be so ashamed of Daddy, former gambler, retired clerk of a "gook suey" store, because of the time when I was six and saw him humiliated on Grant Avenue by two white cops, I know you haven't even been listening to me when I have repeatedly said that I am not ashamed of him, not you, not who we are. When you ask, "Are you so angry because you are unhappy?" I know that we are not talking to each other. Not with understanding, although many words have passed between us, many hours, many afternoons at that round table with Daddy out in the front room watching television, and drifting out every once in a while to say "Still talking?" and getting more peanuts that are so bad for his health.

We talk and we talk and I feel frustrated by your censorship. I know it is unintentional and unconscious. But whatever I have told you about the classes I was teaching, or the stories I was working on, you've always forgotten within a month. Maybe you can't listen—because maybe when you look in my eyes, you will, as you've always done, sense more than what we're actually saying, and that makes you fearful. Do you see your repressed anger manifested in me? What doors would groan wide open if you heard my words with complete understanding? Are you afraid that your daughter is breaking out of our shackles, and into total anarchy? That your daughter has turned into a crazy woman who advocates not only equality for Third World people, for women, but for gays as well? Please don't shudder, Ma, when I speak of homosexuality. Until we can all present ourselves to the world in our completeness, as fully and beautifully as we see ourselves naked in our bedrooms, we are not free.

After what seems like hours of talking, I realize it is not talking at all, but the filling up of time with sounds that say, "I am your daughter, you are my mother, and we are keeping each other company, and that is enough." But it is not enough because my life has been formed by your life. Together we have lived one hundred and eleven years in this country as yellow women, and it is not enough to enunciate words and words and words and then to have them only mean that we have been keeping each other company. I desperately want you to understand me and my work, Ma, to know what I am doing! When you distort what I say, like thinking I am against all "Caucasians" or that I am ashamed of Dad, then I feel anger and more frustration and want to slash out, not at you, but at those external forces which keep us apart. What deepens the chasms between us are our different reactions to those forces. Yours has been one of silence, self-denial, self-effacement; you believing it is your fault that you never fully experienced self-pride and freedom of choice. But listen, Ma, only with a deliberate consciousness is my reaction different from yours.

When I look at you, there are images: images of you as a little ten-year-old Korean girl, being sent alone from Shanghai to the United States, in steerage with only one skimpy little dress, being sick and lonely on Angel Island for three months; then growing up in a "Home" run by white missionary women. Scrubbing floors on your hands and knees, hauling coal in heavy metal buckets up three flights of stairs, tending to the younger children, putting hot bricks on your cheeks to deaden the pain from the terrible toothaches you always had. Working all your life as maid, waitress, salesclerk, office worker, mother. But throughout there is an image of you as strong and courageous, and persevering: climbing out of windows to escape from the Home, then later, from an abusive first husband. There is so much more to these images than I can say, but I think you know what I mean. Escaping out of windows offered only temporary respites; surviving is an everyday chore. You gave me, physically, what you never had, but there was a spiritual, emotional legacy you passed down which was reinforced by society: self-contempt because of our race, our sex, our sexuality. For deeply ingrained in me, Ma, there has been that strong, compulsive force to sink into self-contempt, passivity, and despair. I am sure that my fifteen years of alcohol abuse have not been forgotten by either of us, nor my suicidal depressions.

Now, I know you are going to think that I hate and despise you for your self-hatred, for your isolation. But I don't. Because in spite of your withdrawal, in spite of your loneliness, you have not only survived, but been beside me in the worst of times when your company meant everything in the world to me. I just need more than that now, Ma. I have taken and taken from you in terms of needing you to mother me, to be by my side, and I need, now, to take from you two more things: understanding and support for who I am now and my work.

We are Asian American women and the reaction to our identity is what causes the chasms instead of connections. But do you realize, Ma, that I could never have reacted the way I have if you had not provided for me the opportunity to be free of the binds that have held you down, and to be in the process of self-affirmation? Because of your life, because of the physical security you have given me: my education, my full stomach, my clothed and starched back, my piano and dancing lessons—all those gifts you never received—I saw myself as having worth; now I begin to love myself more, see our potential, and fight for just that kind of social change that will affirm me, my race, my sex, my heritage. And while I affirm myself, Ma, I affirm you.

Today, I am satisfied to call myself either an Asian American Feminist or Yellow Feminist. The two terms are inseparable because race and sex are an integral part of me. This means that I am working with others to realize pride in culture and women and heritage (the heritage that is the exploited yellow immigrant: Daddy and you). Being a Yellow Feminist means being a community activist and a humanist. It does not mean "separatism," either by cutting myself off from non-Asians or men. It does not mean retaining the same power structure and substituting women in positions of control held by men. It does mean fighting the whites and the men who abuse us, straight-jacket us and tape our mouths; it means changing the economic class system and psychological forces (sexism, racism, and homophobia) that really hurt all of us. And I do this, not in isolation, but in the community.

We no longer can afford to stand back and watch while an insatiable elite ravages and devours resources that are enough for all of us. The obstacles are so huge and overwhelming that often I do become cynical and want to give up. And if I were struggling alone, I know I would never even attempt to put into action what I believe in my heart, that (and this is primarily because of you, Ma) Yellow Women are strong and have the potential to be powerful and effective leaders.

I can hear you asking now, "Well, what do you mean by 'social change and leadership'? And how are you going to go about it?" To begin with, we must wipe out the circumstances that keep us down in silence and self-effacement. Right now, my techniques are education and writing. Yellow Feminist means being a core for change, and that core means having the belief in our potential as human beings. I will work with anyone, support anyone, who shares my sensibility, my objectives. But there are barriers to unity: white women who are racist, and Asian American men who are sexist. My very being declares that those two groups do not share my complete sensibility. I would be fragmented, mutilated, if I did not fight against racism and sexism together.

And this is when the pain of the struggle hits home. How many white women have taken on the responsibility to educate themselves about Third World people, their history, their culture? How many white women really think about the stereotypes they retain as truth about women of color? But the perpetuation of dehumanizing stereotypes is really very helpful for whites; they use them to justify their giving us the lowest wages and all the work they don't want to perform. Ma, how can we believe things are changing when as a nurse's aide during World War II, you were given only the tasks of changing the bed linen, removing bed pans, taking urine samples, and then only three years ago as a retired volunteer worker in a local hospital, white women gave themselves desk jobs and gave you, at sixty-nine, the same work you did in 1943? Today you speak more fondly of being a nurse's aide during World War II and how proud you are of the fact that the Red Cross showed its appreciation for your service by giving you a diploma. Still in 1980, the injustices continue. I can give you so many examples of groups which are "feminist" in which women of color were given the usual least important tasks, the shitwork, and given no say in how that group is to be run. Needless to say, those Third World women, like you, dropped out, quit.

Working in writing and teaching, I have seen how white women condescend to Third World women, reasoning that because of our oppression, which they know nothing about, we are behind them and their "progressive ideas" in the struggle for freedom. They don't even look at history! At the facts! How we as Asian American women have always been fighting for more than mere survival, but were never acknowledged because we were in our communities, invisible, but not inaccessible.

And I get so tired of being the instant resource for information on Asian American women. Being the token representative, going from class to class, group to group, bleeding for white women so they can have an easy answer and then—and this is what really gets to me—they usually leave to never continue their education about us on their own.

To the racist white female professor who says, "If I have to watch everything I say I wouldn't say anything," I want to say, "Then get out of teaching."

To the white female poet who says, "Well, frankly, I believe that politics and poetry don't necessarily have to go together," I say, "Your little taste of white privilege has deluded you into thinking that you don't have to fight against sexism in this society. You are talking to me from your own isolation and your own racism. If you feel that you don't have to fight for me, that you don't have to speak out against capitalism, the exploitation of human and natural resources, then you in your silence, your inability to make connections, are siding with a system that will eventually get you, after it has gotten me. And if you think that's not a political stance, you're more than simply deluded, you're crazy!"

This is the same white voice that says, "I am writing about and looking for themes that are 'universal.' " Well, most of the time when "universal" is used, it is just a euphemism for "white": white themes, white significance, white culture. And denying minority groups their rightful place and time in US history is simply racist.

Yes, Ma, I am mad. I carry the anger from my own experience and the anger you couldn't afford to express, and even that is often misinterpreted no matter how hard I try to be clear about my position. A white woman in my class said to me a couple of months ago, "I feel that Third World women hate me and that *they* are being racist; I'm being stereotyped, and I've never been part of the ruling class." I replied, "Please try to understand. Know our history. Know the racism of whites, how deep it goes. Know that we are becoming ever more intolerant of those people who let their ignorance be their excuse for their complacency, their liberalism, when this country (this world!) is going to hell in a handbasket. Try to understand that our distrust is from experience, and that our distrust is power*less*. Racism is an essential part of the status quo, power*ful*, and continues to keep us down. It is a rule taught to all of us from birth. Is it no wonder that we fear there are no exceptions?"

And as if the grief we go through working with white women weren't enough—so close to home, in our community, and so very painful, is the lack of support we get from some of our Asian American brothers. Here is a quote from a rather prominent male writer ranting on about a Yellow "sister":

> . . . I can only believe that such blatant sucking off of the identity is the work of a Chinese American woman, another Jade Snow Wong Pochahontas yellow. Pussywhipped again. Oh, damn, pussywhipped again.

Chinese American woman: "another Jade Snow Wong Pochahontas yellow." According to him, Chinese American women sold out—are contemptuous of their culture, pathetically strain all their lives to be white, hate Asian American men, and so marry white men (the John Smiths)—or just like Pochahontas: we rescue white men while betraying our fathers; then marry white men, get baptized, and go to dear old England to become curiosities of the civilized world. Whew! Now, that's an indictment! (Of all women of color.) Some of the male writers in the Asian American community seem never to support us. They always expect us to support them, and you know what? We almost always do. And Yellow men? Are they kidding? We go to their readings, buy and read and comment on their books, and try to keep up a dialogue. And they accuse us of betrayal, are resentful because we do readings together as Women, and so often do not come to our performances. And all the while we hurt because we are rejected by our brothers. The Pochahontas image used by a Chinese American man points out a tragic truth: the white man and his ideology are still over us and between us. These men of color, with clear vision, fight the racism in white society, but have bought the white male definition of "masculinity": men only should take on the leadership in the community because the qualities of "originality, daring, physical courage, and creativity" are "traditionally masculine."[1]

Some Asian men don't seem to understand that by supporting Third World women and fighting sexism, they are helping themselves as well. I understand all too clearly how dehumanized Dad was in this country. To be a Chinese man in America is to be a victim of both racism and sexism. He was made to feel he was without strength, identity, and purpose. He was made to feel soft and weak, whose only job was to serve whites. Yes, Ma, at one time I was ashamed of him because I thought he was "womanly." When those two white cops said, "Hey, fat boy, where's our meat?" he left me standing there on Grant Avenue while he hurried over to his store to get it; they kept complaining, never satisfied, "That piece isn't good enough. What's the matter with you, fat boy? Don't you have respect? Don't wrap that meat in newspapers either; use the good stuff over there." I didn't know that he spent a year and a half on Angel Island; that we could never have our right names; that he lived in constant fear of being deported; that, like you, he worked two full-time jobs most of his life; that he was mocked and ridiculed because he speaks "broken English." And Ma, I was so ashamed after that experience when I was only six years old that I never held his hand again.

Today, as I write to you of all these memories, I feel even more deeply hurt when I realize how many people, how so many people, because of racism and sexism, fail to see what power we sacrifice by not joining hands.

But not all white women are racist, and not all Asian American men are sexist. And we choose to trust them, love and work with them. And there are visible changes. Real tangible, positive changes. The changes I love to see are those changes within ourselves.

Your grandchildren, my children, Emily and Paul. That makes three generations. Emily loves herself. Always has. There are shades of self-doubt but much less than in you or me. She says exactly what she thinks, most of the time, either in praise or in criticism of herself or others. And at sixteen she goes after whatever she wants, usually center stage. She trusts and loves people, regardless of race or sex (but, of course, she's cautious), loves her community and works in it, speaks up against racism and sexism in school. Did you know that she got Zora Neale Hurston and Alice Walker on her reading list for a Southern Writers class when there were only white authors? That she insisted on changing a script done by an Asian American man when she saw that the depiction of the character she was playing was sexist? That she went to a California State House Conference to speak out for Third World students' needs?

And what about her little brother, Paul? Twelve years old. And remember, Ma? At one of our Saturday Night Family Dinners, how he lectured Ronnie (his uncle, yet!) about how he was a male chauvinist? Paul told me once how he knew he had to fight to be Asian American, and later he added that if it weren't for Emily and me, he wouldn't have to think about feminist stuff, too. He says he can hardly enjoy a movie or TV program anymore because of the sexism. Or comic books. And he is very much aware of the different treatment he gets from adults: "You have to do everything right," he said to Emily, "and I can get away with almost anything."

Emily and Paul give us hope, Ma. Because they are proud of who they are, and they care so much about our culture and history. Emily was the first to write your biography because she knows how crucial it is to get our stories in writing.

Ma, I wish I knew the histories of the women in our family before you. I bet that would be quite a story. But that may be just as well, because I can say that *you* started something. Maybe you feel ambivalent or doubtful about it, but you did. Actually, you should be proud of what you've begun. I am. If my reaction to being a Yellow Woman is different than yours was, please know that that is not a judgment on you, a criticism or denial of you, your worth. I have always supported you, and as the years pass, I think I begin to understand you more and more.

In the last few years, I have realized the value of Homework: I have studied the history of our people in this country. I cannot tell you how proud I am to be a Chinese/Korean American Woman. We have such a proud heritage, such a courageous tradition. I want to tell everyone about that, all the particulars that are left out in the schools. And the full awareness of being a woman makes me want to sing. And I do sing with other Asian Americans and women, Ma, anyone who will sing with me.

I feel now that I can begin to put our lives in a larger framework. Ma, a larger framework! The outlines for us are time and blood, but today there is breadth possible through making connections with others involved in community struggle. In loving ourselves for who we are—American women of color—we can make a vision for the future where we are free to fulfill our human potential. This new framework will not support repression, hatred, exploitation and isolation, but will be a human and beautiful framework, created in a community, bonded not by color, sex or class, but by love and the common goal for the liberation of mind, heart, and spirit.

Ma, today, you are as beautiful and pure to me as the picture I have of you, as a little girl, under my dresser-glass.

I love you,
Merle

Note

1. Frank Chin, Jeffrey Paul Chan, Lawson Fusao Inada, and Shawn Wong, eds., *AIIEEEE! An Anthology of Asian American Writers* (Washington, DC: Howard University Press, 1974).

I Come with No Illusions

Mirtha N. Quintanales

Columbus, Ohio
December 27, 1979

Querida Chabela (Isabel Yrigoyen),

. . . Woman love. Never knew it would be so hard to leave anyone. Even though it means everything to me to move on, to finally embark on this self-healing journey. Torn by guilt. My lover. Working-class "white" woman from a small town. She has no more privileges than I do. As alone as I am. She is not my enemy. World upside down.

. . . What lies ahead? A mystery. Do not dare even consider the possibility of a love relationship with a Latina, a Cuban woman, even to dream that I could find such partnership . . . family. Work. It is my life. It is all I have. It is what now ultimately propels me to make this move. You, my friends, will sweeten my life. I know that. But I come to you with no illusions. I join you because I must. Give of myself to those who can give to me of themselves. Sisters. Sharing. I look for, expect nothing more. Is there really something more?

Setting myself up? Closing up, putting up barriers? Perhaps. Perhaps just trying to be "my own woman." Perhaps just trying to be one, not one-half. Can I find happiness "alone"? Americans tell me that I should strive for this blessed state of self-contentment as "one" if I intend to survive. Yet often I have doubts. Is this the kind of world I want to live in? A world where ultimately only the "I" matters? Millions of people living in self-constructed little boxes, Incommunicado.

I ponder over the meaning and possible repercussions of the choices I am about to make. What does it mean to say to myself that only other Latina, bicultural lesbian women can satisfy my needs? What are the implications of separating myself from American women and creating a separate community with women I identify as my counterparts?

It means, for one thing, that I am admitting failure. Failure to adjust, adapt, change, transcend cultural differences. Yet this is not only a personal failure. It is one which I share with millions. The reality of ethnic minority enclaves throughout the world tells me a great deal about the process I am going through. It is neither unique nor new. And ultimately it may have a lot more to do with "success" than with failure. It is after all, a survival strategy—particularly in the context of a power imbalance between "natives" and "foreigners"—where the latter are in a better bargaining position as a *group* than as scattered individuals fighting their own personal battles.

For myself—as a Latina lesbian/feminist, it also means a real narrowing of options and privileges. I have extremely limited resources. No money, no access to power, no legitimacy. If there are many like me I do not know. Nor is it going to be easy for me to connect with them if I should learn that there are. Their resources are likely to be as limited as mine. This is a socio-economic, political reality that acts as a barrier to the formation of a strong and visible community. Not only the "social goodies" (money, power, fame, and other minor privileges) but life's necessities (a job, a roof over my head . . .) depend on my ties, my interactions with American men and women. To say "I do not like the nature of this tie with the powerful" is dangerous; for the implications are that I may strive to break free from it and in doing so reduce my chances of making it in this society.

But what of human feeling? It is, after all, great personal need, not political analysis that drives me to take this stand, to turn away from my American sisters and put all my energies into creating a community with my Latina sisters. What is the nature and significance of this need? Is it true that love knows no boundaries? Or that being "human" somehow means being ultimately undifferentiated—"all alike"? Perhaps one of the greatest lessons I have learned is that in fact "human nature," bound as it is to "culture," implies variability and difference. Yes, we all need to eat and sleep, keep ourselves warm, protect ourselves from harm, be nurtured into maturity; touch and be touched, etc. But, how we choose to meet these needs varies and changes from time to time, place to place and is dependent both on history and the particular set of environmental circumstances contextual to our lives. What both puzzles me and distresses me is the degree to which we seem to be "culture bound." As if "setting the cultural mold" implied never quite being able to break free from it. At least not completely. This seems to be particularly true in the most private activities of our lives—how we express and share feeling in the context of our intimate interpersonal relationships. The wonder of it! And the pain . . .

Con mucho cariño, tu amiga
Mirtha

I Paid Very Hard for My Immigrant Ignorance

Mirtha N. Quintanales

Columbus, Ohio
January, 1980

Dear Barbara (Smith),

Thanks for your letter. I can appreciate your taking the time to write. It can get *so* difficult for busy people to keep up with correspondence . . . I only hope that you have taken some time to rest, gather your energies. I'm just beginning to emerge from a several-week period of semi-hermitdom myself. I, too, was exhausted. Too much work, too many responsibilities—often the worry of not moving fast enough, or too fast to have any kind of an impact. After a brief peaceful interlude, the pressures are beginning to build again. Oh well . . .

I wanted to tell you about my visit to San Francisco, about coming together with my Latina lesbian/feminist sisters. The joy and the pain of finding each other, of realizing how long we've "*done without*," of how difficult it's going to be to heal ourselves, to find our voices . . . But how perfectly wonderful to finally have a family, a community. Yet I find that there is too much to tell. Cannot easily compress it all in a letter. How I wish that we could meet and talk! So much of the Black lesbian/feminist experience speaks to our own . . . I passed around all the literature you'd handed out at conferences—including *Conditions 5*. And the Latina sisters were amazed. Lorraine Bethel's "What Chou Mean We White Girl?" was especially telling . . . Many of our feelings given form, meaning. Please let her know that her work has been very helpful to us—particularly in sorting out what we want and don't want in our relationships with white, mainstream American feminists. Yes, there is a lot we can learn from each other.

But Barbara, I am worried. At the moment I am in the process of organizing a roundtable for the NWSA[1] conference, on the topic of racial and ethnic minority lesbians in the US. There are two other women involved—a Greek friend of mine from Berkeley, and a Black woman from San Francisco. And I feel the tension building. The Greek woman's many attempts to "connect" with Third World lesbians and "Women of Color" (most poignantly at last year's conference) have been met with outright rejection. Unfortunately, being loud, aggressive and very Greek-

148

identified, she has found a great deal of rejection in white, mainstream lesbian/feminist circles as well. Clearly she does not fit there either.

The Black woman's commitments, from what I can gather, are understandably with Third World women, women of color. And I am quite uncomfortably in the middle. As a Third World, Caribbean woman I understand what it means to have grown up "colonized" in a society built on slavery and the oppression of imperialist forces. As an immigrant and a cultural minority woman who happens to be white-skinned, I empathize with the pain of ethnic invisibility and the perils of passing (always a very tenuous situation—since acknowledgment of ethnic ties is inevitably accompanied by stereotyping, prejudice, and various kinds of discrimination—the problem is not just personal, but "systemic," "political"—one more reality of American "life"). How to reconcile these different kinds of "primary emergencies": race and culture? Of course this kind of conflict tends to obscure the issue of class and its relationship to race and ethnicity so important for the understanding of the dilemma.

Not all Third World women are "women of color"—if by this concept we mean exclusively "non-white." I am only one example. And not all women of color are really Third World—if this term is only used in reference to underdeveloped or developing societies (especially those not allied with any superpower). Clearly then it would be difficult to justify referring to Japanese women, who are women of color, as Third World women. Yet, if we extend the concept of Third World to include internally "colonized" racial and ethnic minority groups in this country, so many different kinds of groups could be conceivably included, that the crucial issue of social and institutional racism and its historic tie to slavery in the US could get diluted, lost in the shuffle. The same thing would likely happen if we extended the meaning of "women of color" to include all those women in this country who are victims of prejudice and discrimination (in many respects), but who nevertheless hold racial privileges and may even be racists.

I don't know what to think anymore. Things begin to get even more complicated when I begin to consider that many of us who identify as "Third World" or "Women of Color" have grown up as, or are fast becoming, "middle class" and highly educated, and therefore more privileged than many of our white, poor and working-class sisters. Sometimes I get angry at my lover because she does not seem to relate to my being a "Cuban" lesbian. And yet, can I really relate to the fact that she grew up in a very small town, in a working-class family—with little money, few other resources, little encouragement to get an education, etc.? Yes . . . and no. There have been times in my life when my family had little money or food. There have been times in my life when I lived from day to day not knowing if I would be alive "tomorrow"—not knowing really how it felt to plan for "next month," or "next year."

Yet, even though I grew up having to heat my bathwater and sleep in a very lumpy bed, even though I grew up often being ashamed of bringing my friends home because our furniture was old and dilapidated, I went to private schools, spent summers at the beach, traveled, had plenty of toys and books to read; took music and dancing lessons, went horseback riding—my parents being very conscious of, and being very *able* to give us the best (if not always in terms of material comforts) that their middle-class resources gave them access to—including the services of a long string of nurse-maids (my mother worked, and in Cuba often the maids had maids—even if it meant putting little girls to work as servants and baby-tenders—economic exploitation galore!).

Yes, I have suffered in this country. I have been the victim of blatant prejudice and institutional discrimination. As an ethnic minority woman and a lesbian I have lived in the margins, in fear, isolated, disconnected, silent and in pain. Nevertheless, those early years of relatively "blissful" middle-class childhood (although I have to say that after age 7 it was *hell*—political violence and death always lurking) in my own country where I was simply part of the "mainstream" if not a little better off because of my father's professional status, have served me as a "cushion" throughout my life. Even in the United States, as an essentially middle-class (and white-skinned) woman, I have had "opportunities" (or have known how to make them for myself) that my very white, working-class American lover has never had.

Having managed to graduate from college (one out of three in her graduating high school class who managed to make it to college) against tremendous odds, she is still struggling with the fact that she may never really learn the ropes of surviving well in mainstream, middle-class American society. And, need I add that mainstream white, middle-class American feminism is as insensitive to her needs as it is to mine?

I realize that I cannot fight everybody's battles. But need I create false enemies in order to wage my own? I am a bit concerned when a Latina lesbian sister generalizes about/puts down the "white woman"— especially if she herself has white skin. In the midst of this labeling, might she not dismiss the fact of her own white privileges—regardless of her identification with Black, Native American, and other Third World women of color? Might she not dismiss the fact that she may often be far better off than many white women? I cannot presume to know what it is really like to be a Black woman in America, to be racially oppressed.

I cannot presume to know what it is really like to grow up American "White Trash" and destitute.

But I am also a bit concerned when a Black sister generalizes about/dismisses all non-black women, or all women who are not strictly "women of color" or strictly "Third World." If you are not WASP in this country, if you or your family have known the immigrant experience or ghetto life, you are likely to be very much acquainted with the social, economic political reality of internal colonization. Yes, racism is a BIG MONSTER we all need to contend with—regardless of our skin color and ethnic affiliation. But I think we need to keep in mind that in this country, in this world, racism is used *both* to create false differences among us *and* to mask very very significant ones—cultural economic, political . . . And yes, those who have been racially oppressed must create separatist spaces to explore the meaning of their experiences—to heal themselves, to gather their energies, their strength, to develop their own voices, to build their armies. And yes, those of us who have not been victims of racial oppression must come to terms with our own racism, our own complicity with this system that discriminates and oppresses on the basis of skin color and body features. And of course it would be irresponsible liberal folly to propose that social and institutional racism could be eliminated by simply "becoming" personally non-racist, by becoming "integrated" in our private lives . . . How ridiculous for white folk to think that a long history of slavery (and every other kind of oppression) and an *ongoing* and *insidious* reality of social, economic, political exploitation could be magically transcended through a few individual choices . . . And even if everybody's skin should suddenly turn black, it would be quite impossible to truly know what it means to have grown up—generation after generation—Black and female in America. Of course our skin is not likely to "turn," and so regardless of how "conscious" we claim to be of the "Black experience" in America, we shall always be limited by our own history and the reality of our white skin and the privileges it automatically confers on us.

Ironically, when a Black American sister (or anyone for that matter) puts me, or other ethnic women of this society in the same category with the socially dominant White American Woman on the basis of lighter-than-black skin color, she is in fact denying my history, my culture, my identity, my very being, my pain and my struggle. She, too, is being *personally* racist. When she fails to recognize that the "social privileges" of lighter-than-black ethnic-minority lesbians in this society are almost totally dependent on our denial of who we are, on our *ethnic death*, she also falls prey to the racist mythology that color differences are the end-all indications of social inequality. That those who happen to have the "right" skin color are not only all alike but all hold the same social privileges. Yes, lighter-than-black skin color *may* confer on some ethnic minority women the option of becoming "assimilated," "integrated" in mainstream American society. But is this really a privilege when it always means having to become invisible, ghost-like, identity-less, community-less, totally alienated? The perils of "passing" as white American are perils indeed. It should be easy enough at least for *lesbians* to understand the meaning of being and yet not being, of "merging" and yet remaining utterly alone and in the margins of our society.

And while it is true that a lesbian/feminist community and culture have emerged, while it is true that Black, Latina and other Third World/lesbians "of color" have begun to speak up, it is not true that we have yet engaged in a truly un-biased, unprejudiced *dialogue*. We are still measuring each other by the yardstick of the White, Capitalist, Imperialist, Racist American Patriarch. *We are still seeing radical differences when they don't exist and not seeing them when they are critical.* And most disastrously, we are failing to recognize much of what we *share*. Is it not possible for us to recognize, respect and settle our differences; to validate our various groups' struggles and need for separate spaces, and yet to open our eyes to the fact that divided we are only likely to succeed at defeat?

It is pure folly to think that a small group of Latina or Black or Chinese American lesbians can, on its own, create a feminist revolution. It is pure folly to think that middle-class WASP feminists can do so . . .

Barbara, I ache to live with and love with my Latina lesbian/feminist sisters—to speak "Spanglish," to eat arroz con frijoles, to dance salsa, to openly talk sex and flirt with one another; to secretly pray to Yemayá, Changó, Oshún, and the Virgen de Guadalupe. I run to them for refuge, for dear life!

But when I meet you and other Black lesbian sisters—and am moved by what we seem to share, I ache for you also. I spend time with Stacy (Anastasia) and other Southern European/North African/Mediterranean lesbian sisters—and am stirred by what we seem to have in common, I feel deep yearning for them . . . I read the words of other ethnic American lesbian sisters and I find that I understand them and want to share in these women's lives. And I live, love and work with working-class sisters. Have lived, loved and worked in the poor urban ghettos of Chicago and Boston. Have spent some time in the poor, rural, isolated mountains of New Mexico. Have traveled to Latin American countries, to India, Thailand, Taiwan, Hong Kong, Japan—feeling the pain of my poor and hard-working sisters—struggling against all odds to stay alive, to live with dignity. I cannot sleep sometimes—haunted by the memories of such all-encompassing poverty—the kind of poverty that even poor Americans could not begin to conceive. India. India was the unraveling. How insignificant our troubles seem in the United States . . . How ridiculously small my own struggles . . . I don't feel guilt or shame, but this nausea . . . To find us squabbling over who may or may not be called a feminist, who may or may not join or take part in this or that particular political group, etc., etc. The privilege of having feminist "groups"—most women in the world just eat shit. And lesbians—who really knows the fate of most lesbians in the world, especially the Third World?

Is it not possible for all of us here in America to turn *right now* to *all* the sisters of the world—to form a common, human-woman-lesbian bond?

I have lost some sleep lately pondering over this race/culture/class problem . . . We've got to do *something*! Many of us Latinas are non-white—as a matter of fact, most of us are racially mixed to various degrees. Ask a Black or "mulatto" Puerto Rican woman what her identity is, though, and most likely she will tell you *"Puerto Rican."* All Chinese American women are non-white. But ask any of them what her identity is. She will not tell you "yellow," she will tell you Chinese, or Chinese American. Many African peoples are "Black," but ask a Nigerian, an Ethiopian, etc., what her identity is, and she will tell you "Nigerian," or "Ethiopian," or whatever . . . Obviously "Black Culture" is an American phenomenon. Many of us don't really understand this. I know I didn't for a long time. When I first came to this country I just assumed that Black people were simply American (for that matter I just assumed *all* Americans shared the same kind of "American Culture"). I grew up with people of all kinds of skin color—but we were all *Cuban* and understood each other, even though we *could* recognize the most minute "color differences," even though we *could* recognize class differences. How was I supposed to know—given the propaganda—that there was no such thing as a "melting pot"? How was I supposed to know that racism was so widespread and so deeply ingrained in American society? I was *shocked* in my sophomore year in college when several Black women implied that I was a racist when I said I could not figure out what was different about being Black or Yellow, or White, or Red in the United States. I could understand not knowing about a "culture," but not knowing about a "race"? Was "race" per se so important? Was it really linked to a "culture"? This was a weird notion to me indeed!

Well I paid very hard for my immigrant ignorance. I'm still paying—even though I have learned a great deal since then about American sub-cultures and about American racism. Many of my Latina sisters have had similar experiences, and the big question is always there—Will we ever really be accepted by our Black American sisters? I cannot really convey the pain—especially in those of us who *are* Afro-Hispanic-American but light skinned—of seeing so much of ourselves in, and of being so drawn to, African-American women, and yet feeling that we are very likely to be denied a connection, to be rejected. The fucking irony of it! Racism. It has so thoroughly poisoned Americans of all colors that many of us can simply not see beyond it. I'm sorry about this long letter Barbara—especially this last part. But I have not been able to get over this pain. I used to have this recurrent dream (for years) that I would alternately become black and white and black and white over and over and over again . . . It felt really good. But I've never quite figured out all of what it meant . . . Well, take care Barbara.

In sisterhood,
Mirtha

Note

1. National Women's Studies Association.

Earth-Lover, Survivor, Musician

Naomi Littlebear Moreno

The following is an excerpt from a letter in response to Cherríe's request that Naomi write an essay on "language & oppression" as a Chicana.

January, 1980

Cherríe,

I have a clear image in my mind about the things we talked about, your anger about language, identification—given the brief acquaintance, I personally could relate to a lot of what you were saying—i realize that those feelings had a lot to do with why i wrote the book i'm sending you[1]—that was a very important time in my life. However I realize now that it wasn't for me exactly the most balanced part of my life. It was only a time in which i hurt so bad i had to shake off the dust of one too many insults in order to carry on. Nonetheless, my criticism, analysis, etc., did not come from a natural place in me. It was not the "voice of my mothers" nor did it completely reflect the way i was brought up to be. I wrote that book as a brown woman's retort to white *people*, white middle-class leftists who were trying to redirect my spirit. I was *supposed* to be the angry chicana speaking her vengeance against whites, against the capitalist system.

> *I am a sad chicana lesbian woman who is a woman-identified earth lover, survivor, musician—music and beauty are my tools against my aches and pains—striving to bring peace into an otherwise tumultuous past.*

I am not the scholar analyst you are—which I totally respect. I'm clear about why i am and how i am—*i cannot extricate the lesbian from my soul no more than i could the chicana—i have always been both.*

The woman I am right now is not struggling with language—this time—i am closest and clearest right now about violence—i am haunted by dreams from my childhood and not-too-distant past. I could not adequately write about language unless i was right there with the problem, as you seem to be—you are fairly bursting with reasons and important thoughts, insights into our mutual experience with the degradation and denial that came with our language loss (abduction?).

Imagine the process you would have to go thru if I asked you to write me a paper on violence in the barrios and how that affected your

155

personal life? *I need to feel control of my own life—violence has on some deep level rendered me helpless and given me a deep fear of being powerless*—our language being stripped from us creates similar fears. I need to figure out what is closest to me. I have done some work in exorcising the demons of communication—my current observation is that i feel comfortable with words again, except when i try to make scientific discoveries—that is me reacting to male energy that says women are stupid & emotional.

My emotions & intuitions are there for a purpose. They are honest perceptions. I don't have to try to be grassroots. I do have to try to relate my straight feminist politics.

Wanting to be loving and have a family is my connection with my culture. I am doing that. Going to meetings is not part of my ethnic background.

I got real turned around when i got involved with leftist politics. I am now trying to piece my life together, discard the violence & humiliations, accept that i am a complete person with nothing lacking. My mind and heart are capable of deciding what's best for me.

For once in my life i have to let my self deserve a home, food on the table, and a handful of loving friends—this is a time of healing and taking the blame of the rapes and attempted rapes, the child beatings i received, taking all that pain off my shoulders and giving it back to whom it belongs.

I want you to accept me as i accept you. Be an amiga, not a comrade to me. I will send you more words if you like but right now the hurt's all around me and i feel like flying away. I will fight back with music, but don't ask me to fight with words. Trust my instincts, my knowledge—i am not a sheltered little wetback—i've been through so much pain that i've popped out the other side. *We* have been thru so much pain that now we have no place to put that pain but to leave it out of our lives—because the pain was given to do its worst damage by festering in our soul, by growing comfortable in our flesh that we more often hurt each other 'tho infested by the same disease.

I have no solution but to go on. I will not carry the stigma that so many have tried to burden me with. These words are mine because this now is *my* language—13 years of English, 13 years of Spanish—that's when I flipped out—the day of my two "children's" anniversary. I was prompted by devils—clinical radicals who instructed me in self-autopsy. Please applaud my victory over those fuckers—it is *your* victory as well—remember they think we're all related. We're not at all where they expected us to be—we just slipped through—because we knew damn well it was a lie.

I refuse to be separated from your life by these words. I read you loud & clear: the story-telling, my crazy aunts, the laughter, deep-hearted joy, celebrating *anything* with a six-pack of beer.[2]

I remember. And as long as i know you too were once there—it is something that can warm us both this winter.

Because i haven't seen my cousins in years.

That is what i miss, that is what i'm looking for.

March 23, 1980

Now that the ice has melted and the flowers begin to bloom i welcome the season of growing. Thank you for sharing with me. I do believe we have in common—the cultural rip-off, the anger, the wisdom, the fullness of life.

. . . I have started this letter many times, wanting to send you these stories. I appreciated your letter very much. It's still on my desk reminding me how hard we are working to be visible. We are touring again, maybe we'll meet.

Notes

1. *The Dark of the Moon.* (Portland: Olive Press, 1977). Book of essays & poetry on life in the barrio, and the topics of the Church, Family, Education & the Left.
2. Here Naomi is referring to experiences Cherríe describes in her essay "La Guëra." *(Editors' note, 1981)*

V

Speaking in Tongues

The Third World Woman Writer

Theresa Hak Kyung Cha, *Aveugle Voix (Blind Voice)*, 1975
Black & white photograph, image #3, 9.75" × 6.5"
University of California, Berkeley Art Museum and Pacific Film Archive
Gift of the Theresa Hak Kyung Cha Foundation

Speaking in Tongues

The Third World Woman Writer

Who am I, a poor Chicanita from the sticks, to think I could write?

—Gloria Anzaldúa

As first generation writers, we defy the myth that the color of our skins prevents us from using the pen to create. We come from that history, yes; as Gabrielle Daniels conveys in her poem of the silenced writings of "Millicent Fredericks." But, the face of "American" Literature is radically changing as women of color begin to publish in and out of the mainstream. Still, it is not enough to have our books published. We must also actively engage in establishing the criteria and the standards by which our work can be viewed. As Barbara Smith laid the ground-work in developing literary criticism for Black women in "Toward a Black Feminist Criticism,"[1] here Norma Alarcón plants the seed which germinates a feminist criticism involving the history, mythology, and writings of La Chicana. This article represents the kind of literary criti-cism that is beginning to appear in every segment of the Third World women's community.

We are Third World women writers, so similar yet so different—similar in the issues we confront, different in approach and style. What we have in common is our love of writing and a love of the literature of women of color. In our common struggle and in our writing we reclaim our tongues. We wield a pen as a tool, a weapon, a means of survival, a magic wand that will attract power, that will draw self-love into our bodies.

And though often we may feel ambivalent about our devotion to the female self, we continue to swim *fearless with the length of our own bodies* (Wong) in a sea of words. We continue to swim toward that raft and lifeline which is ourself—ourself as mother, ourself as hero. What we choose finally is to *cultivate our colored skins*.

a teacher taught me
more than she knew
patting me on the head
putting words in my head
—"pretty little Indian girl!"
  saving them—
  going to give them
  back to her one day . . .

—Anna Lee Walters[2]

A woman who writes has power. A woman with power is feared. In the eyes of the world this makes us dangerous beasts.

Notes

1. *Conditions* 2 (October 1977).
2. Dexter Fisher, ed., *The Third Woman: Minority Women Writers in the US.* (Boston: Houghton Mifflin, 1980), 109.

Speaking in Tongues
A Letter to Third World Women Writers[1]

Gloria Anzaldúa

21 mayo 80

Dear mujeres de color, companions in writing—

I sit here naked in the sun, typewriter against my knee trying to visualize you. Black woman huddles over a desk on the fifth floor of some New York tenement. Sitting on a porch in south Texas, a Chicana fanning away mosquitos and the hot air, trying to arouse the smoldering embers of writing. Indian woman walking to school or work lamenting the lack of time to weave writing into your life. Asian American, lesbian, single mother, tugged in all directions by children, lover or ex-husband, and the writing.

It is not easy writing this letter. It began as a poem, a long poem. I tried to turn it into an essay but the result was wooden, cold. I have not yet unlearned the esoteric bullshit and pseudo-intellectualizing that school brainwashed into my writing.

How to begin again. How to approximate the intimacy and immediacy I want. What form? A letter, of course.

My dear *hermanas*, the dangers we face as women writers of color are not the same as those of white women though we have many in common. We don't have as much to lose—we never had any privileges. I wanted to call the dangers "obstacles" but that would be a kind of lying. We can't *transcend* the dangers, can't rise above them. We must go through them and hope we won't have to repeat the performance.

Unlikely to be friends of people in high literary places, the beginning woman of color is invisible both in the white male mainstream world and in the white women's feminist world, though in the latter this is gradually changing. The *lesbian* of color is not only invisible, she doesn't even exist. Our speech, too, is inaudible. We speak in tongues like the outcast and the insane.

Because white eyes do not want to know us, they do not bother to learn our language, the language which reflects us, our culture, our spirit. The schools we attended or didn't attend did not give us the skills for writing nor the confidence that we were correct in using our class and ethnic languages. I, for one, became adept at, and majored in English to spite, to show up, the arrogant racist teachers who thought all Chicano children were dumb and dirty. And Spanish was not taught in grade school. And Spanish was not required in High School. And though now I write my poems in Spanish as well as English I feel the rip-off of my native tongue.

> I *lack imagination* you say
>
> *No*. I lack language.
> The language to clarify
> my resistance to the literate.
> Words are a war to me.
> They threaten my family.
>
> To gain the word
> to describe the loss
> I risk losing everything.
> I may create a monster
> the word's length and body
> swelling up colorful and thrilling
> looming over my *mother*, characterized.
> Her voice in the distance
> *unintelligible illiterate*.
> These are the monster's words.[2]
>
> —Cherríe Moraga

Who gave us permission to perform the act of writing? Why does writing seem so unnatural for me? I'll do anything to postpone it—empty the trash, answer the telephone. The voice recurs in me: *Who am I, a poor Chicanita from the sticks, to think I could write?* How dare I even consider becoming a writer as I stooped over the tomato fields bending, bending under the hot sun, hands broadened and calloused, not fit to hold the quill, numbed into an animal stupor by the heat.

How hard it is for us to *think* we can choose to become writers, much less feel and believe that we can. What have we to contribute, to give? Our own expectations condition us. Does not our class, our culture as well as the white man tell us writing is not for women such as us?

The white man speaks: *Perhaps if you scrape the dark off of your face. Maybe if you bleach your bones. Stop speaking in tongues, stop writing left-handed. Don't cultivate your colored skins nor tongues of fire if you want to make it in a right-handed world.*

Man, like all the other animals, fears and is repelled by that which he does not understand, and mere difference is apt to connote something malign.[3]

I think, yes, perhaps if we go to the university. Perhaps if we become male-women or as middle class as we can. Perhaps if we give up loving women, we will be worthy of having something to say worth saying. They convince us that we must cultivate art for art's sake. Bow down to the sacred bull, form. Put frames and metaframes around the writing. Achieve distance in order to win the coveted title "literary writer" or "professional writer." Above all do not be simple, direct, nor immediate.

Why do they fight us? Because they think we are dangerous beasts? Why *are* we dangerous beasts? Because we shake and often break the white's comfortable stereotypic images they have of us: the Black domestic, the lumbering nanny with twelve babies sucking her tits, the slant-eyed Chinese with her expert hand—"They know how to treat a man in bed"—the flat-faced Chicana or Indian, passively lying on her back, being fucked by the Man a la La Chingada.

The Third World woman revolts: *We revoke, we erase your white male imprint. When you come knocking on our doors with your rubber stamps to brand our faces with DUMB, HYSTERICAL, PASSIVE PUTA, PERVERT, when you come with your branding irons to burn MY PROPERTY on our buttocks, we will vomit the guilt, self-denial and race-hatred you have force-fed into us right back into your mouth. We are done being cushions for your projected fears. We are tired of being your sacrificial lambs and scapegoats.*

I can write this and yet I realize that many of us women of color who have strung degrees, credentials and published books around our necks like pearls that we hang on to for dear life are in danger of contributing to the invisibility of our sister-writers. "La Vendida," the sell-out.

The danger of selling out one's own ideologies. For the Third World woman, who has, at best, one foot in the feminist literary world, the temptation is great to adopt the current feeling-fads and theory fads, the latest half truths in political thought, the half-digested new age psychological axioms that are preached by the white feminist establishment. Its followers are notorious for "adopting" women of color as their "cause" while still expecting us to adapt to *their* expectations and *their* language.

How dare we get out of our colored faces. How dare we reveal the human flesh underneath and bleed red blood like the white folks. It takes tremendous energy and courage not to acquiesce, not to capitulate to a definition of feminism that still renders most of us invisible. Even as I write this I am disturbed that I am the only Third World woman writer in this handbook [*Words in Our Pockets*]. Over and over I have found myself to be the only Third World woman at readings, workshops, and meetings.

We cannot allow ourselves to be tokenized. We must make our own writing and that of Third World women the first priority. We cannot educate white women and take them by the hand. Most of us are willing to help, but we can't do the white woman's homework for her. That's an energy drain. More times than she cares to remember, Nellie Wong, Asian American feminist writer, has been called by white women wanting a list of Asian American women who can give readings or workshops. We are in danger of being reduced to purveyors of resource lists.

Coming face to face with one's limitations. There are only so many things I can do in one day. Luisah Teish addressing a group of predominantly white feminist writers had this to say of Third World women's experience:

> If you are not caught in the maze that (we) are in, it's very difficult to explain to you the hours in the day we do not have. And the hours that we do not have are hours that are translated into survival skills and money. And when one of those hours is taken away it means an hour *not* that we don't have to lie back and stare at the ceiling or an hour that we don't have to talk to a friend. For me it's a loaf of bread.

Understand.
My family is poor.
Poor. I can't afford
a new ribbon. The risk
of this one is enough
to keep me moving
through it, accountable.
The repetition like my mother's
stories retold, *each* time
reveals more particulars
gains more familiarity.

You can't get me in your car so fast.[4]

—*Cherríe Moraga*

Complacency is a far more dangerous attitude than outrage.[5]
—*Naomi Littlebear Morena*

Why am I compelled to write? Because the writing saves me from this complacency I fear. Because I have no choice. Because I must keep the spirit of my revolt and myself alive. Because the world I create in the writing compensates for what the real world does not give me. By writing I put order in the world, give it a handle so I can grasp it. I write because life does not appease my appetites and hunger. I write to record what others erase when I speak, to rewrite the stories others have miswritten about me, about you. To become more intimate with myself and you. To discover myself, to preserve myself, to make myself, to achieve self-autonomy. To dispel the myths that I am a mad prophet or a poor suffering soul. To convince myself that I am worthy and that what I have to say is not a pile of shit. To show that I *can* and that I *will* write, never mind their admonitions to the contrary. And I will write about the unmentionables, never mind the outraged gasp of the censor and the audience. Finally, I write because I'm scared of writing but I'm more scared of not writing.

Why should I try to justify why I write? Do I need to justify being Chicana, being woman? You might as well ask me to try to justify why I'm alive.

The act of writing is the act of making soul, alchemy. It is the quest for the self, for the center of the self, which we women of color have come to think of as "other"—the dark, the feminine. Didn't we start writing to reconcile this other within us? We knew we were different, set apart, exiled from what is considered "normal," white-right. And as we internalized this exile, we came to see the alien within us and too often, as a result, we split apart from ourselves and each other. Forever after we have been in search of that self, that "other" and each other. And we return, in widening spirals and never to the same childhood place where it happened, first in our families, with our mothers, with our fathers. The writing is a tool for piercing that mystery but it also shields us, gives a margin of distance, helps us survive. And those that don't survive? The waste of ourselves: so much meat thrown at the feet of madness or fate or the state.

24 mayo 80

It is dark and damp and has been raining all day. I love days like this. As I lie in bed I am able to delve inward. Perhaps today I will write from that deep core. As I grope for words and a voice to speak of writing, I stare at my brown hand clenching the pen and think of you thousands of miles away clutching your pen. You are not alone.

Pen, I feel right at home in your ink doing a pirouette, stirring the cobwebs, leaving my signature on the window panes. Pen, how could I ever have feared you. You're quite house-broken but it's your wildness I am in love with. I'll have to get rid of you when you start being predictable, when you stop chasing

dustdevils. The more you outwit me the more I love you. It's
when I'm tired or have had too much caffeine or wine that
you get past my defenses and you say more than what I had
intended. You surprise me, shock me into knowing some part
of me I'd kept secret even from myself.

–Journal entry

In the kitchen Maria and Cherríe's voices falling on these pages. I
can see Cherríe going about in her terry cloth wrap, barefoot, washing
the dishes, shaking out the tablecloth, vacuuming. Deriving a certain
pleasure watching her perform those simple tasks, I am thinking *they
lied, there is no separation between life and writing.*

The danger in writing is not fusing our personal experience and
world view with the social reality we live in, with our inner life, our history, our economics, and our vision. What validates us as human beings
validates us as writers. What matters to us is the relationships that are
important to us whether with our self or others. We must use what is
important to us to get to the writing. *No topic is too trivial.* The danger
is in being too universal and humanitarian and invoking the eternal to
the sacrifice of the particular and the feminine and the specific historical moment.

The problem is to focus, to concentrate. The body distracts, sabotages
with a hundred ruses, a cup of coffee, pencils to sharpen. The solution
is to anchor the body to a cigarette or some other ritual. And who has
time or energy to write after nurturing husband or lover, children and
often an outside job? The problems seem insurmountable and they are,
but they cease being insurmountable once we make up our mind that
whether married or childrened or working outside jobs we are going to
make time for the writing.

Forget the room of one's own—write in the kitchen, lock yourself
up in the bathroom. Write on the bus or the welfare line, on the job
or during meals, between sleeping or waking. I write while sitting on
the John. No long stretches at the typewriter unless you're wealthy or
have a patron—you may not even own a typewriter. While you wash the
floor or clothes listen to the words chanting in your body. When you're
depressed, angry, hurt, when compassion and love possess you. When
you cannot help but write.

Distractions all—that I spring on myself when I'm so deep into
the writing when I'm almost at that place, that dark cellar where some
"thing" is liable to jump up and pounce on me. The ways I subvert the
writing are many. The way I don't tap the well nor learn how to make
the windmill turn.

Eating is my main distraction. Getting up to eat an apple danish. That I've been off sugar for three years is not a deterrent nor that I have to put on a coat, find the keys and go out into the San Francisco fog to get it. Getting up to light incense, to put a record on, to go for a walk—anything just to put off the writing.

Returning after I've stuffed myself. Writing paragraphs on pieces of paper, adding to the puzzle on the floor, to the confusion on my desk making completion far away and perfection impossible.

26 mayo 80

Dear mujeres de color, I feel heavy and tired and there is a buzz in my head—too many beers last night. But I must finish this letter. My bribe: to take myself out to pizza.

So I cut and paste and line the floor with my bits of paper. My life strewn on the floor in bits and pieces and I try to make some order out of it—working against time, psyching myself up with decaffeinated coffee, trying to fill in the gaps.

Leslie, my housemate, comes in gets on hands and knees to read my fragments on the floor and says, "It's good, Gloria." And I think: *I don't have to go back to Texas, to my family of land, mesquites, cactus, rattlesnakes and roadrunners. My family, this community of writers. How could I have lived and survived so long without it? And I remember the isolation, re-live the pain again.*

"To assess the damage is a dangerous act,"[6] writes Cherríe Moraga. To stop there is even more dangerous.

It's too easy, blaming it all on the white man or white feminists or society or on our parents. What we say and what we do ultimately comes back to us, so let us own our responsibility, place it in our own hands and carry it with dignity and strength. No one's going to do my shitwork, I pick up after myself.

It makes perfect sense to me now how I resisted the act of writing, the commitment to writing. To write is to confront one's demons, look them in the face and live to write about them. Fear acts like a magnet; it draws the demons out of the closet and into the ink in our pens.

The tiger riding our backs (writing) never lets us alone. *Why aren't you riding, writing, writing?* It asks constantly till we begin to feel we're vampires sucking the blood out of too fresh an experience; that we are sucking life's blood to feed the pen. Writing is the most daring thing that I have ever done and the most dangerous. Nellie Wong calls writing "the three-eyed demon shrieking the truth."[7]

Writing is dangerous because we are afraid of what the writing reveals: the fears, the angers, the strengths of a woman under a triple or quadruple oppression. Yet in that very act lies our survival because a woman who writes has power. And a woman with power is feared.

> What did it mean for a black woman to be an artist in our grandmother's time? It is a question with an answer cruel enough to stop the blood.[8]
>
> —Alice Walker

I have never seen so much power in the ability to move and transform others as from that of the writing of women of color.

In the San Francisco area, where I now live, none can stir the audience with their craft and truthsaying as do Cherríe Moraga (Chicana), Genny Lim (Asian American), and Luisah Teish (Black). With women like these, the loneliness of writing and the sense of powerlessness can be dispelled. We can walk among each other talking of our writing, reading to each other. And more and more when I'm alone, though still in communion with each other, the writing possesses me and propels me to leap into a timeless, spaceless no-place where I forget myself and feel I am the universe. *This* is power.

It's not on paper that you create but in your innards, in the gut and out of living tissue—*organic writing* I call it. A poem works for me *not* when it says what I want it to say and *not* when it evokes what I want it to. It works when the subject I started out with metamorphoses alchemically into a different one, one that has been discovered, or uncovered, by the poem. It works when it surprises me, when it says something I have repressed or pretended not to know. The meaning and worth of my writing is measured by how much *I* put myself on the line and how much nakedness I achieve.

> Audre said we need to speak up. Speak loud, speak unsettling things and be dangerous and just fuck, hell, let it out and let everybody hear whether they want to or not.[9]
>
> —Kathy Kendall

I say mujer mágica, empty yourself. Shock yourself into new ways of perceiving the world, shock your readers into the same. Stop the chatter inside their heads.

Your skin must be sensitive enough for the lightest kiss and thick enough to ward off the sneers. If you are going to spit in the eye of the world, make sure your back is to the wind. Write of what most links us with life, the sensation of the body, the images seen by the eye, the expansion of the psyche in tranquility: moments of high intensity, its movement, sounds, thoughts. *Even though we go hungry we are not impoverished of experiences.*

> I think many of us have been fooled by the mass media, by society's conditioning that our lives must be lived in great explosions, by "falling in love," by being "swept off our feet," and by the sorcery of magic genies that will fulfill our every wish, our every childhood longing. Wishes, dreams, and fantasies are important parts of our creative lives. They are the steps a writer integrates into her craft. They are the spectrum of resources to reach the truth, the heart of things, the immediacy and the impact of human conflict.[10]

—Nellie Wong

Many have a way with words. They label themselves seers but they will not see. Many have the gift of tongue but nothing to say. Do not listen to them. Many who have words and tongue have no ear, they cannot listen and they will not hear.

There is no need for words to fester in our minds. They germinate in the open mouth of the barefoot child in the midst of restive crowds. They wither in ivory towers and in college classrooms.

Throw away abstraction and the academic learning, the rules, the map and compass. Feel your way without blinders. To touch more people, the personal realities and the social must be evoked—not through rhetoric but through blood and pus and sweat.

Write with your eyes like painters, with your ears like musicians, with your feet like dancers. You are the truthsayer with quill and torch. Write with your tongues of fire. Don't let the pen banish you from yourself. Don't let the ink coagulate in your pens. Don't let the censor snuff out the spark, nor the gags muffle your voice. Put your shit on the paper.

We are not reconciled to the oppressors who whet their howl on our grief. We are not reconciled.

Find the muse within you. The voice that lies buried under you, dig it up. Do not fake it, try to sell it for a handclap or your name in print.

Love,
Gloria

Notes

1. Originally written for *Words in Our Pockets* (San Francisco: Bootlegger), The Feminist Writer's Guild Handbook.
2. Cherríe L. Moraga, poem "It's the Poverty," in *Loving in the War Years* (Boston: South End Press, 1983), 62–63.
3. Alice Walker, ed., "What White Publishers Won't Print," *I Love Myself When I Am Laughing—A Zora Neal Hurston Reader* (New York: Feminist Press, 1979), 169.
4. Moraga, "It's the Poverty."
5. Naomi Littlebear Morena, *The Dark of the Moon*, (Portland: Olive Press, 1977), 36.
6. Cherríe L. Moraga's essay, "La Güera," in this volume.
7. Nellie Wong, "Flows from the Dark of Monsters and Demons: Notes on Writing," in *Radical Women Pamphlet* (San Francisco, 1979).
8. Alice Walker, "In Search of Our Mother's Gardens: The Creativity of Black Women in the South," *MS*, May 1974, 60.
9. Letter from Kathy Kendall, March 10, 1980, concerning a writer's workshop given by Audre Lorde, Adrienne Rich, and Meridel LeSeur.
10. Wong, "Flows from the Dark of Monsters and Demons," 88.

Millicent Fredericks

Gabrielle Daniels

Millicent Fredericks is part of my anthology of forgotten Third World women celebrated in poetry, *A Woman Left Behind*. She was Anais Nin's housemaid, and the quotes about her and on black people in general are the original ones from Anais' Diary.

Millicent has been on my mind since I first read the Diaries while getting my B.A. (I am going for my Master's now.) One day it just poured out. I haven't been able to find a publisher for her, because some people will not touch it. Too much for them to take, I guess. Too damn bad. All our saints have a few taints of sin . . .

Millicent Fredericks was a black woman from Antigua, who married an American black man and had four children. He had a trade as a tailor that he refused to implement after a while. Millicent was an alien, therefore she could not teach school as she had in Antigua. The only way out was housework. As far as I know she remained the sole support of her family. As noted in the Diaries of Anais Nin, one son was shot up in a gang war.

Here were two women, one black and one white, both educated and silenced in their own ways, yet could not help each other because of race and class differences.

Anais could not get beyond the fact of Millicent's blackness and poverty and suffering. The stench of the patrona just reeks about her:

> I would like to write the life of Millicent. But saint's lives are difficult to do . . . A Negro is a concept . . . Millicent perhaps . . . becomes a symbol of what they have to endure . . . the very first day she came to me sent by my mother and she sat sewing, the thread rolled to the floor and I picked it up for her . . . This gesture established the quality of our relationship . . . I would like to devote my life to the recognition of the Negro's equality, but I always feel ineffectual in political battles . . . one can only win by force or trickery . . . she has fine features, which a Gauguin would have enjoyed painting . . .
>
> —from *The Diary of Anais Nin*

Only for the sake of art
Millicent, do you rise
tall from the ink
in the pupils you sought
dark and wide
taking you in like the letters
you would have performed
scratched indelibly on slated memories, chalk dust
gold on your fingers. A teacher.

From A to B
from Antigua to Harlem
is no giant step. Brown syrup
from the cane stills of home
stick like skin
adheres to the sharpened ribs of shanty girls
running careless like your husband from responsibility
catches white heat rubbing shoulders
on the New York trolley, the floors and windows
sucking the strength from your maid's fingers
your teats dribbling the same tar sweetness on
to your smacking children the same curse.

Beyond introductions
the thread of your lives intersected,
ran from the tangled nest in the sewing basket.
The spools dared equality. Two aliens
two mothers well met, living on little thanks.
The pin money feebly spread out
for Dad and his drink, Patchen
a pair of shoes for the youngest, the press
Pressure. Glimpses in the lilt of clipped English
from both sides of the ocean:
Harlem clubs, black street gangs cutting up
a son, the broken families and the literati
dining on themselves
The mending to be done, the mending of words
the hunger knit in the growling guts of the mind
Publish, publish our cries.

You the ministrant
above the small white fact

which was but one seam
pinched in emergency in the creeping taxi
is your last conscious scene.

No curtain calls in the proceeding pages
in the wake of her saving move to California,
you continue
to rummage through days-old bread,
trickle down shops. The killing routine
she admired of you, and because of you
escaped to write, to cable Henry
ever the last sum. "The writer," she said,
"must be served and taken care of,"
lessening the time
you could afford for breath
to clean your own home for Sunday meetin'

Perhaps to dust off your teacher's diploma
with more care.

No islander, despite her praise
Gauguin could not have traced
the furrows in your face,
the buried seeds waiting in vain
for spotlight to flower
a smile, Madonna, smile please . . .

In your uniform
you were like everyone of them
at war to survive
and then like no other. I have learned
from such self-denial,
martyrs and saints are made
or forgotten.

In Search of the Self as Hero

Confetti of Voices on New Year's Night—
a Letter to Myself

Nellie Wong

You want to run away and hide now, become a breeze beneath a willow tree, a breath from the dragon's mouth, a blade of grass struggling skyward to shoot above the ground, not to be squashed like an ant, not to be forgotten perhaps like an Asian prostitute. These past few days now, that have become years of memories and dreams, of work and struggle, of becoming and living, you shiver in the fleece of your inkblue robe, wondering why you tiptoe down the stairs to write, to face your typewriter like a long, lost friend, welcoming her this New Year's Night.

You don't question the urgency to write, to express yourselves, your innocence and naïveté, your conflicts and passions, your doubts and beliefs as a woman, a writer, a feminist, a poet, an Asian American, a secretary, a thlee yip nui, a wife, trying to learn the business of life: the act of loving. You have come away from a weekend of workshops at the Modern Language Association conference, absorbed the words and thoughts of writers like yourselves, provoked by the hate and love directed at a book by Maxine Hong Kingston. *The Woman Warrior: A Girlhood among Ghosts*—for you a book of brilliance, of love and anger, becoming an art form, a testimony and vision of one Chinese American woman's world.

Ah, but you ask, *who determines Chinese American culture, Asian American sensibility?* These opponents to the art of Maxine Hong Kingston, or to the confetti of voices fluttering from the past, voices still yet to be heard, to be written down?

Who are you who has written a book of poems, who has stored away over ten years of fiction, poems and prose? Who are you who describes herself as an Asian American Feminist, who works and writes toward that identity, that affinity, that necessary self-affirming love? And you ask yourselves if you must retreat, scared rabbits, into the forests of your own imagination, your own prisons and clearings, your entanglements of words versus concepts, of dreams versus reality, of expression versus interpretation, of language versus life, knowing in all your sensibilities as a woman writer that you face the struggles head-on. You know there is no retreat now, no avoiding the confrontations, the debates and disagreements between what is art and what is not art which for you also means: what is Asian American feminist art and politics?

If you sing too often of woe, yours or your sisters', you may be charged with being "too personal," "too autobiographical," too much a woman who cries out, who acknowledges openly, shamelessly, the pain of living and the joy of becoming free. You believe, almost too simply, that you are establishing your own traditions, becoming your own role model, becoming your own best friend, your own accessible hero. In so doing you do not deny human relationships, but acknowledge them, want them and fight for them. And you are angered by the arrogance of some articles that would tell you that Virginia Woolf is your spiritual mother, your possible role model, for the work you have to do: to write. And why are you angered except for the fact that she was white and privileged, yet so ill that she walked into the sea.

And now you have discovered Ding Ling, China's most prolific woman writer, a feminist, a communist, a loving, fighting woman, whose stories gleam, bright lights in the dark of China's past. Ding Ling, imprisoned for expressing her anguish, her love and compassion for China's women, for recording the conditions of their lives. Ding Ling, attacked for her feminism, supposedly bourgeois, individualistic, impeding the movement of communism in her native land. Now there is information trickling out that she is writing again, silenced for so many years. Now you want to search for more of her work, jewels you want to hold in your own hands. Now you want to share her work, to discover the links between the women of China and the women of Chinese America, to find the grandmothers you wish to adopt.

In your search you do not deny the writings of Hisaye Yamamoto, or Wakako Yamauchi, Jade Snow Wong or Maxine Hong Kingston, Jessica Hagedorn or Mei-Mei Berssenbrugge. However, you deny these women as role models because your experiences are not theirs. Their experiences are not yours though you assimilate them because the range of human experience tickles your solitariness, your desire to become pluralistic, a free spirit soaring into the north and south poles of everywoman's existence. You respect these writers, your contemporaries, and yet you do not only hear their voices simply because you must carve out your own destiny: a woman hero, an adventurer, a doer, a singer, an actor, fearless with the length of your own body, the depth of your dark seeing eyes, the sounds of your typewriter keys. And you ask: *where have you gone and what have you done?* You don't have the time to count the poems, the stories, the outpourings of grief and joy, but they are there in your file cabinet, they are there in your mind, and they are there flowing through your bloodstream. They are there as surely as you awaken each morning and shower and shower, happy as a hummingbird, content to let the water fall over your body, splash it and splash it, while you soap your ears and underarms, while you shampoo your hair, while you have a few moments alone to let the thoughts and impulses pour into song, rhythm, poems, life.

Could you have become a recluse, simply an observer of life, content to roam by the sea, thinking and dreaming and stopping to eat only when you had to? Could you have become a hobo, an alcoholic, a sleeping princess, content to live through the deeds and accomplishments of others? And what is this adventure, this hunger, that roars in you now, as a woman, a writer, an Asian American, a feminist? And why? And what is this satisfaction, this self-assuredness, of individuality, or spirit, of aloneness? And finally, what is this thrust toward community, toward interaction with women and men, this arrow toward creativity, toward freedom?

You have the support of friends and sister writers. You have the love of your husband and your siblings, and yet you turn from them, run with this force, this necessity, this light toward art, toward politics and writing. In the doing and expressing, in the organizing, cutting and filing, in the hours you spend in your study on a bright Sunday afternoon, you wonder why it seems simple to remove yourselves from other people. You think you could have become a minister or a nun, judging and commenting on philosophy, on morality, on the complexities of human life, on the injustice of human beings oppressing other human beings. You have no answers. You have questions and more questions about violence against women, against children, against ethnic minorities, against gays. You only understand that you must try to answer your questions. You think at times you can answer them alone, but that is impossible because you live and work as a social being in this material, physical and economic world.

If you desire freedom, total freedom, you ask, does it mean that you must die? You are unafraid, but you think of the dead, of the dying. Of women like Sylvia Plath and Anne Sexton, writers who killed themselves, poets you've admired; of two Asian American teenaged sisters who committed suicide because their father opposed their dating Hispanic boys. You think of your cousin who hung himself in Las Vegas, his hearing gone, his son alienated from him. You think of your father who died of cirrhosis of the liver, who brought your mother and three sisters to America. You think of your mother who died of stomach cancer, who desired her own fur coat, her own grandson; and of Bok Gung, a cook, a gentle old man, a pioneer, a grandfather, who died at home in his rented room above Hamburger Joe's in Oakland's Chinatown. And is the question that of mortality and how you desire to become immortal, and not be a fool, a real human being? You a mortal, you a woman, who does not want to be small in any sense of the word. You a poet, you a feminist, who seeks beauty in and beyond the ordinariness of the everyday world.

You talk of children and yet you have none. You talk of writing and leaving a part of yourselves to daughters and sons, their daughters and sons, so they will discover for themselves the heart and minds of Asian Americans, particularly the women who are struggling in this fight for freedom. You don't understand why you have this vision, of leaving work, signs and clues, knowledge and art, stones, however rough or polished, for people you will never know. You realize you will be gone when the questions of the future arise like wildflowers on the plains of this earth. You want to be a part of a legacy and so you write and write, questioning and exploring, not knowing if what you write will become a part of America's freedom song, not knowing if there is a rainbow.

You believed once in your own passivity, your own powerlessness, your own spiritual malaise. You are now awakening in the beginnings of a new birth. Not born again, but born for the first time, triumphant and resolute, out of experience and struggle, out of a flowing, living memory, out of consciousness and will, facing, confronting, challenging head-on the contradictions of your lives and the lives of people around you. You believe now in the necessity and beauty of struggle: that feminism for you means working for the equality and humanity of women and men, for children, for the love that is possible.

You rub your legs in this cold room. You shiver when you recall your own self-pity when you had no date on New Year's Eve, when you regretted the family gathering because it reminded you that you stood out, a woman without a man, a woman without children. Now you are strengthened, encouraged by the range of your own experiences as a writer, a feminist, an organizer, a secretary. Now you are fired by your own needs, by the needs of your sisters and brothers in the social world, by your journey toward solidarity against tyranny in the workplace, on the streets, in our literature and in our homes. You are fueled by the clarity of your own sight, heated by your own energy to assert yourselves as a human being, a writer, a woman, an Asian American, a feminist, a clerical worker, a student, a teacher, not in loneliness and isolation, but in a community of freedom fighters. Your poems and stories will do some of the work for you, but poems and stories alone aren't enough. Nothing for you is ever enough and so you challenge yourselves, again and again, to try something new, to help build a movement, to organize for the rights of working people, to write a novel, a play, to create a living theater that will embody your dreams and vision, energy in print, on stage, at work that will assert the will of an independent, freedom-loving woman, that will reflect a sensibility of Asian America, of feminism, of sharing food and wealth with all the people, with all your kin.

And you will not stop working and writing because you care, because you refuse to give up, because you won't submit to the forces that will silence you, a cheong hay poa, a long steam woman, a talker, a dancer who moves with lightning. And you are propelled by your sense of fair play, by your respect for the dead and the living, by your thlee yip American laughter and language, by your desire to help order the chaotic world that you live in, knowing as the stars sparkle on this New Year's night that you will not survive the work that still needs to be done in the streets of Gold Mountain.

Chicana's Feminist Literature

A Re-vision through Malintzin/
or Malintzin Putting Flesh Back on the Object

Norma Alarcón

Malintzin (or La Malinche) was an Aztec noble woman who was presented to Cortés upon landing in Veracruz in 1519. She subsequently served Cortés as lover, translator and tactical advisor. She is a controversial figure in the Conquest of Mexico. Her name is often called forth to reenact, symbolically, the Conquest or any conquest. Part of this drama, analogically so, is now being played out also in Aztlán.

Malintzin's history, her legend and subsequent mythic dimensions as evil goddess and creator of a new race—the mestizo race—embroils her in a family quarrel, where many male members often prefer to see her as the mother-whore, bearer of illegitimate children, responsible for the foreign Spanish invasion; and where female members attempt to restore balance in ways that are sometimes painfully ambivalent, and at other times attempt to topple the traditional patriarchal mythology through revision and re-vision.[1]

This essay will explore the traditional image of Malintzin in Chicano culture and will provide examples of the ways contemporary Chicana feminist writers have reacted to and used this image in their work.

In our patriarchal mythological pantheon, there exists even now a woman who was once real. Her historicity, her experience, her true flesh and blood were discarded. A Kantian, dualistic male consciousness stole her and placed her on the throne of evil, like Dante's upside down frozen Judas, doomed to moan and bemoan. The woman is interchangeably called by three names: Malintzin, Malinche, Marina. Malintzin's excruciating life in bondage was of no account, and continues to be of no account. Her almost half century of mythic existence, until recent times mostly in the oral traditions, had turned her into a handy reference point not only for controlling, interpreting or visualizing women, but also to wage a domestic battle of stifling proportions.

Unlike Eve whose primeval reality is not historically documentable and who supposedly existed in some past edenic time, Malintzin's betrayal of our supposed pre-Columbian paradise is recent and hence almost palpable. This almost-within-reach past heightens romantic nostalgia; and as a consequence, hatred for Malintzin and women becomes as vitriolic as the American Puritans' loathing of witches-women.

The focus of the betrayal is not a lofty challenge to a "god" who subsequently unleashed evil upon the world as punishment. Disobedience to a "god" might place the discussion at times on an ideal plane and relieve tension momentarily as one switches from an intense dialogue about one's body to a "rarified" field at least in terms of the vocabulary used. However, the male myth of Malintzin is made to see betrayal first of all in her very sexuality, which makes it nearly impossible at any given moment to go beyond the vagina as the supreme site of evil until proven innocent by way of virginity or virtue, the most pawnable commodities around.[2]

Because the myth of Malintzin pervades not only male thought but ours too as it seeps into our own consciousness in the cradle through their eyes as well as our mothers', who are entrusted with the transmission of culture, we may come to believe that indeed our very sexuality condemns us to enslavement. An enslavement which is subsequently manifested in self-hatred. All we see is hatred of women. We must hate her too since love seems only possible through extreme virtue whose definition is at best slippery.

The poet Alma Villanueva must have realized, understood the insidiousness of the hate syndrome. Her whole book *Bloodroots* is a song to the rejection of self-loathing. The poem "I sing to myself" states:

> I could weep and rage
> against the man who never
> stroked my fine child hair
> who never felt the pride of
> my femininity . . .[3]

It is not just the father that is a source of pain; a mother figure appears also. The mother is impotent to help the daughter. All of her energies seem directed, spent in her desire and need for man, a factor that repulses and attracts the daughter. Love for mother is an ambivalence rooted in the daughter's sense of abandonment by her mother and her apparently enormous and irrational need:

> Never finding a breast to rest
> and warm myself . . .[4]

As the daughter proceeds to repeat her mother's experience, she ironically discovers and affirms a "mounting self/love" as a combative force against the repetition of the mother's abnegation, and irrational need of and dependency on men. Self-love as a tool of survival, however, leads the male lover to reject her. Her conclusion leaves no doubt as to what woman may be forced to do:

> I/woman give birth:
> and this time to
> myself [5]

The sexual abuse experienced leaves the daughter no choice but to be her own mother, to provide her own supportive, nurturing base for the physical and psychic survival. To escape the cycle of loathing and self-loathing, Villanueva's woman has no alternative, even though she would have wanted more options, but to first love the self and then proceed to regenerate and nurture it by becoming her own mother. She is forced to transform the self into both mother and daughter and rejects the male flesh which at this point in time "is putrid and bitter." He must be transfigured.

The end effect could be seen as narcissistic, a perennial accusation directed at woman's literature. Yet, if it be narcissistic, never has a motive force for it been revealed so tellingly and clearly, never have the possible roots been exposed so well: starvation for self-reflection in the other: man or woman.

The male myth of Malintzin, in its ambivalent distaste and fear of the so-called "enigmatic feminine," echoes in this poem as it does in many Mexican/Chicana's poems, even when her name is not mentioned. The pervasiveness of the myth is unfathomable, often permeating and suffusing our very being without conscious awareness.

The myth contains the following sexual possibilities: woman is sexually passive, and hence at all times open to potential use by men whether it be seduction or rape. The possible use is double-edged: That is, the use of her as pawn may be intracultural, "amongst us guys," or intercultural, which means if we are not using her then "they" must be using her. Since woman is seen as highly pawnable, nothing she does is perceived as a choice. Because Malintzin aided Cortés in the Conquest of the New World, she is seen as concretizing woman's sexual weakness and interchangeability, always open to sexual exploitation. Indeed, as long as we continue to be seen in that way we are earmarked to be abusable matter, not just by men of another culture, but all cultures including the one that breeds us.

Lorna Dee Cervantes addresses herself to the latter point in her poem "Baby you cramp my style." In the poem Malintzin is mentioned by her other name: Malinche. The poet is asked to bestow her sexual favors; the lover's tone implies that her body/self is as available as the mythic Malinche is thought to be by male consciousness:

> You cramp my style, baby
> when you roll on top of me
> shouting, "Viva La Raza!"
> at the top of your prick.
>
> . . .
>
> Come on Malinche
> Gimme some more![6]

He cramps her style; she refuses sexual exploitation for herself and her daughters yet to come, in a way Malintzin could not do because of the constraints of the slave society into which she was born.

The Mexican poet Rosario Castellanos reminds us in "Malinche"[7] that Malintzin was sold into slavery by complicitous parents to enhance her brother's inheritance. The mother eager to please her new husband agrees to sell her daughter, and therefore enchains her destiny. Castellanos speculates, in the poem, that this is the result of the mother's own self-loathing. A mother who cannot bear to see herself reflected in her daughter's mirror/sexuality prefers to shatter the image/mirror, negate the daughter and thereby perpetuate rejection and negation.

Bernal Díaz del Castillo, a brilliant chronicler of the Conquest with a great eye for detail, reveals to us that when Malintzin re-encounters her mother and brother years later and during the very process of the Conquest, she is merely polite. It seems that Malintzin, instead of offering them protection within the folds of the victorious, leaves them to their own devices for survival in an embattled country. In a way she condemns them to servitude just as she had been condemned. Why is there no forgiveness? Within what context can we analyze Malintzin's behavior at this point? We have a reversal, the daughter negates the mother.

Within the complex mother-daughter relationship, the mother keeps bearing quite a bit of the responsibility for the daughter's emotional starvation, abandonment or enslavement and yet paradoxically both are subordinate and subjected to a male culture and tradition. Perhaps our sexual identification with our mothers leads us to expect greater understanding from her as well a psychic/sexual protection. Villanueva tells us it is a false expectation—mothers are powerless, looking to satisfy their own hunger through men, which is agonizing for the daughter: "her pain haunted me for years."[8]

Simone Weil suggests that the conscious slave is much superior, and I would add that a woman who is conscious of being perceived as pawn is much superior. I doubt that the historical Malintzin was a truly conscious slave. In her ambiance slavery was a cultural norm, it was not unusual for men or women to be royalty one day and slave, vanquished or sacrificial victim the next. It was a norm within which she had to seek accommodation. It is also quite possible that what is seen as Malintzin's allegiance to Cortés—hence purposeful betrayal of "her people"—may be explained by Weil's perception of the slave–master relationship. She says, ". . . the thought of being in absolute subjection as somebody's plaything is a thought no human being can sustain: so if a man (I add woman) is left with no means at all of escaping constraint he (she) has no alternative except to persuade himself (herself) that he (she) is doing voluntarily the very things he (she) is forced to do; in other words, he (she) substitutes devotion for obedience . . . devotion of this kind rests upon self-deception, because the reasons for it will not bear inspection."[9]

In our religiously permeated and oriented indo-hispanic minds, it is often the case that devotion is equated with obedience and vice versa, particularly for women and children, so that disobedience is seen as a lack of devout allegiance, and not necessarily as a radical questioning of our forms of life. This factor makes it almost impossible to sense a shift from obedience to devotion; they have been one and the same for hundreds of years. As such, we are a greater unconscious prey to subjugation which we then proceed to call devotion/love. To be obedient/devoted is proof of love, especially for women and children.

Consciously and unconsciously the Mexican/Chicano patriarchal perspective assigns the role of servitude to woman particularly as heterosexual relationships are conceived today and in the past. In an "Open Letter to Carolina . . . or Relations between Men and Women" the Chicano poet Abelardo Delgado testifies as follows: "Octavio Paz in *El Laberinto de la Soledad*[10] has much to say as to how we as Chicanos see our women . . . For now let it suffice to say that as far as our wives and mothers we make saints of them but remain always in search of a lover with macho characteristics (*sic*)."[11] Obviously when the wife or would-be-wife, the mother or would-be-mother questions out loud and in print the complex "servitude/devotion/love," she will be quickly seen as false to her "obligation" and duty, hence a traitor. Delgado also points to the creation of a different category of women—macho-lover—who will provide comforts beyond those that fall within the purview of wives and mothers. What is a macho/lover kind of woman?

Delgado goes on to tell Carolina that "All it takes is a simple refusal on the part of women to be abused by us men." However, he cautions about the manner in which it is done, "You must show them all that your mind is on par or above theirs. You must be careful that you do this with some grace, dignity and humility . . . Men might accept your challenges a few times and let it go but if our ego happens to be wounded, then watch out, Carolina, because what follows is a cold rejection and a new assigned role as a feme-macho."[12] (Will this new role of a "feme-macho" then provide the macho/lovers that are sought above and beyond the wife and mother?)

It seems that what is wanted here is for all women to be a kind of Sor Juana,[13] which leaves out the majority of us who are not fortunate enough to be a woman of genius. But because we know Sor Juana's dreadful fate as a result of her intellectual endeavors, we also know that genius is hardly enough. Even a genius needs a political base, a constituency. Since many Mexican/Chicana poets' challenges are straightforward, not humble, I shudder to think at our marginalization; how are we being shunned?

When our subjection is manifested through devotion we are saints and escape direct insult. When we are disobedient, hence undevout, we are equated with Malintzin; that is, the *myth* of male consciousness, not the *historical* figure in all her dimensions doomed to live in chains (regardless of which patriarchy might have seemed the best option for survival).

Carmen Tafolla's poem "La Malinche"[14] makes it quite clear that Malintzin as woman is dispossessed of herself by every male ideology with which she was connected. Tafolla would simply like to see Malintzin recognized as a visionary and founder of a people. Yet as I have noted, the realities that this figure encompasses are much too complex to simply replace them with the notion of a matriarch. However, each implicit or explicit poem on Malintzin emphasizes the pervasive preoccupation and influence of the myth and women's need to demythify.

The mythic aspects of disavowal, and the historical ambiance of Malintzin merge in Chicanas' literature to bring out the following sexual political themes: 1) to choose among extant patriarchies is not a choice at all; 2) woman's abandonment and orphanhood and psychic/emotional starvation occur even in the midst of tangible family; 3) woman is a slave, emotionally as well as economically; 4) women are seen not just by one patriarchy but by all as rapeable and sexually exploitable; 5) blind devotion is not a feasible human choice (this is further clarified by the telling absence of poems by women to the Virgin of Guadalupe, while poems by men to her are plentiful); 6) when there is love/devotion it is at best deeply ambivalent as exemplified by Rina Rocha in "To the penetrator":

> I hate the love
> I feel for you.[15]

Feminist women agree with Hegel, despite his relentless use of man as universal, that the subject depends on external reality. If she is to be fully at home this external reality must reflect back to her what she actually is or would want to be. When we don't participate in creating our own defined identity and reality as women, when the material and spiritual realities do not reflect us as contributors to the shaping of the world, we may feel as in Judy Lucero's poem, "I speak in an illusion":

> I speak but only in an illusion
> For I see and I don't
>
> It's me and It's not
> I hear and I don't
>
> These illusions belong to me
> I stole them from another
>
> Care to spend a day in my House of Death?
> Look at my garden . . . are U amazed?
>
> No trees, no flowers, no grass . . . no gardens . . .
>
> I love and I don't
> I hate and I don't
> I sing and I don't
> I live and I don't
>
> For I'm in a room of clouded smoke
> And a perfumed odor
>
> Nowhere can I go and break these bonds
> Which have me in an illusion
>
> But the bonds are real.[16]

Feminism is a way of saying that nothing in patriarchy truly reflects women unless we accept distortions—mythic and historical. However, as Chicanas embrace feminism they are charged with betrayal *a la* Malinche.

Often great pains are taken to explain that our feminism assumes a humanistic nuance. The charge remains as a clear image imprinted on Chicanas (and I believe most Third World women, in this country or outside of it) by men. It continues to urge us to make quantum leaps towards a male ideologized humanism devoid of female consciousness. The lure of an ideal humanism is seductive, especially for spiritual women such as we have often been brought up to be; but without female consciousness and envisioning how as women we would like to exist in the material world, to leap into humanism without repossessing ourselves may be exchanging one male ideology for another.

As women we are and continue to be tokens everywhere at the present moment. Everywhere in a Third World context, women invited to partake in the feast of modeling humanism can be counted among the few; and those few may be enjoying what Adrienne Rich calls "a false power which masculine society offers to a few women who 'think like men' on condition that they use it to maintain things as they are. This is the meaning of female tokenism: that power withheld from the vast majority of women is offered to the few."[17]

Even as we concern ourselves with Third World women's economic exploitation, we have to concern ourselves with psychosexual exploitation and pawnability at the hands of one's brother, father, employer, master, political systems and sometimes, sadly so, powerless mothers. As world politics continue the histrionics of dominance and control attempting to figure out just who indeed will be the better macho in the world map, macho politics' last priority is the quality of our lives as women or the lives of our children.

Notes

1. Insofar as feminine symbolic figures are concerned, much of the Mexican/ Chicano oral tradition as well as the intellectual are dominated by La Malinche/Llorona and the Virgin of Guadalupe. The former is a subversive feminine symbol which often is identified with La Llorona, the latter a feminine symbol of transcendence and salvation. The Mexican/Chicano cultural tradition has tended to polarize the lives of women through these national (and nationalistic) symbols thereby exercising almost sole authority over the control, interpretation and visualization of women. Although the material on both figures is vast, the following serve as guides to past and present visions and elucidations: Eric Wolf, "The Virgin of Guadalupe: A Mexican National Symbol," *Journal of American Folklore* 71 (1958): 34–39; Américo Paredes, "Mexican Legendry and the Rise of the Mestizo: A Survey," in *American Folk Legend*, edited by Wayland D. Hand (Berkeley: University of California

Press, 1971), 97–107; Richard M. Dorson's foreword to *Folktales of Mexico*, edited by Américo Paredes (Chicago: University of Chicago Press, 1970), esp. xvi–xxxvii; and Octavio Paz, "The Songs of La Malinche," in *The Labryinth of Solitude*, translated by Lysander Kemp (New York: Grove Press, 1961), 65–88. Paz takes the traditional male perspective of woman as enigma and mystery and then proceeds to disclose the culture's (men's) mentality vis-à-vis these figures. Women in their assigned roles as transmitters of the culture have often adhered to these views, however, they have not created them.

2. Bertrand Russell in *Marriage and Morals* affirms that the conception of female virtues has been built up in order to make the patriarchal family as we have known it possible.

3. Alma Villanueva, "I sing to myself," in *Third Chicano Literary Prize: Irvine 1976–77* (Irvine, CA: Dept. of Spanish and Portuguese, University of California, Irvine, 1977), 99–101.

4. Ibid., 100.

5. Ibid., 101.

6. *El Fuego de Aztlán* 1, no. 4 (Summer 1977): 39.

7. *Poesía no eres tú* (México: Fondo de Cultura Económica, 1972), 295–297.

8. Villanueva, op. cit., 99.

9. Simone Weil, *First and Last Notebooks*, translated by Richard Rees (London: Oxford University Press, 1970), 41.

10. See note 1 for my commentary on this text.

11. *Revista Chicano-Riqueña* 6, no. 2 (Spring 1978): 35.

12. Ibid., 38.

13. Sor Juana Inés de la Cruz is a famous poet-nun of the Mexican Colonial Period. A highly creative and intellectual woman, she was forced by the church to abandon her writing after penning a treatise that challenged a prelate's notions on the nature of Love and Christ.

14. *Canto al Pueblo: An Anthology of Experience* (San Antonio, Texas: Penca Books, 1978), 38–39.

15. *Revista Chicano-Riqueña* 3, no. 2 (Spring 1975): 5.

16. *De Colores* 2, no. 1 (Winter 1973): 52.

17. "On Priviledge, Power and Tokenism," *MS*, September 1979, 43.

Ceremony for Completing a Poetry Reading

Chrystos

This is a give-away poem
You have come gathering
You have made a circle with me
of the places where I have wandered
I want to give you the first daffodil opening from the earth I have sown
to give you warm loaves of bread
baked in soft mounds like breasts
In this circle I pass each of you a shell from our mother sea
Hold it in your spirit & hear the stories she will tell you
I have wrapped your faces around me, a warm robe
Let me give you ribbonwork leggings, dresses sewn with elk teeth
moccasins woven with red & sky blue porcupine quills
I give you blankets woven of flowers & roots
Come closer
I have more to give   this   basket is very large
I have stitched it of your kind words
Here is a necklace of feathers & bones
a sacred meal of choke cherries
Take this mask of bark which keeps out the evil ones
This basket is only the beginning
There is something in my arms for all of you
I offer you
this memory of sunrise seen through ice crystals
Here, an afternoon of looking into the sea from high rocks
Here, a red-tailed hawk circling over our heads
One of its feathers drops for your hair
May I give you this round stone which holds an ancient spirit
This stone will soothe you
Within this basket is something you have been looking for
all of your life
Come take it
Take as much as you want
I give you seeds of a new way
I give you the moon shining on a fire of singing women
I give you the sound of our feet dancing

I give you the sound of our thoughts flying
I give you the sound of peace
moving into your faces & sitting down
Come
this is a give away poem
I cannot go home
until you have taken everything
and the basket which held it

When my hands are empty
I will be full

VI

El Mundo Zurdo

The Vision

Liliana Wilson, *Los desaparecidos en el cielo (The Disappeared in Heaven)*, 1977
Pencil on paper, 7" × 5"
Collection of Cynthia Pérez

El Mundo Zurdo

The Vision

Coming into spirituality the way I did changed the christian myth that there is nothing we can do—we are totally powerless. I found out that when there was trouble, my people did not say "o.k., we can't fight, we just have to let god handle it." They went and made sacrifices, they evoked their gods and goddesses, they became possessed, and they went out there and they fought. You learn to take power when there is a presence behind you.

—Luisah Teish

We, the women here, take a trip back into the self, travel to the deep core of our roots to discover and reclaim our colored souls, our rituals, our religion. We reach a spirituality that has been hidden in the hearts of oppressed people under layers of centuries of traditional god-worship. It emerges from under the veils of La Virgen de Guadalupe and unrolls from Yemaya's ocean waves whenever we need to be uplifted from or need the courage to face the tribulations of a racist patriarchal world where there is no relief. Our spirituality does not come from outside ourselves. It emerges when we listen to the "small still voice" (Teish) within us which can empower us to create actual change in the world.

The vision of our spirituality provides us with no trap door solution, no escape hatch tempting us to "transcend" our struggle. We must act in the everyday world. Words are not enough. We must perform visible and public acts that may make us more vulnerable to the very oppressions we are fighting against. But our vulnerability *can* be the source of our power—**if we use it.**

As Third World women, we are especially vulnerable to the many-headed demon of oppression. We are the women on the bottom. Few oppressions pass over us. To work toward the freedom of our own skin and souls would, as Combahee states, ". . . mean that everyone else would have to be free since our freedom would necessitate the destruction of *all* systems of oppression." The love we have for our common maligned bodies and souls must burgeon out in *lucha*, in struggle. As Teish points out, we must work toward diminishing the possibility of being locked up in a padded cell, of being battered or raped. Our feelings of craziness and powerlessness that Combahee speaks of are induced by the shit society dumps on us rather than stemming from being born ugly or evil as the patriarchal shrinks would have us believe. We must not believe the story *they* tell about us. We must recognize the effects that our external circumstances of sex, class, race and sexuality have on our perception of ourselves—even in our most private unspoken moments.

The vision of radical Third World Feminism necessitates our willingness to work with those people who would feel at home in *El Mundo Zurdo, the left-handed world*: the colored, the queer, the poor, the female, the physically challenged. From our blood and spirit connections with these groups, we women on the bottom throughout the world can form an international feminism. For separatism by race, nation, or gender will not do the trick of revolution. *Autonomy*, however, is *not* separatism. We recognize the right and necessity of colonized peoples throughout the world, including Third World women in the US, forming independent movements toward self-government. But ultimately, we must struggle together. *Together* we form a vision that spans from the self-love of our colored skins, to the respect of our foremothers who kept the embers of revolution burning, to our reverence for the trees—the final reminder of our rightful place on this planet.

The change evoked on these pages is material as well as psychic. Change requires a lot of heat. It requires both the alchemist and the welder, the magician and the laborer, the witch and the warrior, the myth-smasher and the myth-maker.

Hand in Hand, we brew and forge a revolution.

Give Me Back

Chrystos

that anger bone mal mama
that rattle painted red, painted fresh blood, slaughtered enemy
hung with strong feathers, guts of vipers
I'll knock down this old long house this weary war horse
these dry rituals called
how are you
I want that brown thigh bone
carved with eagle beak
that club   dig it out of the dirt

mal mama spirit stole my bones   put them in her burying jug
sealed me up in wax & ashes
I crack out
arrange my bones in their naming places
I take what I want
shaking my sacred hair   dancing out taboo
I mark out the space I am
with knives

La Prieta

Gloria Anzaldúa

When I was born, Mamágrande Locha inspected my buttocks looking for the dark blotch, the sign of indio, or worse, of mulatto blood. My grandmother (Spanish, part German, the hint of royalty lying just beneath the surface of her fair skin, blue eyes and the coils of her once blond hair) would brag that her family was one of the first to settle in the range country of south Texas.

Too bad mi'jita was morena, *muy prieta*, so dark and different from her own fair-skinned children. But she loved mi'jita anyway. What I lacked in whiteness, I had in smartness. But it *was* too bad I was dark like an Indian.

"Don't go out in the sun," my mother would tell me when I wanted to play outside. "If you get any darker, they'll mistake you for an Indian. And don't get dirt on your clothes. You don't want people to say you're a dirty Mexican." It never dawned on her that, though sixth-generation American, we were still Mexican and that all Mexicans are part Indian. I passed my adolescence combatting her incessant orders to bathe my body, scrub the floors and cupboards, clean the windows and the walls.

And as we'd get into the back of the "patrón's" truck that would take us to the fields, she'd ask, "Where's your gorra (sunbonnet)?" La gorra—rim held firm by slats of cardboard, neck flounce flowing over my shoulders—made me feel like a horse with blinders, a member of the French Foreign Legion, or a nun bowed down by her wimple.

One day in the middle of the cotton field, I threw the gorra away and donned a sombrero. Though it didn't keep out the Texas 110° sun as well as the bonnet, I could now see in all directions, feel the breeze, dry the sweat on my neck.

When I began writing this essay, nearly two years ago, the wind I was accustomed to suddenly turned into a hurricane. It opened the door to the old images that haunt me, the old ghosts and all the old wounds. Each image a sword that cuts through me, each word a test. Terrified, I shelved the rough draft of this essay for a year.

I was terrified because in this writing I must be hard on people of color who are the oppressed victims. I am still afraid because I will have to call us on a lot of shit like our own racism, our fear of women and sexuality. One of my biggest fears is that of betraying myself, of consuming myself with self-castigation, of not being able to unseat the guilt that has ridden on my back for years.

These my two hands
quick to slap my face
before others could slap it[1]

But above all, I am terrified of making my mother the villain in my life rather than showing how she has been a victim. Will I be betraying her in this essay for her early disloyalty to me?

With terror as my companion, I dip into my life and begin work on myself. Where did it begin, the pain, the images that haunt me?

Images That Haunt Me

When I was three months old tiny pink spots began appearing on my diaper. "She's a throwback to the Eskimo," the doctor told my mother. "Eskimo girl children get their periods early." At seven I had budding breasts. My mother would wrap them in tight cotton girdles so the kids at school would not think them strange beside their own flat brown mole nipples. My mother would pin onto my panties a folded piece of rag. "Keep your legs shut, Prieta." This, the deep dark secret between us, her punishment for having fucked before the wedding ceremony, my punishment for being born. And when she got mad at me she would yell, "He batallado más contigo que con todos los demás y no lo agradeces!" (I've taken more care with you than I have with all the others and you're not even grateful.) My sister started suspecting our secret—that there was something "wrong" with me. How much can you hide from a sister you've slept with in the same bed since infancy?

What my mother wanted in return for having birthed me and for nurturing me was that I submit to her without rebellion. Was this a survival skill she was trying to teach me? She objected not so much to my disobedience but to my questioning her right to demand obedience from me. Mixed with this power struggle was her guilt at having borne a child who was marked "con la seña," thinking she had made me a victim of her sin. In her eyes and in the eyes of others I saw myself reflected as "strange," "abnormal," "QUEER." I saw no other reflection. Helpless to change that image, I retreated into books and solitude and kept away from others.

The whole time growing up I felt that I was not of this earth. An alien from another planet—I'd been dropped on my mother's lap. But for what purpose?

One day when I was about seven or eight, my father dropped on my lap a 25¢ pocket western, the only type of book he could pick up at a drugstore. The act of reading forever changed me. In the westerns I read, the house servants, the villains and the cantineras (prostitutes) were all Mexicans. But I knew that the first cowboys (vaqueros) were Mexicans, that in Texas we outnumbered the Anglos, that my grandmother's ranch lands had been ripped off by the greedy Anglo. Yet in the pages of these books, the Mexican and Indian were vermin. The racism I would later recognize in my school teachers and never be able to ignore again I found in that first western I read.

My father dying, his aorta bursting while he was driving, the truck turning over, his body thrown out, the truck falling on his face. Blood on the pavement. His death occurred just as I entered puberty. It irrevocably shattered the myth that there existed a male figure to look after me. How could my strong, good, beautiful godlike father be killed? How stupid and careless of God. What if chance and circumstance and accident ruled? I lost my father, God, and my innocence all in one bloody blow.

Every 24 days, raging fevers cooked my brain. Full flowing periods accompanied cramps, tonsillitis, and 105° fevers. Every month a trip to the doctors. "It's all in your head," they would say. "When you get older and get married and have children the pain will stop." A monotonous litany from the men in white all through my teens.

The bloodshed on the highway had robbed my adolescence from me like the blood on my diaper had robbed childhood from me. And into my hands unknowingly I took the transformation of my own being.

Nobody's going to save you.
No one's going to cut you down
cut the thorns around you.
No one's going to storm
the castle walls nor
kiss awake your birth,
climb down your hair,
nor mount you
onto the white steed.

There is no one who
will feed the yearning.
Face it. You will have
to do, do it yourself.[2]

My father dead, my mother and I turned to each other. Hadn't we grown together? We were like sisters—she was 16 when she gave birth to me.

Though she loved me she would only show it covertly—in the tone of her voice, in a look. Not so with my brothers—there it was visible for all the world to see. They were male and surrogate husbands, legitimate receivers of her power. Her allegiance was and is to her male children, not to the female.

Seeing my mother turn to my brothers for protection, for guidance—a mock act. She and I both knew she wouldn't be getting any from them. Like most men they didn't have it to give, instead needed to get it from women. I resented the fact that it was OK for my brothers to touch and kiss and flirt with her, but not for my sister and me. Resenting the fact that physical intimacy between women was taboo, dirty.

Yet she could not discount me. "Machona—india ladina" (masculine—wild Indian), she would call me because I did not act like a nice little Chicanita is supposed to act: later, in the same breath she would praise and blame me, often for the same thing—being a tomboy and wearing boots, being unafraid of snakes or knives, showing my contempt for women's roles, leaving home to go to college, not settling down and getting married, being a política, siding with the Farmworkers. Yet, while she would try to correct my more aggressive moods, my mother was secretly proud of my "waywardness." (Something she will never admit.) Proud that I'd worked myself through school. Secretly proud of my paintings, of my writing, though all the while complaining because I made no money out of it.

Vergüenza (Shame)

. . . being afraid that my friends would see my momma, would know that she was loud—her voice penetrated every corner. Always when we came into a room everyone looked up. I didn't want my friends to hear her brag about her children. I was afraid she would blurt out some secret, would criticize me in public. She always embarrassed me by telling everyone that I liked to lie in bed reading and wouldn't help her with the housework.

. . . eating at school out of sacks, hiding our "lonches" papas con chorizo behind cupped hands and bowed heads, gobbling them up before the other kids could see. Guilt lay folded in the tortilla. The Anglo kids laughing—calling us "tortilleros," the Mexican kids taking up the word and using it as a club with which to hit each other. My brothers, sister and I started bringing white bread sandwiches to school. After a while we stopped taking our lunch altogether.

There is no beauty in poverty, in my mother being able to give only one of her children lunch money. (We all agreed it should go to Nune, he was growing fast and was always hungry.) It was not very romantic for my sister and me to wear the dresses and panties my mother made us out of flour sacks because she couldn't afford store-bought ones like the other mothers.

Well, I'm not ashamed of you anymore, Momma.

My heart, once bent and cracked, once
ashamed of your China ways.
Ma, hear me now, tell me your story
again and again.

—Nellie Wong, "From a Heart of Rice Straw,"
Dreams of Harrison Railroad Park

It was not my mother's fault that we were poor and yet so much of my pain and shame has been with our both betraying each other. But my mother has always been there for me in spite of our differences and emotional gulfs. She has never stopped fighting; she is a survivor. Even now I can hear her arguing with my father over how to raise us, insisting that all decisions be made by both of them. I can hear her crying over the body of my dead father. She was 28, had had little schooling, was unskilled, yet her strength was greater than most men's, raising us single-handed.

After my father died, I worked in the fields every weekend and every summer, even when I was a student in college. (We only migrated once when I was seven, journeyed in the back of my father's red truck with two other families to the cotton fields of west Texas. When I missed a few weeks of school, my father decided this should not happen again.) . . . the planes swooping down on us, the fifty or a hundred of us falling onto the ground, the cloud of insecticide lacerating our eyes, clogging our nostrils. Nor did the corporate farm owners care that there were no toilets in the wide open fields, no bushes to hide behind.

Over the years, the confines of farm and ranch life began to chafe. The traditional role of la mujer was a saddle I did not want to wear. The concepts "passive" and "dutiful" raked my skin like spurs, and "marriage" and "children" set me to bucking faster than rattlesnakes or coyotes. I took to wearing boots and men's jeans and walking about with my head full of visions, hungry for more words and more words. Slowly I unbowed my head, refused my state and began to challenge the way things were. But it's taken over thirty years to unlearn the belief instilled in me that white is better than brown—something that some people of color *never* will unlearn. And it is only now that the hatred of myself, which I spent the greater part of my adolescence cultivating, is turning to love.

La Muerte, the Frozen Snow Queen

I dig a grave, bury my first love, a German Shepherd. Bury the second, third, and fourth dog. The last one retching in the backyard, going into convulsions from insecticide poisoning. I buried him beside the others, five mounds in a row crowned with crosses I'd fashioned from twigs.

No more pets, no more loves—I court death now.

. . . Two years ago on a fine November day in Yosemite Park, I fall on the floor with cramps, severe chills and shaking that go into spasms and near convulsions, then fevers so high my eyes feel like eggs frying. Twelve hours of this. I tell everyone, "It's nothing, don't worry, I'm alright." The first four gynecologists advise a hysterectomy. The fifth, a woman, says wait.

. . . Last March my fibroids conspired with an intestinal tract infection and spawned watermelons in my uterus. The doctor played with his knife. La Chingada ripped open, raped with the white man's wand. My soul in one corner of the hospital ceiling, getting thinner and thinner, telling me to clean up my shit, to release the fears and garbage from the past that are hanging me up. So I take La Muerte's scythe and cut away my arrogance and pride, the emotional depressions I indulge in, the head trips I do on myself and other people. With her scythe I cut the umbilical cord shackling me to the past and to friends and attitudes that drag me down. Strip away—all the way to the bone. Make myself utterly vulnerable.

. . . I can't sleep nights. The mugger said he would come and get me. There was a break in the county jail and I just know he is broken out and is coming to get me because I picked up a big rock and chased him, because I got help and caught him. How *dare* he drag me over rocks and twigs, the skin on my knees peeling, how *dare* he lay his hands on my throat, how *dare* he try to choke me to death, how *dare* he try to push me off the bridge to splatter my blood and bones on the rocks 20 feet below. His breath on my face, our eyes only inches apart, our bodies rolling on the ground in an embrace so intimate we could have been mistaken for lovers.

That night terror found me curled up in my bed. I couldn't stop trembling. For months terror came to me at night and never left me. And even now, seven years later, when I'm out in the street after dark and I hear running footsteps behind me, terror finds me again and again.

No more pets, no more loves.

. . . one of my lovers saying I was frigid when he couldn't bring me to orgasm.

. . . bringing home my Peruvian boyfriend and my mother saying she did not want her "Prieta" to have a "mojado" (wetback) for a lover.

. . . my mother and brothers calling me puta when I told them I had lost my virginity and that I'd done it on purpose. My mother and brothers calling me jota (queer) when I told them my friends were gay men and lesbians.

. . . Randy saying, "It's time you stopped being a nun, an ice queen afraid of living." But I did not want to be a snow queen regal with icy smiles and fingernails that ripped her prey ruthlessly. And yet, I knew my being distant, remote, a mountain sleeping under the snow, is what attracted him.

A woman lies buried under me,
interred for centuries, presumed dead.

A woman lies buried under me.
I hear her soft whisper
the rasp of her parchment skin
fighting the folds of her shroud.
Her eyes are pierced by needles
her eyelids, two fluttering moths.[3]

I am always surprised by the image that my white and non-Chicano friends have of me, surprised at how much they *do not* know me, at how I do not allow them to know me. They have substituted the negative picture the white culture has painted of my race with a highly romanticized, idealized image. "You're strong," my friends said, "a mountain of strength."

Though the power may be real, the mythic qualities attached to it keep others from dealing with me as a person and rob me of my being able to act out my other selves. Having this "power" doesn't exempt me from being prey in the streets nor does it make my scrambling to survive, to feed myself, easier. To cope with hurt and control my fears, I grew a thick skin. Oh, the many names of power—pride, arrogance, control. I am not the frozen snow queen but a flesh and blood woman with perhaps too loving a heart, one easily hurt.

I'm not invincible, I tell you. My skin's as fragile as a baby's. I'm brittle bones and human, I tell you. I'm a broken arm.

You're a razor's edge, you tell me. Shock them shitless. Be the holocaust. Be the black Kali. Spit in their eye and never cry. Oh broken angel, throw away your cast, mend your wing. Be not a rock but a razor's edge and burn with falling (Journal Entry, Summer Solstice, 1978).

Who Are My People?

I am a wind-swayed bridge, a crossroads inhabited by whirlwinds. Gloria the facilitator, Gloria the mediator, straddling the walls between abysses. "Your allegiance is to La Raza, the Chicano movement," say the members of my race. "Your allegiance is to the Third World," say my Black and Asian friends. "Your allegiance is to your gender, to women," say the feminists. Then there's my allegiance to the Gay movement, to the socialist revolution, to the New Age, to magic and the occult. And there's my affinity to literature, to the world of the artist. What am I? *A third world lesbian feminist with Marxist and mystic leanings.* They would chop me up into little fragments and tag each piece with a label.

You say my name is ambivalence? Think of me as Shiva, a many-armed and legged body with one foot on brown soil, one on white, one in straight society, one in the gay world, the man's world, the women's, one limb in the literary world, another in the working class, the socialist, and the occult worlds. A sort of spider woman hanging by one thin strand of web.

Who, me confused? Ambivalent? Not so. Only your labels split me.

Years ago, a roommate of mine fighting for gay rights told MAYO, a Chicano organization, that she and the president were gay. They were ostracized. When they left, MAYO fell apart. They too, being forced to choose between the priorities of race, sexual preference, or gender.

In the streets of this gay mecca, San Francisco, a Black man at a bus stop yells, "Hey Faggots, come suck my cock." Randy yells back, "You goddamn nigger, I worked in the Civil Rights movement ten years so you could call me names." Guilt gagging in his throat with the word, nigger. . . . a white woman waiting for the J-Church streetcar sees Randy and David kissing and says, "You should be ashamed of yourselves. Two grown men—disgusting."

. . . Randy and David running into the house. The hair on the back of my neck rises, something in their voices triggers fear in me. Three Latino men in a car had chased them as they were walking home from work. "Gay boys, faggots," they yelled throwing a beer bottle. Getting out of their car, knife blades reflect the full moon. . . . Randy and David hitting each other in the hall. Thuds on the wall—the heavy animal sounds.

. . . Randy pounding on my door one corner of his mouth bleeding, his glasses broken, blind without them, he crying, "I'm going to kill him, I'm going to kill the son of a bitch."

The violence against us, the violence within us, aroused like a rabid dog. Adrenaline-filled bodies, we bring home the anger and the violence we meet on the street and turn it against each other. We sic the rabid dog on each other and on ourselves. The black moods of alienation descend, the bridges we've extended out to each other crumble. We put the walls back up between us.

Once again it's faggot-hunting and queer-baiting time in the city. "And on your first anniversary of loving each other," I say to Randy, "and they had to be Latinos," feeling guilt when I look at David. Who is my brother's keeper, I wonder—knowing I have to be, we all have to be. We are all responsible. But who exactly *are* my people?

I identify as a woman. Whatever insults women insults me.

I identify as gay. Whoever insults gays insults me.

I identify as feminist. Whoever slurs feminism slurs me.

That which is insulted I take as part of me, but there is something too simple about this kind of thinking. Part of the dialectic is missing. What about what I do not identify as?

I have been terrified of writing this essay because I will have to own up to the fact that I do not exclude whites from the list of people I love, two of them happen to be gay males. For the politically correct stance we let color, class, and gender separate us from those who would be kindred spirits. So the walls grow higher, the gulfs between us wider, the silences more profound. There is an enormous contradiction in being a bridge.

Dance to the Beat of Radical Colored Chic

This task—to be a bridge, to be a fucking crossroads for goddess' sake.

During my stint in the Feminist Writers' Guild many white members would ask me why Third World women do not come to FWG meetings and readings. I should have answered, "Because their skins are not as thick as mine, because their fear of encountering racism is greater than mine. They don't enjoy being put down, ignored, not engaged in equal dialogue, being tokens. And, neither do I." Oh, I know, women of color are hot right now and hip. Our afro-rhythms and latin salsas, the beat of our drums is in. White women flock to our parties, dance to the beat of radical colored chic. They come to our readings, take up our cause. I have no objections to this. What I mind is the pseudo-liberal ones who suffer from the white women's burden. Like the monkey in the Sufi story, who upon seeing a fish in the water rushes to rescue it from drowning by carrying it up into the branches of a tree. She takes a missionary role. She attempts to talk *for* us—what a presumption! This act is a rape of our tongue and our acquiescence is a complicity to that rape. We women of color have to stop being modern medusas—throats cut, silenced into a mere hissing.

Where Do We Hang the Blame?

The pull between what is and what should be.

Does the root of the sickness lie within ourselves or within our patriarchal institutions? Did our institutions birth and propagate themselves and are we merely their pawns? Do ideas originate in human minds or do they exist in a "no-osphere," a limbo space where ideas originate without our help? Where do we hang the blame for the sickness we see around us—around our own heads or around the throat of "capitalism," "socialism," "men," "white culture"?

If we do not create these institutions, we certainly perpetuate them through our inadvertent support. What lessons do we learn from the mugger?

Certainly racism is not just a white phenomenon. Whites are the top dogs and they shit on the rest of us every day of our lives. But casting stones is not the solution. Do we hand the oppressor thug the rocks he throws at us? How often do we people of color place our necks on the chopping block? What are the ways we hold out our wrists to be shackled? Do we gag our own mouths with our "dios lo manda" resignation? How many times before the cock crows do we deny ourselves, shake off our dreams, and trample them into the sand? How many times do we fail to help one another up from the bottom of the stairs? How many times have we let someone else carry our crosses? How still do we stand to be crucified?

It is difficult for me to break free of the Chicano cultural bias into which I was born and raised, and the cultural bias of the Anglo culture that I was brainwashed into adopting. It is easier to repeat the racial patterns and attitudes, especially those of fear and prejudice, that we have inherited than to resist them.

Like a favorite old shoe that no longer fits we do not let go of our comfortable old selves so that the new self can be worn. We fear our power, fear our feminine selves, fear the strong woman within, especially the black Kali aspect, dark and awesome. Thus we pay homage not to the power inside us but to the power outside us, masculine power, external power.

I see Third World peoples and women not as oppressors but as accomplices to oppression by our unwittingly passing on to our children and our friends the oppressor's ideologies. I cannot discount the role I play as accomplice, that we all play as accomplices, for we are not screaming loud enough in protest.

The disease of powerlessness thrives in my body, not just out there in society. And just as the use of gloves, masks, and disinfectants fails to kill this disease, government grants, equal rights opportunity programs, welfare, and foodstamps fail to uproot racism, sexism, and homophobia. And tokenism is not the answer. Sharing the pie is not going to work. I had a bite of it once and it almost poisoned me. With mutations of the virus such as these, one cannot isolate the virus and treat it. The whole organism is poisoned.

I stand behind whatever threatens our oppression. I stand behind whatever breaks us out of our bonds, short of killing and maiming. I stand with whatever and whoever breaks us out of our limited views and awakens our atrophied potentials.

How to turn away from the hellish journey that the disease has put me through, the alchemical nights of the soul. Torn limb from limb, knifed, mugged, beaten. My tongue (Spanish) ripped from my mouth, left voiceless. My name stolen from me. My bowels fucked with a surgeon's knife, uterus and ovaries pitched into the trash. Castrated. Set apart from my own kind, isolated. My life-blood sucked out of me by my role as woman nurturer—the last form of cannibalism.

El Mundo Zurdo (the Left-Handed World)[4]

The pull between what is and what should be. I believe that by changing ourselves we change the world, that traveling El Mundo Zurdo path is the path of a two-way movement—a going deep into the self and an expanding out into the world, a simultaneous recreation of the self and a reconstruction of society. And yet, I am confused as to how to accomplish this.

I can't discount the fact of the thousands that go to bed hungry every night. The thousands that do numbing shitwork eight hours a day each day of their lives. The thousands that get beaten and killed every day. The millions of women who have been burned at the stake, the millions who have been raped. Where is the justice to this?

I can't reconcile the sight of a battered child with the belief that we choose what happens to us, that we create our own world. *I cannot resolve* this in myself. I don't know. I can only speculate, try to integrate the experiences that I've had or have been witness to and try to make some sense of why we do violence to each other. In short, I'm trying to create a religion not out there somewhere, but in my gut. I am trying to make peace between what has happened to me, what the world is, and what it should be.

"Growing up I felt that I was an alien from another planet dropped on my mother's lap. But for what purpose?"

The mixture of bloods and affinities, rather than confusing or unbalancing me, has forced me to achieve a kind of equilibrium. Both cultures deny me a place in *their* universe. Between them and among others, I build my own universe, *El Mundo Zurdo*. I belong to myself and not to any one people.

I walk the tightrope with ease and grace. I span abysses. Blindfolded in the blue air. The sword between my thighs, the blade warm with my flesh. I walk the rope—an acrobat in equipoise, expert at the Balancing Act.

The rational, the patriarchal, and the heterosexual have held sway and legal tender for too long. Third World women, lesbians, feminists, and feminist-oriented men of all colors are banding and bonding together to right that balance. Only *together* can we be a force. I see us as a network of kindred spirits, a kind of family.

We are the queer groups, the people that don't belong anywhere, not in the dominant world nor completely within our own respective cultures. Combined we cover so many oppressions. But the overwhelming oppression is the collective fact that we do not fit, and because we do not fit *we are a threat*. Not all of us have the same oppressions, but we empathize and identify with each other's oppressions. We do not have the same ideology, nor do we derive similar solutions. Some of us are leftists, some of us practitioners of magic. Some of us are both. But these different affinities are not opposed to each other. In El Mundo Zurdo I with my own affinities and my people with theirs can live together and transform the planet.[5]

Notes

1. From my poem "The Woman Who Lived Forever." All subsequent unacknowledged poems will be from my own writings.
2. From "Letting Go." Now published in *Borderlands/La Frontera: The New Mestiza* (San Francisco: Aunt Lute, 2nd edition, 1999), 186–188. *(Editor, 2015)*
3. From "A Woman Lies Buried under Me."
4. This section consists of notes "Towards a Construction of El Mundo Zurdo," an essay in progress.
5. Much of Gloria Anzaldúa's unpublished writings can be found in her archives: The Gloria Evangelina Anzaldúa Papers, located at the Nettie Lee Benson Library, Latin American Collection at the University of Texas, Austin.

A Black Feminist Statement

Combahee River Collective[1]

We are a collective of Black feminists who have been meeting together since 1974.[2] During that time we have been involved in the process of defining and clarifying our politics, while at the same time doing political work within our own group and in coalition with other progressive organizations and movements. The most general statement of our politics at the present time would be that we are actively committed to struggling against racial, sexual, heterosexual, and class oppression and see as our particular task the development of integrated analysis and practice based upon the fact that the major systems of oppression are interlocking. The synthesis of these oppressions creates the conditions of our lives. As Black women we see Black feminism as the logical political movement to combat the manifold and simultaneous oppressions that all women of color face.

We will discuss four major topics in the paper that follows: (1) the genesis of contemporary Black feminism; (2) what we believe, i.e., the specific province of our politics; (3) the problems in organizing Black feminists, including a brief herstory of our collective; and (4) Black feminist issues and practice.

1. The Genesis of Contemporary Black Feminism

Before looking at the recent development of Black feminism we would like to affirm that we find our origins in the historical reality of Afro-American women's continuous life-and-death struggle for survival and liberation. Black women's extremely negative relationship to the American political system (a system of white male rule) has always been determined by our membership in two oppressed racial and sexual castes. As Angela Davis points out in "Reflections on the Black Woman's Role in the Community of Slaves," Black women have always embodied, if only in their physical manifestation, an adversary stance to white male rule and have actively resisted its inroads upon them and their communities in both dramatic and subtle ways. There have always been Black women activists—some known, like Sojourner Truth, Harriet Tubman, Frances E. W. Harper, Ida B. Wells Barnett, and Mary Church Terrell, and thousands upon thousands unknown—who had a shared awareness of how their sexual identity combined with their racial identity to make their whole life situation and the focus of their political struggles unique. Contemporary Black feminism is the outgrowth of countless generations of personal sacrifice, militancy, and work by our mothers and sisters.

A Black feminist presence has evolved most obviously in connection with the second wave of the American women's movement beginning in the late 1960s. Black, other Third World, and working women have been involved in the feminist movement from its start, but both outside reactionary forces and racism and elitism within the movement itself have served to obscure our participation. In 1973 Black feminists, primarily located in New York, felt the necessity of forming a separate Black feminist group. This became the National Black Feminist Organization (NBFO).

Black feminist politics also have an obvious connection to movements for Black liberation, particularly those of the 1960s and 1970s. Many of us were active in those movements (civil rights, Black nationalism, the Black Panthers), and all of our lives were greatly affected and changed by their ideology, their goals, and the tactics used to achieve their goals. It was our experience and disillusionment within these liberation movements, as well as experience on the periphery of the white male left, that led to the need to develop a politic that was antiracist, unlike those of white women, and antisexist, unlike those of Black and white men.

There is also undeniably a personal genesis for Black feminism; that is, the political realization that comes from the seemingly personal experiences of individual Black women's lives. Black feminists and many more Black women who do not define themselves as feminists have all experienced sexual oppression as a constant factor in our day-to-day existence. As children we realized that we were different from boys and that we were treated differently. For example, we were told in the same breath to be quiet both for the sake of being "ladylike" and to make us less objectionable in the eyes of white people. As we grew older we became aware of the threat of physical and sexual abuse by men. However, we had no way of conceptualizing what was so apparent to us, what we *knew* was really happening.

Black feminists often talk about their feelings of craziness before becoming conscious of the concepts of sexual politics, patriarchal rule, and most importantly, feminism—the political analysis and practice that we women use to struggle against our oppression. The fact that racial politics and indeed racism are pervasive factors in our lives did not allow us, and still does not allow most Black women, to look more deeply into our own experiences and, from that sharing and growing consciousness, to build a politics that will change our lives and inevitably end our oppression. Our development must also be tied to the contemporary economic and political position of Black people. The post World War II generation of Black youth was the first to be able to minimally partake of certain educational and employment options, previously closed completely to Black people. Although our economic position is still at the very bottom of the American capitalistic economy, a handful of us have been able to gain certain tools as a result of tokenism in education and employment which potentially enable us to more effectively fight our oppression.

A combined antiracist and antisexist position drew us together initially, and as we developed politically we addressed ourselves to heterosexism and economic oppression under capitalism.

2. What We Believe

Above all else, our politics initially sprang from the shared belief that Black women are inherently valuable, that our liberation is a necessity not as an adjunct to somebody else's but because of our need as human persons for autonomy. This may seem so obvious as to sound simplistic, but it is apparent that no other ostensibly progressive movement has ever considered our specific oppression as a priority or worked seriously for the ending of that oppression. Merely naming the pejorative stereotypes attributed to Black women (e.g., mammy, matriarch, Sapphire, whore, bulldagger), let alone cataloguing the cruel, often murderous, treatment we receive, indicates how little value has been placed upon our lives during four centuries of bondage in the Western hemisphere. We realize that the only people who care enough about us to work consistently for our liberation is us. Our politics evolve from a healthy love for ourselves, our sisters and our community which allows us to continue our struggle and work.

This focusing upon our own oppression is embodied in the concept of identity politics. We believe that the most profound and potentially the most radical politics come directly out of our own identity, as opposed to working to end somebody else's oppression. In the case of Black women this is a particularly repugnant, dangerous, threatening, and therefore revolutionary concept because it is obvious from looking at all the political movements that have preceded us that anyone is more worthy of liberation than ourselves. We reject pedestals, queenhood, and walking ten paces behind. To be recognized as human, levelly human, is enough.

We believe that sexual politics under patriarchy is as pervasive in Black women's lives as are the politics of class and race. We also often find it difficult to separate race from class from sex oppression because in our lives they are most often experienced simultaneously. We know that there is such a thing as racial-sexual oppression which is neither solely racial nor solely sexual, e.g., the history of rape of Black women by white men as a weapon of political repression.

Although we are feminists and lesbians, we feel solidarity with progressive Black men and do not advocate the fractionalization that white women who are separatists demand. Our situation as Black people necessitates that we have solidarity around the fact of race, which white women of course do not need to have with white men, unless it is their negative solidarity as racial oppressors. We struggle together with Black men against racism, while we also struggle with Black men about sexism.

We realize that the liberation of all oppressed peoples necessitates the destruction of the political-economic systems of capitalism and imperialism as well as patriarchy. We are socialists because we believe the work must be organized for the collective benefit of those who do the work and create the products, and not for the profit of the bosses. Material resources must be equally distributed among those who create these resources. We are not convinced, however, that a socialist revolution that is not also a feminist and antiracist revolution will guarantee our liberation. We have arrived at the necessity for developing an understanding of class relationships that takes into account the specific class position of Black women who are generally marginal in the labor force, while at this particular time some of us are temporarily viewed as doubly desirable tokens at white-collar and professional levels. We need to articulate the real class situation of persons who are not merely raceless, sexless workers, but for whom racial and sexual oppression are significant determinants in their working/economic lives. Although we are in essential agreement with Marx's theory as it applied to the very specific economic relationships he analyzed, we know that his analysis must be extended further in order for us to understand our specific economic situation as Black women.

A political contribution which we feel we have already made is the expansion of the feminist principle that the personal is political. In our consciousness-raising sessions, for example, we have in many ways gone beyond white women's revelations because we are dealing with the implications of race and class as well as sex. Even our Black women's style of talking/testifying in Black language about what we have experienced has a resonance that is both cultural and political. We have spent a great deal of energy delving into the cultural and experiential nature of our oppression out of necessity because none of these matters has ever been looked at before. No one before has ever examined the multilayered texture of Black women's lives. An example of this kind of revelation/conceptualization occurred at a meeting as we discussed the ways in which our early intellectual interests had been attacked by our peers, particularly Black males. We discovered that all of us, because we were "smart," had also been considered "ugly," i.e., "smart-ugly." "Smart-ugly" crystallized the way in which most of us had been forced to develop our intellects at great cost to our "social" lives. The sanctions in the Black and white communities against Black women thinkers are comparatively much higher than for white women, particularly ones from the educated middle and upper classes.

As we have already stated, we reject the stance of lesbian separatism because it is not a viable political analysis or strategy for us. It leaves out far too much and far too many people, particularly Black men, women, and children. We have a great deal of criticism and loathing for what men have been socialized to be in this society: what they support, how they act, and how they oppress. But we do not have the misguided notion that it is their maleness, per se—*i.e.*, their biological maleness—that makes them what they are. As Black women we find any type of biological determinism a particularly dangerous and reactionary basis upon which to build a politic. We must also question whether lesbian separatism is an adequate and progressive political analysis and strategy, even for those who practice it, since it so completely denies any but the sexual sources of women's oppression, negating the facts of class and race.

3. Problems in Organizing Black Feminists

During our years together as a Black feminist collective we have experienced success and defeat, joy and pain, victory and failure. We have found that it is very difficult to organize around Black feminist issues, difficult even to announce in certain contexts that we are Black feminists. We have tried to think about the reasons for our difficulties, particularly since the white women's movement continues to be strong and to grow in many directions. In this section we will discuss some of the general reasons for the organizing problems we face and also talk specifically about the stages in organizing our own collective.

The major source of difficulty in our political work is that we are not just trying to fight oppression on one front or even two, but instead to address a whole range of oppressions. We do not have racial, sexual, heterosexual, or class privilege to rely upon, nor do we have even the minimal access to resources and power that groups who possess any one of these types of privilege have.

The psychological toll of being a Black woman and the difficulties this presents in reaching political consciousness and doing political work can never be underestimated. There is a very low value placed upon Black women's psyches in this society, which is both racist and sexist. As an early group member once said, "We are all damaged people merely by virtue of being Black women." We are dispossessed psychologically and on every other level, and yet we feel the necessity to struggle to change the condition of all Black women. In "A Black Feminist's Search for Sisterhood," Michele Wallace arrives at this conclusion:

> We exist as women who are Black who are feminists, each stranded for the moment, working independently because there is not yet an environment in this society remotely congenial to our struggle—because, being on the bottom, we would have to do what no one else has done: we would have to fight the world.[3]

Wallace is pessimistic but realistic in her assessment of Black feminists' position, particularly in her allusion to the nearly classic isolation most of us face. We might use our position at the bottom, however, to make a clear leap into revolutionary action. If Black women were free, it would mean that everyone else would have to be free since our freedom would necessitate the destruction of all the systems of oppression.

Feminism is, nevertheless, very threatening to the majority of Black people because it calls into question some of the most basic assumptions about our existence, i.e., that sex should be a determinant of power relationships. Here is the way male and female voices were defined in a Black nationalist pamphlet from the early 1970s:

> We understand that it is and has been traditional that the man is the head of the house. He is the leader of the house/nation because his knowledge of the world is broader, his awareness is greater, his understanding is fuller and his application of this information is wiser . . . After all, it is only reasonable that the man be the head of the house because he is able to defend and protect the development of his home . . . Women cannot do the same things as men—they are made by nature to function differently. Equality of men and women is something that cannot happen even in the abstract world. Men are not equal to other men, i.e., ability, experience or even understanding. The value of men and women can be seen as in the value of gold and silver—they are not equal but both have great value. We must realize that men and women are a complement to each other because there is no house/ family without a man and his wife. Both are essential to the development of any life.[4]

The material conditions of most Black women would hardly lead them to upset both economic and sexual arrangements that seem to represent some stability in their lives. Many Black women have a good understanding of both sexism and racism, but because of the everyday constrictions of their lives cannot risk struggling against them both.

The reaction of Black men to feminism has been notoriously negative. They are, of course, even more threatened than Black women by the possibility that Black feminists might organize around our own needs. They realize that they might not only lose valuable and hard-working allies in their struggles but that they might also be forced to change their habitually sexist ways of interacting with and oppressing Black women. Accusations that Black feminism divides the Black struggle are powerful deterrents to the growth of an autonomous Black women's movement.

Still, hundreds of women have been active at different times during the three-year existence of our group. And every Black woman who came, did so out of a strongly-felt need for some level of possibility that did not previously exist in her life.

When we first started meeting early in 1974 after the NBFO first eastern regional conference, we did not have a strategy for organizing, or even a focus. We just wanted to see what we had. After a period of months of not meeting, we began to meet again late in the year and started doing an intense variety of consciousness-raising. The overwhelming feeling we had was that after years and years we had finally found each other. Although we were not doing political work as a group, individuals continued their involvement in lesbian politics, sterilization abuse and abortion rights work, Third World Women's International Women's Day activities, and support activity for the trials of Dr. Kenneth Edelin, Joan Little, and Inéz García. During our first summer, when membership had dropped off considerably, those of us remaining devoted serious discussion to the possibility of opening a refuge for battered women in a Black community. (There was no refuge in Boston at that time.) We also decided around that time to become an independent collective since we had serious disagreements with NBFO's bourgeois-feminist stance and their lack of a clear political focus.

We also were contacted at that time by socialist feminists, with whom we had worked on abortion rights activities, who wanted to encourage us to attend the National Socialist Feminist Conference in Yellow Springs. One of our members did attend and despite the narrowness of the ideology that was promoted at that particular conference, we became more aware of the need for us to understand our own economic situation and to make our own economic analysis.

In the fall, when some members returned, we experienced several months of comparative inactivity and internal disagreements which were first conceptualized as a lesbian-straight split but which were also the result of class and political differences. During the summer those of us who were still meeting had determined the need to do political work and to move beyond consciousness-raising and serving exclusively as an emotional support group. At the beginning of 1976, when some of the women who had not wanted to do political work and who also had voiced disagreements stopped attending of their own accord, we again looked for a focus. We decided at that time, with the addition of new members, to become a study group. We had always shared our reading with each other, and some of us had written papers on Black feminism for group discussion a few months before this decision was made. We began functioning as a study group and also began discussing the possibility of starting a Black feminist publication. We had a retreat in the late spring which provided a time for both political discussion and working out interpersonal issues. Currently we are planning to gather together a collection of Black feminist writing. We feel that it is absolutely essential to demonstrate the reality of our politics to other Black women and believe that we can do this through writing and distributing our work. The fact that individual Black feminists are living in isolation all over the country, that our own numbers are small, and that we have some skills in writing, printing, and publishing makes us want to carry out these kinds of projects as a means of organizing Black feminists as we continue to do political work in coalition with other groups.

4. Black Feminist Issues and Projects

During our time together we have identified and worked on many issues of particular relevance to Black women. The inclusiveness of our politics makes us concerned with any situation that impinges upon the lives of women, Third World, and working people. We are of course particularly committed to working on those struggles in which race, sex and class are simultaneous factors in oppression. We might, for example, become involved in workplace organizing at a factory that employs Third World women or picket a hospital that is cutting back on already inadequate health care to a Third World community, or set up a rape crisis center in a Black neighborhood. Organizing around welfare and daycare concerns might also be a focus. The work to be done and the countless issues that this work represents merely reflect the pervasiveness of our oppression.

Issues and projects that collective members have actually worked on are sterilization abuse, abortion rights, battered women, rape and health care. We have also done many workshops and educationals on

Black feminism on college campuses, at women's conferences, and most recently for high school girls.

One issue that is of major concern to us and that we have begun to publicly address is racism in the white women's movement. As Black feminists we are made constantly and painfully aware of how little effort white women have made to understand and combat their racism, which requires among other things that they have a more than superficial comprehension of race, color, and black history and culture. Eliminating racism in the white women's movement is by definition work for white women to do, but we will continue to speak to and demand account- ability on this issue.

In the practice of our politics we do not believe that the end always justifies the means. Many reactionary and destructive acts have been done in the name of achieving "correct" political goals. As feminists we do not want to mess over people in the name of politics. We believe in collective process and a nonhierarchical distribution of power within our own group and in our vision of a revolutionary society. We are commit- ted to a continual examination of our politics, as they develop through criticism and self-criticism, as an essential aspect of our practice. In her introduction to *Sisterhood Is Powerful* Robin Morgan writes:

> I haven't the faintest notion what possible revolutionary role white heterosexual men could fulfill, since they are the very embodiment of reactionary-vested-interest-power.

As Black feminists and lesbians we know that we have a very definite revolutionary task to perform and we are ready for the lifetime of work and struggle before us.

Notes

1. The Combahee River Collective is a Black feminist group in Boston whose name comes from the guerilla action conceptualized and led by Harriet Tub- man on June 2, 1863, in the Port Royal region of South Carolina. This action freed more than 750 slaves and is the only military campaign in American history planned and led by a woman.
2. This statement is dated April, 1977.
3. Michele Wallace, "A Black Feminist's Search for Sisterhood," *Village Voice*, (July 28, 1975), 6–7.
4. Mumininas of Committee for Unified Newark, Mwanamke Mwananchi (The Nationalist Woman), Newark, NJ, 1971, 4–5. From *Capitalist Patriarchy and the Case for Socialist Feminism*, edited by Zillah Eisenstein (New York: Monthly Review Press, 1978).

The Welder

Cherríe Moraga

[handwritten: daily life (mundane]

[handwritten: common woman]

I am a welder.
Not an alchemist.
I am interested in the blend
of common elements to make
a common thing.

No magic here.
Only the heat of my desire to fuse
what I already know
exists. Is possible.

We plead to each other,
we all come from the same rock
we all come from the same rock
ignoring the fact that we bend
at different temperatures
that each of us is malleable
up to a point.

[handwritten: same yet different]

Yes, fusion *is* possible
but only if things get hot enough—
all else is temporary adhesion,
patching up.

[handwritten: conversations begin]

It is the intimacy of steel melting
into steel, the fire of our individual
passion to take hold of ourselves
that makes sculpture of our lives,
builds buildings.

And I am not talking about skyscrapers,
merely structures that can support us
without fear
of trembling.

For too long a time
the heat of my heavy hands

219

has been smoldering
in the pockets of other
people's business—
they need oxygen to make fire.

I am now
coming up for air.
Yes, I *am*
picking up the torch.

I am the welder.
I understand the capacity of heat
to change the shape of things.
I am suited to work
within the realm of sparks
out of control.

agency

I am the welder.
I am taking the power
into my own hands.

O.K. Momma, Who the Hell Am I?

An Interview with Luisah Teish

Gloria Anzaldúa

Part One: "There was this rumbling in the background . . ."

G: *Teish, in Numerology you can derive what your mission or life path is by adding the day of your birth, the month and the year and reducing it to a single digit number. The number corresponds with a Tarot card. According to this system you are a 19-10 and 1, the "genius." What do you see as your task in this life and how did you find that out?*

T: I've had a series of experiences that point the way. It's as if I was given a road map, and started traveling at different points. There is a travel consultant that meets me and says okay, now you go this way. The big vision, which I call my reformation, happened in Fall 1974. I was in a terrible situation. I was coming out of having been deeply steeped in the Black Power movement. I had spent since 1970 quite a bit of time trying to ignore feminist teachings. There was this rumbling in the background saying that women ought to consider the position of women. I'm here screaming at the top of my lungs that Black people have to be free, you see. And over here I'm hearing people saying women have to be free too; there's a certain kind of oppression women suffer. But because it was primarily white women in the movement and white women who were vocalizing at the time, for a while I went along with the idea that, well, what they're talking about is only relevant to white women. At the same time, in my personal life I was being mistreated by people who claim to be about the fight for freedom. That contradiction was staring me in my face. My inner self was telling me, "You have marched, you have demonstrated, and you have fought for freedom, and Malcolm said 'freedom by any means necessary.'"

And yet I'm taking certain kinds of crap off of my brothers, you know. Why doesn't this apply clean across the board? And it put me in a position where I felt literally crippled. I felt like I had nowhere to turn and nothing really to do. Other things that had happened in my life—I was broke, underemployed, pregnant. I had had a child that died, went through a whole number of things and came to the position that if I didn't have the right to fight to create a world that I could live in, if I could not have the right to fight absolutely everybody for the kind of world that I could live in—then I wouldn't live. I wouldn't live in a world where I would have to pretend to be inferior so that some man would look superior. I wouldn't live where somebody got a better break than me only because their skin was lighter.

But at the same time I didn't feel that I had enough power to really fight it. So I became suicidal. At the time I was taking Valium at the suggestion of a gynecologist who had a terrible reputation. You go in with a vaginal infection and they give you Valium, you know what I mean? And I'm on these Valiums and I'm saying I'm not going to live this kind of life, and I look around and I decided that I'm going to leave here. I lay down to die and my soul raised up out of my chest and sits up on the ceiling. She has a long debate with me about why am I trying to check out of here. And I tell her why I'm trying to check out and she says "no, no, no, no, you are going to live and you are going to fight, and I'm going to show you what you are going to do."

I lay there and here comes this parade of visions. Sometimes it was pictures, sometimes it was words—bold white letters traced in black. And she was telling me to go fight. Essentially, she was telling me to fight for my right to be a free woman. She was telling me to fight for my right to create beauty in the way that I see it. You know, when you're in the theatre there's always a struggle with people's art being junk and Hollywood and Broadway being the place to get to. She made it clear for me that my work had to have substance. There's no sense in me trying to play Miss Cupie Doll; I'm not one of the June Taylor dancers. I am the person who is going to work with the folk movement. Part of my assignment is legitimizing, bringing to life, the value of folk knowledge. And so I see myself using my art for the rest of my life, using my art to illuminate the culture of the common people.

Just about everything that I have done since 1973 has been the outgrowth of this spiritual prompting. Once I accepted my role—that I am an important person with a purpose—I have listened to that still small voice and she says things to me. You must always confront that which you fear. You gain strength by that, you see. And there's a bit of magic here.

I went through a period of time when I seriously thought I was going to lose my mind. That was because I was accepting, not what my goddess said my role was, but what other people said my role ought to be. Putting on false clothes. She said take them off. And there I was naked and I said, "O.K., Momma, who the hell am I?" You know? And she says, "You're a person who has been afraid of going crazy. You should do something about that." So the natural thing you must do is—that anything you want to be spared of, you must work toward diminishing the possibility of it happening to you. And if it can happen to somebody else, it can happen to you, you know. So I can't afford to just walk around worried that I individually am going to be locked up for no reason. I have to make sure that *nobody* can be locked up for no reason. You have to eliminate the fear not only in yourself but the real basis for that fear.

So consequently, my work with the battered women shelters and my work with rape are basically an attempt to protect myself. It's about my own survival instinct and understanding that my destiny is infinitely tied with that of everybody else. You know there's a reason why we're here together on this same planet at this point in time.

Part Two: "I see the reemergence of the women's movement as the manifestations of the desires of the goddess energy."

T: The thing that I'm feeling very intuitively about is that something important is going on at this point in time, not only in my life but in the lives of women in general and in the life of writing. There are times when I look at what human history has been and I say, oh, okay, there have always been people like us who get a momentum started and then it dies down and nothing becomes of it. And it's a hundred years or so before those thoughts are resurrected. But there's a little voice in my ears that insists that I continue. It insists that something really important is happening here, something that is going to have an effect here for years. Something that is going to make a significant change in the world.

G: *Sí, I see it in terms of the left-handed world coming into being. For centuries now, ever since the industrial age or maybe even before, it has always been a world of the intellect, reasoning, the machine. Here women were stuck with having tremendous powers of intuition experiencing other levels of reality and other realities yet they had to sit on it because men would say, well, you're crazy. All of a sudden there's a reemergence of the intuitive energies—and they are very powerful. And if you apply them in your life on the personal and political plane then that gives you a tremendous amount of energy—it's almost like a volcano erupting. We have yet to learn how to control that power. And we're scared of it.*

T: I think too that it's part of the balance that always goes on in nature. It's like technology, which is purely masculine, material, and all about aggressive-conquering power, has taken itself to the point of sleeping on the self-destruct button and now it's as if the mother goddess is coming in and saying, "Wait a minute son, hold it boy. Now there are other things; there is life. I've allowed you to play with your death machines long enough. Now be quiet, cool down, I have to clean the situation up." And I definitely see the reemergence of the women's movement as the manifestations of the desires of the goddess energy.

G: *What part does feminist spirituality have in taking back our own power?*

T: It is slowly doing a lot. Feminist spirituality had a real problem because most revolutionary circles have considered spirituality a no-no area. Because the male god and the institutionalized church has been so counterrevolutionary, there has been the temptation to say that there is nothing but the material world, and this is all we should deal with. Okay? So slowly but surely the people who are in tune with both the need for revolution and understanding of the spiritual world are beginning to say, "Hey, these worlds are not diametrically opposed to each other. Look, these two can work together." But now we are tapping our powers in self-defense. We are using our power in self-defense. For example if you look in Z. Budapest's book *The Feminist Book of Lights and Shadows*, you will see a charm for how to combat a racist. We use our spiritual power now to understand that this man does not have the right to overpower me, and because I know that this is right, I'm calling on that force to stand up to him. When we reclaim women's blood we increase our power.

Every time a sister learns that she is not born to live in a world of fear, to be dominated, every time a sister sits down with a glass of water in front of her and understands that she is intimately tied to water and that all life is tied to water, she is gradually building an inner strength that gives her armor to go out and fight the world.

For centuries we heard woman is no good, we have been beat down, we have been made lethal, we have had to recycle our strength in other ways. But now, because we have a spiritual understanding that this myth is bull, we have the nerve to test our strength. In testing it we will find out what it is, how much of it we have, and how much we can do with it. *See, we're coming out of the shadow.*

We have to use our strength to break the chain. And there are concrete, very very concrete things we can do. Like I teach a lot of wealth charms because a lot of women who come to my workshops are working-class women who have no money, you know. So yes, we do a lot of charms to pull money out of the rich and have it rechanneled into our hands. We do a lot of healing on each other so I can keep my sister out of the hands of that nice "happy" man over there. It's very small, but we have to recapture what is going to keep us alive. Because we have to keep alive.

If you take medicine for example, the man is always putting down herbal remedies because they're too available to everybody. Because if you find out you can heal yourself on your own, without him, he's out of the job. So you've got to come to him to give him a chance to run his Frankenstein experiments on you, you see. It's like that Indian proverb that if you give a man a fish, he eats for a day. If you teach the man to fish he eats forever. They're into "Here, here little momma, big daddy's gonna do this for you, take a crumb here (*snap*), take a crumb there." And I'm saying, I'm the one that baked the bread, baby. You can't do that no more.

G: *You have spoken many times about the different charms you use for healing. Would you give an example of each one of those?*

T: Sure. It's really good that you asked because right now I'm putting together notes for a book that I want to do on women's spirituality[1] that would be a combination of my own personal experiences and certain historical information, but mostly a book of charms. When I came into this I would not give anybody a charm that I had not experimented with myself. That's something you don't get from your local doctor. He uses a rat and then transposes it to a human.

Two charms that I think are especially important to women are those involving water and those involving earth. Fire and light are important, but water and earth charms seem to work very very fast. It's interesting that most of my charms require cooperation from one other person.

Let us say that we have a situation where we have two women who find themselves in dire, dire poverty, you know. We can put the principle of water to work in a charm called "pouring the money." That is, you know that you are going to run out of money soon, you know what's coming. Each day, for seven days, you come into your house and you take whatever small change you have, and you put it into a bowl. Preferably you should have two bowls, a white bowl and a green bowl. And then with the new moon, especially a new moon in an earth sign or a water sign is best, you sit down with the money you've saved, you sit down with a candle, green or white, and you take something that is the symbol of wealth for you. Sometimes I use one of the cards from the Tarot deck, other times I will use a dollar bill, other times I will use a picture of the thing I want to buy. If it's groceries I put pictures of food there, if it's clothes I use pictures of the pair of shoes I'd like to buy. You put water in the bowl with the money, and you pour the water and the money into one bowl and you state what you need. The other woman pours the money into the other bowl and she states what she needs. You continue to do this, you see, for some time depending on how much you need.

One night I did it with a sister in LA from sunset to sunrise, when the moon was no longer visible. And in the period of time between the new moon and the full moon several very interesting things happened.

She got a check from these people she used to work for. She hadn't worked for them in a year, their bookkeeper looked on the books and decided that they hadn't sent her some back pay. They sent it to her, right? I was a waitress at a health food restaurant at the time, and the other waitress decided that she wanted some vacation so I got to work her hours—the tips increased, right? And that was a small amount of money to take us out of the starving stage and put us back on our feet. That's a small one. It depends on how much energy you put into it and what you need it for. It's important that you know what you need it for because *the spirit deals in need.*

But we live in a world where you think I gotta have so many things, dollars in my hand and that is just not true, you know. The energy that is out there that created the universe gave us everything we need. If we treated the earth properly there would be enough for everybody to eat. You know that bullshit about over-population is a crock. A misdistribution, you know.

Another earth charm that I really like is paralleling your growth with that of a plant. If I'm getting ready to write a book, the first day that I lay the first page out, I go out to get either a seedling or a baby plant. I put it near that place where I'm working with the water. I feed the plant and I work page two. I clip the plant today and I work page three. I spray the plant today and I work page four. So that there is a direct relationship between my growth and the growth of that plant.

G: *But that's scary because what if the plant starts dying?*

T: If the plant starts dying then you have to reconsider the way you're operating, you see. And we do a lot of stuff around fear. In reality the two basic emotions are fear and love and everything else is an aspect of one of those. Fear has been *drummed* into us. Fear has been drummed into us like nothing else. If you don't go ask this expert then you're supposed to be afraid. Once you go see the infallible expert nothing can go wrong anymore. A lot of times messages are coming through to us and we receive them with fear because we've been trained to be fearful and that fear is the thing that ruins the charm. My plant dying would be for me the sign that I've come to a point of stagnation, you know. I've got to go back to the root of the problem. I've got to take the plant out of its pot, look at it, see what is not being done. I've got to lay that book down and read what is missing. And you can set things up that way so that it is parallel. Overcoming certain fears is so easy. It amazed me when I found out how to do it.

It's really interesting that right now I'm speaking with a woman who is in her early thirties and is having her first sexual experience. And some of the things that she worries about I forgot that I used to worry about because I've gone through enough of a process of cleaning myself—out of old guilt and false responsibility and false senses of oppression. Speaking with her I find that I am going to have to put her through the same thing that I've been through.

You are a woman, you are human, you have the right to be sexual, you have the right to be sexual with whomever you see fit to be sexual with. You know, the false sense of morality has been designed, if you look at it, to keeping women's power in check. That comes through real clear on the psychic level. Look at all the taboos around women's blood. Women's blood contains the seed of new life. That is the power of the creator. Yet you travel from circle to circle and they tell you women's blood is this evil thing. Then life itself has to be an evil thing. And I just feel that patriarchy has made the god concept so lopsided, that man is all positive and woman is all negative and that is bullshit, you know. Day cannot be day without night.

G: *What do you think men hold against women most?*

T: Well, specifically, the question of women's blood. It's the one thing we have that they don't. Now, the uterus, the vaginal blood, the power of creation, the nurturing power that we have, the sustaining power that we have is something that *they* don't have. And when I look into the folklore of Louisiana, when I look into the charms and the spells I find that the charms involving women's blood are the charms designed to overpower men. That's how women's blood was used.

G: *Even the love potions?*

T: Yeah, it's for bending his will. You use women's blood to bend man's will. Of course there is a great taboo against it. As long as they (men) are involved. That's like Superman outlawing Kryptonite; of course he will.

G: *Teish, I always felt when I was growing up that women had the power, that women were strong, that women were the nurturers, and they pretended that they didn't have it, that the men did; it was a conspiracy. Men don't have it. So here is a woman using rituals and charms to bend men's power, when actually she could be straightening up her own.*

T: We have now become *victims of our own benevolence*. We see certain weaknesses. We are accustomed to mothering, raising, nurturing, looking for potential, speeding the imagination with children. We have seen the child in men and nurtured it in the same way. So now you have the son growing up thinking that he can slap the mother who nursed him. I see that happen a number of times. Before I liberated myself it was part of my culture. You go out to dinner and the man didn't have enough money you slip it under the table so it looks like he paid for it. You learn how to suggest subtly that this or that be done and then when he follows your advice and it works you praise him for having such a wonderful idea. Bull. Bull. The whole hog. I'm not doing that anymore. The goddess is not doing that anymore. The trial is coming to an end. The grace period is slowly drawing to a close. The queen is about to move on the chess board.

G: *It's about time.*

T: Now I'm saying that the period where the goddess allows the little boy, allows her son to go rampaging through the universe, is coming to a close. She's saying, "Johnny, you've misbehaved long enough. Now mother's going to whip you."

G: *Another thing I want to ask you is what kind of world do you want to live in and when do you see this kind of world existing on the physical plane?*

T: Well, it's not in my lifetime. I know that. That's the sad thing about it. It is not in my lifetime. I'm into a world where people are judged by the wealth of their soul, not their pockets. You know what I mean? I want each person to have what they've earned *by right of consciousness*, you see. The basis of it is what you can conceive mentally—the infinite power will give you the substance to create it, you see. There has been entirely too much rip-off for me. There have been too many people who have tilled the soil and not eaten the fruit. There have been too many people that have written the poems and not gotten the praise. There have been too many people that have created the invention and then been used by the machine. That has to stop.

I am shooting for a world where everybody eats, where everybody has decent housing, where everybody has their basic necessities and the freedom to be who they are. The freedom to express the spirit that is inside of them. What is all this bowing and scraping to these various two-legged authorities, you know? The only person I'm willing to bow to is the spirit. And in my faith you don't scrape in front of them, see.

Our fates *are* tied. We have this strange notion on this planet that our fates are *not* tied. If it were not so we would not be here together. It's that simple. But there's this refusal to understand, so we create these false classes. I'm richer than she is. I'm a different color than that one. I'm taller than that one. That's all bull. We all eat and shit in the same manner. And until I meet someone with green blood who eats food and has no wastes coming out of him, who never cries, who never has to sleep—when I meet somebody like that, I may consider them superior. At first I'll consider them different. I'll have to test it to see if they are in fact superior. That's all I'm after—*everybody's right to express the spirit that lives in them.*

G: *That would be a beautiful world. I kind of think that we will see that kind of world in our lifetime. Or at least it's beginnings. Otherwise it's going to be the end of us because we're poisoning ourselves and our world pretty fast.*

T: Yeah. That's another job that women spiritualists are taking over. We seem to realize, because of our intimate connection with earth, that she is sending us the message. She's not going to tolerate any more of that. I don't know what the geologists think, they may have their theories of air getting trapped under the earth and that's why St. Helens was blowing. The woman is blowing to tell you that *she is mad* and it's that simple.

G: *According to the Mayan calendar we are in El Quinto Sol (The Fifth World Sun) and that this world will end by earthquake and fire on December 24, 2011. I guess it parallels the end of the Piscean Age and the beginning of the Aquarian. The sixth sun, which the Mayans call "Consciousness," will follow the fifth one.*

T: I believe it. It's really, really obvious when the water is messed up and the air is messed up and the mountain begins to rumble, that is a real indication: "Johnny, put your toy down; pay attention to your health; momma's about to explode." But they won't listen because they're blinded by greed. They are blinded by this grabby, grabby . . .

G: *And they're very insecure, peeny little beings, they're very scared they're going to lose their power.*

T: Exactly. And they ignore the one who is power. Where would their power be if earth decides she's had it?

Part Three: Smashing the Myth

G: *What are the particular barriers or struggles involved in Third World Women's spirituality?*

T: You have to understand that first and foremost, the greater part of our problem as Third World people is that for a long time we internalized a lot that *we are nobody with nothing.* You know, God is white therefore the all-powerful is on the side of the one who is in power.

    I remember quite some years ago when I was in St. Louis I was doing a lot of demonstrating and stuff. There was this old Black woman I was talking to and trying to get her to go to a demonstration with me, you know. It was down by the old courthouse by the St. Louis arch and she said to me, she said, "You know, there's a chopping block in there where they used to sell niggers." She said, "Now if you go down there and take a look you will see that the blood is still on that chopping block. It's stained in the wood, you know. You can't be going down and telling these white folks what to do." I said, "Oh yes, I can. I have some power, they have to hear me. I'm not going to just lay down and die, dada dadada." And she said to me, "Chile, don't you know god suffered the Indians to die so that the white men could have this land." And I blew my stack. Because there it was right there, you know.

G: *Believing in the white man's conditioning, in their shit.*

T: *My* gods tell me that things are not that absolute, that there is always a struggle of power going on and that I must struggle for this power.

The basic problem that we have had was believing somebody else's story about us—*what we can and cannot do, who we can and cannot be.* As Third World people we needed it more than anybody because we have been kept down for so long and this is the thing that's so hard for people to accept. Most Third World people on the surface seem to have accepted the rigidity of Christianity, yet certain true things still survive. And what we've got to do is *feed that which has survived,* build on that which has survived till our gods and goddesses speak. "Oh, yes, my children are strong now, they are ready now. Give them a total green light. Let's go, ya'll." You know the baby goes from crawling to walking. We've come out of an infancy of oppression into our own power because there's enough archeological evidence that everybody at one point or another had a great civilization. Every people alive had a great civilization until this man came along whose environment tricked him, you know. It was the snow, I feel, that was responsible for the unusual aggression of the Europeans and their chance encounter with gunpowder, you see, from the East. Put those two things together and here comes this big conquering hero.

G: *And also fear I think, fear had a great deal to do with it, fear of not surviving made him more aggressive. Made him take up weapons for defense, become cold, reasoning.*

When you said that that which has survived through the ages comes from women's power and spirituality, I was thinking of La Virgen de Guadalupe that my Mamágrande Ramona had on her altar. When the Spaniards took over Mexico they instituted Catholicism, but a lot of my people kept some of the old gods and goddesses by integrating them into the Christian ones. So now La Virgen de Guadalupe contains within her Tonantzin, the Aztec creation goddess. Mexicans attach more power to her than they do to the patriarchal god and his long-suffering son.

T: Yeah. I came into religion in the sixties. We were looking for the history. We were looking for the rhyme and reason behind our struggle. How did things get turned around? How can we reclaim our blackness? And so when you look at what has come down we immediately see the militant aspect, we see this is something that has survived through the threat of death. The whole Black power movement was a very sexist movement, you know, here the main theme was reinstating the Black man, OK. The problem with the Black men, the reason that they couldn't get jobs, and this is another piece of bullshit, was because Black women were too strong. That she was the castrator and that that was what was wrong with us.

G: *What was wrong with you was that you were too strong?*

T: I was too strong. I was not a woman, dada dada da. So I came into the movement, trying to be the perfect African woman. In the process I find out there used to be a cult of women in Africa who were warriors, you know, who cut a man's penis and stuck it in his mouth as a mark that they had done this. I find out that the major god was an androgyne. I learn that the lightning bolt originally belonged to a female deity. I start learning things that whisper of very strong women, you know. I was very confused by it all for awhile, until I accepted a personal message from her. She was telling me that the sexism I was experiencing in the movement religion should not be tolerated anymore and she was laying the responsibility on me to put an end to it. So from there, I had to confront, finally, the "men's room." When I talk about the "men's room," I mean a room in this collective spiritual household where women were not allowed to go, because according to the males we would be struck by lightning if we went in there. So one day I just on my own decided I'm going to walk in there and disprove this myth. I was somewhat scared that hey I *would* get struck by lightning until I had a dream that said, you know, *go. I want you to go, go, go, go. And finally, if you don't go you'll be sorry.* So very nervously I said, "OK momma, this is what you told me to do. I'm a good chile. Please stop the thunder god from hitting me. Please, please momma, I'm depending on you" and I walk on in there and *smash a myth.*

Note

1. The book in progress was *Working the Mother*. Published as *Jambalaya: The Natural Woman's Book of Charms and Practical Rituals* (New York: Harper One, 1985). *(Editor, 2015)*

Brownness

Andrea Canaan

I am brown and I have experienced life as a brown person.[1] Outwardly I have traversed with ease the salons of the white rich, the bayous and lakes of cajun South Louisiana, the hot-white racism of Shreveport, the folksy back-slapping, peculiar institutions of Natchez, the friendly invisible oppression of Bay St. Louis and Ocean Springs, the humid, lazy apathy of New Orleans. With soul intact, identity sure, sense of humanness unchained by myth and ignorance, I have lived my years inside brown skin that didn't show the bruises, the wounds, to anyone.

Since before I can remember, brownness was always compared to whiteness in terms that were ultimately degrading for brownness. Lazy, shiftless, poor, nonhuman, dirty, abusive, ignorant, uncultured, uneducated, were used to convey conscious and unconscious messages that brown was not a good thing to be and the ultimate model of things right and good was white. Yes, white people called me nigger, forced me to drink from separate fountains, would not allow me to sit in the front of the bus. This message, however, was first and most transmitted by brown. There was an all powerful and real knowledge, like the pungent smell of chitterlings cooking on a rainy winter day, that no matter how good, how clean, how pious the brown, they could not equal or reflect the ultimate good and right-white.

Now understand, no brown person acknowledged feeling this way or accepted responsibility for conveying the message. Everyone joked, laughed, and put down white. We put up and revered brown. For all the up brown and down white a black comedy twisted and reversed the jokes, the laughs, and the put-downs back into brown. We welcomed this black comedy routine. We made its scenes our rituals. We claimed the right of self-defacement. We remained degraded inside ourselves and we continued to empower others to control us.

Don't mistake me, brown is not The Oppressor but the victim. But part of our victimization is self-oppression. Our adaptations were creative, the end goal, survival. This peculiar system of degrading self so that outsiders won't hurt us so much has its base in remembered servitude, helplessness and powerlessness combined with the pride and hope that comes from surviving, mixed with the shame of surviving, the humiliation of servitude, and the rage of being considered nonhuman. The system's apex is the reality that while adapting to white language, dress, worship, thought and social interaction we had not gained social acceptance. Further, while sacrificing, working, praying, singing, fighting, and dying for and with white, we had not gained equality, economic security, or freedom. What we had gained was an insidious terrifying, self-negating desire—even need—to be white.

By the time I was a woman, I had all the necessary external survival skills needed, supposedly, to protect me from the rejection and humiliation projected onto me by white media, government, church, and social institutions. I had unending strength, evergrowing intellect, a heart as big as the heavens and earth, a soul more forgiving than gods themselves, and I accepted total responsibility for myself, my own oppressed state, the oppression of the brown man, and the sin of being both brown and woman. This superwoman veneer protected me from the external world much of the time. This superwoman veneer also warded off internal self-reflection needed to assess if indeed I was strong enough to carry such heavy burdens. The evergrowing intellect was an additional burden because the ability to think allows me to look at, if not truly see, options and truth. The open heart and forgiving soul stifled my rightful indignation, gagged my rage, and forced my fears, my needs, my rage, my joys, my accomplishments, inward. The acceptance of total responsibility, real, concrete, or abstract, for myself and others became my ultimate straitjacket, the last and strongest barrier to self. The guilt alone associated with such responsibility should have broken the backs of brown women long ago. The isolation is deafening and support is non-existent. The inherent conflicts of interests of parents, children, husbands, lovers, church, state, and self cry out like sound and fury and we think ourselves crazed because there is a constant buzz in our ears. In this state I began to see, as through a lifting mist, the enemies of self.

Racial memory coursed through my veins. Memories of being snatched away by friend and stranger, stuffed into vessels that traversed vast spaces of water, chained, whipped, branded, hunted and sold by overlapping generational systems of degradation that were supported by male gods, male governments, male-controlled social institutions across the globe, across the centuries. I was sure that the ultimate evil was the white male, and I became afraid of him. It was a survival fear of being fooled by bright promises, hope-laden movement songs, loopholed constitutional amendments and proclamations. Afraid of being enslaved again, afraid of being annihilated this time.

My brown woman community counted our most dangerous enemy as the white woman. Didn't she seduce brown men and cry rape? Didn't her status forever decree our children born out of forced rape by her brothers, sons, husbands, and fathers illegitimate and create a caste system within brown that made light brown better than dark brown and her delicate white, best? Doesn't the hand that rocks the cradle rule the world? Is she not responsible for the actions and sins of her men? Did not her essential evil cause the downfall of her men? Is she not cloaked in sexual mystery so that our brown men cannot resist her? Does she not compete with us for brown men, the centers of our lives, as well as white men, our benevolent, if somewhat distracted and crabby, fathers? Does she not force us to use our bodies as a commodity in the white marketplace in order to feed our babies in order to feed our men?

The mist began to clear. I could no longer justify viewing the white woman as the personification of the evil done to us, the dangerous enemy. I began to look at the things brown women faced with a watchful eye for a power base. What is rape but power? What is racism but power? What is poverty but power? What is sexism but power? What is oppression but power? What is deception but power? What is fear but power? I began to see the enemy as those forces within me that allowed others to control me and those who empowered or sought to empower themselves to control me.

I could see my enemy as my brownness, my community, my mothers and fathers, sisters and brothers. This is logical, given my patterns of self oppression. I could isolate myself from the brown community, claiming my right to be me without concern for our growth and development as a whole. I would, however, be cutting off an essential part of my development to nurture another. I would simply be acknowledging the oppression of my brownness and not that of my femaleness. They are both essential and important, however. The fact is I am brown and female, and my growth and development are tied to the entire community. I must nurture and develop brown self, woman, man, and child. I must address the issues of my own oppression and survival. When I separate them, isolate them, and ignore them, I separate, isolate, and ignore myself. I am a unit. A part of brownness. My health, energy, intellect, and talent are resources of my community. When I fall ill my community is weakened. When my community is invaded by disease I am affected, even killed. I must work both as an individual and as a part of my community in order to survive in order for my community to survive.

It would be very easy to identify white women as my enemy. As long as I do, however, I accept my devalued, oppressed, unliberated woman state. We do not trust her because she is white. We do not seek to know her because we would be betraying our brownness, collaborating with the enemy, whiteness. We do not embrace her because she is woman. And women, we remain believing, are evil beings who started this entire mess in the garden of eden. The problem here is that as we remain isolated and unknowing of woman, any woman, we continue to accept the basis for a part of our oppression. As we trade distrust and irresponsibility we trade off our liberation. It's as if we think liberation a fixed quantity, that there is only so much to go around. That an individual or community is liberated at the expense of another. *When we view liberation as a scarce resource, something only a precious few of us can have, we stifle our potential, our creativity, our genius for living, learning and growing.*

It is hardest to see my enemy as brown men yet in order to see myself clearly I must face the closest threat to my survival for it is he who most rapes me, batters me, devalues my strength, will not allow my weakness. He is closest to me for he is my father, my brother, my son, my man, my lover. I love him, I glory in his maleness and agonize in his degradation. I must refuse to allow him to oppress me while I must be concerned for his survival. This major conflict of interest is basic to brown oppression. Divide and conquer. Choose who is more worthy of liberation. I refuse to play this diabolical self-destructive game. I refuse to play out the superwoman image as I refuse to believe the powerless, weak, politically ineffective, superstud image of the brown man. We are both strong and weak, oppressed and oppressor of each, as well as by the white super culture. Our individual and collective development as men and women will not jeopardize but enhance our liberation. The brown man is not my enemy. Nor I his, but we must recognize that we both contribute to each other's oppression.

It would be easiest of all to see the white male as the enemy. He has the giant share of power. He controls our governments, resources, social institutions, language, education. Essentially he controls the world. To see him as the evil all-powerful enemy, however, forces me to accept little responsibility for my own oppression. It negates my power to change my status. When I accept white male power as inevitable and not within my control, I accept my impotence to acquire power and control for myself, through and for my brown community, through and for my world community. To give to brown, white, men, women, etc., the status of all-powerful is to cloak them in mystery and power. We must focus on those things within us that allow others to control us, know those who would empower themselves to control us and understand that the forces can be brown male or female, white male or female, as well as our selves. We must demystify and know more in depth the world around and in us in order to distinguish friend from foe rather than accepting prefabricated enemies.

The enemy is brownness and whiteness, maleness and femaleness. The enemy is our urgent need to stereotype and close off people, places, and events into isolated categories. Hatred, distrust, irresponsibility, unloving, classism, sexism, and racism, in their myriad forms, cloud our vision and isolate us. This closed and limited view blocks women embracing women, brown women embracing brown women, brown women embracing brown men, brown women embracing white women and women embracing men. We close off avenues of communication and vision so that individual and communal trust, responsibility, loving, and knowing are impossible.

In facing myself, while eliminating my self oppression, I stumble into a terrifying and isolated place. If I reject and question concepts, mores, and values of my brown community, where is my support, where is my family, what becomes of my sense of community . . . peoplehood? While becoming myself, will I become so different, so threatening, that they too will reject me?

I am facing that terror and isolation as are brown women across the globe. When we question ourselves, seek to create harmonious, supportive, nurturing, liberating environments for ourselves, we find the white and brown super cultures ready to wage battle together in order to make us reform, in order to decrease their stress and difficulty in visualizing difference and selfhood as revolution and revolution as positive and necessary for cohabitation on this planet.

The white super culture has not yet erased my brown presence, but it continually seeks to erase my individual freedom to be different, to make decisions and choices for myself. The brown community feels the awful terrifying pressure and transmits urgent messages to me to blend, hide, retreat, in order to survive even at the expense of self. Survive by any means necessary, including self defacement, self negation, and the allowance of powerlessness.

I hold arm raised, fist clenched to the white super culture. I embrace the brown community with respect and deep loving, but with firm insistence that being myself, being different—even radically different from my mothers and fathers, sisters and brothers—is my right, my duty, my way of living a whole and sane existence, accepting the responsibility and consequences of being true to myself in order to be true to my humanness in order to be true to my community.

I send a warning to you white woman. The women's movement, the feminist movement, is not a middle-class clique. It is not an elitist class of white women hiding from men. It is a positive ever-growing movement of women who believe in the equality of all people. Women who are not willing to settle for token change but insist that the economic and political resources and power of this nation this world be distributed equally. It is women being concerned about women and being willing to place women's needs and their development first. It is a battle for

economic, political, and social freedom and not a battle of sexes. It is
not white. It is not racist. It is not classist. It is not closed. Understand
that although we are of the same gender we must cross over miles of
mistrust and cross victimization in order to meet, in order to learn and
grow and work together. Understand that sexism is not the ultimate evil
but a place of unification, a place of commonality, a place from which
to become a political force for women, for humanness.

I challenge you, brown woman. You, who will not interface the
women's movement. You, who say the movement is separatist, white,
lesbian, without glamour. Further, you say you are too liberated and
want to be dependent, protected, shackled to the pedestal. "Ain't you a
woman?" Look at yourself, your community, your country, your world
and ask yourself, who has the least to lose and the most to gain from
economic security, equality, freedom? Who has waited longest, deferred
most, worked hardest, lived poorest, nurtured, encouraged, loved more
while asking the least in return? Who I ask you? Yes, you are correct.
You yourself. Yet who is most oppressed in this land today? No! Don't
put on your visor. It is not the brown man or the third world man. It is
the brown woman, the third world woman. Understand, the people who
are most oppressed in a society have the most investment in that society's
change. It is when that bottom layer becomes a political force for itself
that change will occur. Changes will not only occur for that layer but
will move outward and upward throughout that society. Remember the
civil rights movement? It has reverberated around the world to become a
human rights movement. We are the bottom of the heap, brown women.
We have the most to gain and least to lose. Straight and lesbian among
us, we must fight, learn and grow with, and for, ourselves, our mothers,
daughters, and sisters across this nation across this globe and yes, brown
women, we must fight, learn, grow with, and for our fathers, brothers,
sons, and men.

The buck stops here as it did with a brown woman in Montgomery,
Alabama. *The women's movement is ours.*

Note

1. While I know and identify black, my first knowing of myself before I knew
   much about skin color and its effects was as a brown baby girl looking in
   the mirror of my mother's face. Brown is my color, the very shade of which
   colors my existence both inside the black community and outside of it.

Revolution
It's Not Neat or Pretty or Quick

Pat Parker

The following speech was given at the BASTA conference in Oakland, California, in August 1980. It represented three organizations: The Black Women's Revolutionary Council, the Eleventh Hour Battalion, and the Feminist Women's Health Center in Oakland.

I have been to many conferences: People's Constitutional convention in Washington, DC, Women's Conference on Violence in San Francisco, Lesbian Conference in Los Angeles, International Tribunal on Crimes Against Women in Belgium. I've been to more conferences than I can name and to many I would like to forget, but I have never come to a conference with as much anticipation and feeling of urgency.

We are in a critical time. Imperialist forces in the world are finding themselves backed against the wall; no longer able to control the world with the threat of force. And they are getting desperate. And they should be desperate. What we do here this weekend and what we take from this conference can be the difference, the deciding factor as to whether a group of women will ever again be able to meet not only in this country, but the entire world. We are facing the most critical time in the history of the world. The superpowers cannot afford for us to join forces and work to rid this earth of them, and we cannot afford not to.

In order to leave here prepared to be a strong force in the fight against imperialism we must have a clear understanding of what imperialism is and how it manifests itself in our lives. It is perhaps easier for us to understand the nature of imperialism when we look at how this country deals with other countries. It doesn't take a great amount of political sophistication to see how the interest of oil companies played a role in our relationship with the Shah's Iran. The people of Iran were exploited in order for Americans to drive gas-guzzling monsters. And that is perhaps the difficult part of imperialism for us to understand. The rest of the world is being exploited in order to maintain our standard of living. We who are five percent of the world's population use 40 percent of the world's oil.

As anti-imperialists we must be prepared to destroy all imperialist governments; and we must realize that by doing this we will drastically alter the standard of living that we now enjoy. We cannot talk on one hand about making revolution in this country, yet be unwilling to give up our videotape records and recreational vehicles. An anti-imperialist understands the exploitation of the working class, understands that in order for capitalism to function, there must be a certain percentage that is unemployed. We must also define our friends and enemies based on their stand on imperialism.

At this time, the super powers are in a state of decline. The Iranians rose up and said no to US imperialism; the Afghanis and Eritreans are saying no to Soviet-social imperialism. The situation has become critical and the only resource left is world war between the US and the Soviet Union. We are daily being given warning that war is imminent. To some people, this is no significant change, just escalation. The Blacks, poor whites, Chicanos, and other oppressed people of this country already know we're at war.

And the rest of the country's people are being prepared. The media is bombarding us with patriotic declarations about "our" hostages and "our" embassy in Iran. This government is constantly reminding us of "our" commitment to "our" allies in Israel. Ads inviting us to become the 17 "few," the "chosen," the marine or "fly with the air force," etc., are filling our 18 television screens.

And it doesn't stop there. This system is insidious in its machinations. It's no coincidence that the "right wing" of this country is being mobilized. Media sources are bombarding us with the news of KKK and Nazi party activity. But we who were involved in the civil rights movement are very familiar with these tactics. We remember the revelations of FBI agents, not only infiltrating the Klan but participating in and leading their activities. And we are not for one moment fooled by these manipulations.

The Klan and the Nazis are our enemies and must be stopped, but to simply mobilize around stopping them is not enough. They are functionaries, tools of this governmental system. They serve in the same way as our armed forces and police. To end Klan or Nazi activity doesn't end imperialism. It doesn't end institutional racism; it doesn't end sexism; it does not bring this monster down, and we must not forget what our goals are and who our enemies are. To simply label these people as lunatic fringes and not accurately assess their roles as a part of this system is a dangerous error. These people do the dirty work. They are the arms and legs of the congressmen, the businessmen, the Tri-lateral Commission.

And the message they bring is coming clear. Be a good American—Support registration for the draft. The equation is being laid out in front of us. Good American equals Support Imperialism and war. To this, I must declare—I am not a good American. I do not wish to have the world colonized, bombarded and plundered in order to eat steak.

Each time a national liberation victory is won I applaud and support it. It means we are one step closer to ending the madness that we live under. It means we weaken the chains that are binding the world.

Yet to support national liberation struggles alone is not enough. We must actively fight within the confines of this country to bring it down. I am not prepared to let other nationalities do my dirty work for me. I want the people of Iran to be free. I want the people of Puerto Rico to be free, but I am a revolutionary feminist because I want me to be free. And it is critically important to me that you who are here, that your commitment to revolution is based on the fact that you want revolution for yourself.

In order for revolution to be possible, and revolution *is* possible, it must be led by the poor and working-class people of this country. Our interest does not lie with being a part of this system, and our tendencies to be co-opted and diverted are lessened by the realization of our oppression. We know and understand that our oppression is not simply a question of nationality but that poor and working-class people are oppressed throughout the world by the imperialist powers.

We as women face a particular oppression, not in a vacuum but as a part of this corrupt system. The issues of women are the issues of the working class as well. By not having this understanding, the women's movement has allowed itself to be co-opted and misdirected.

It is unthinkable to me as a revolutionary feminist that some women's liberationists would entertain the notion that women should be drafted in exchange for passage of the ERA. This is a clear example of not understanding imperialism and not basing one's political line on its destruction. If the passage of the ERA means that I am going to become an equal participant in the exploitation of the world; that I am going to bear arms against other Third World people who are fighting to reclaim what is rightfully theirs—then I say Fuck the ERA.

One of the difficult questions for us to understand is just "what is revolution?" Perhaps we have had too many years of media madness with "revolutionary eye makeup and revolutionary tampons." Perhaps we have had too many years of Hollywood fantasy where the revolutionary man kills his enemies and walks off into the sunset with his revolutionary woman who has been waiting for his return. And that's the end of the tale.

The reality is that revolution is not a one step process: you fight— you win—it's over. It takes years. Long after the smoke of the last gun has faded away the struggle to build a society that is classless, that has no traces of sexism and racism in it, will still be going on. We have many examples of societies in our lifetime that have had successful armed revolution. And we have no examples of any country that has completed the revolutionary process. Is Russia now the society that Marx and Lenin dreamed? Is China the society that Mao dreamed? Before and after armed revolution there must be education, and analysis, and struggle. If not, and even if so, one will be faced with coups, counterrevolution and revision.

The other illusion is that revolution is neat. *It's not neat or pretty or quick.* It is a long dirty process. We will be faced with decisions that are not easy. We will have to consider the deaths of friends and family. We will be faced with the decisions of killing members of our own race.

Another illusion that we suffer under in this country is that a single facet of the population can make revolution. Black people alone cannot make revolution in this country. Native American people alone cannot make revolution in this country. Chicanos alone cannot make revolution in this country. Asians alone cannot make revolution in this country. White people alone cannot make revolution in this country. Women alone cannot make revolution in this country. Gay people alone cannot make revolution in this country. And anyone who tries it will not be successful.

Yet it is critically important for women to take a leadership role in this struggle. And I do not mean leading the way to the coffee machine.

A part of the task charged to us this weekend is deciding the direction we must take. First I say let us reclaim our movement. For too long I have watched the white middle class be represented as my leaders in the women's movement. I have often heard that the women's movement is a white middle-class movement.

I am a feminist. I am neither white nor middle class. And the women that I've worked with were like me. Yet I am told that we don't exist, and that we didn't exist. Now I understand that the racism and classism of some women in the movement prevented them from seeing me and people like me. But I also understand that with the aid of the media many middle-class women were made more visible. And this gave them an opportunity to use their skills gained through their privilege to lead the movement into at first reformist and now counterrevolutionary bullshit.

These women allowed themselves to be red-baited and dyke-baited into isolating and ignoring the progressive elements of the women's movement. And I, for one, am no longer willing to watch a group of self-serving reformist idiots continue to abort the demands of revolutionary thinking women. You and I are the women's movement. Its leadership and direction should come from us.

We are charged with the task of rebuilding and revitalizing the dreams of the '60s and turning it into the reality of the '80s. And it will not be easy. At the same time that we must weed reformist elements out of our movement, we will have to fight tooth and nail with our brothers and sisters of the left. For in reality, we are "all products of a decadent capitalist society."

At the same time that we must understand and support the men and women of national liberation struggles—the left (especially upper- and middle-class women) must give up its undying loyalty to the nuclear family. The nuclear family is the basic unit of capitalism and in order for us to move to revolution it has to be destroyed. And I mean destroyed. The male left has duped too many women with cries of genocide into believing it is revolutionary to be bound to babies. As to the question of abortion, I am appalled at the presumptions of men. The question is whether or not we have control of our bodies which in turn means control of our community and its growth. I believe that Black women are as intelligent as white women and we know when to have babies or not. And I want no man regardless of color to tell me when and where to bear children. As long as women are bound by the nuclear family structure we cannot effectively move toward revolution. And if women don't move, it will not happen.

We do not have an easy task before us. At this conference we will disagree; we will get angry; we will fight. This is good and should be welcomed. Here is where we should air our differences but here is also where we should build. In order to survive in this world we must make a commitment to change it; not reform it—revolutionize it. Here is where we begin to build a new women's movement, not one easily co-opted and misdirected by media pigs and agents of this insidious imperialist system. Here is where we begin to build a revolutionary force of women. Judy Grahn in the "She Who" poem says, "When she who moves, the earth will turn over." You and I are the "She Who" and if we dare to struggle, dare to win, this earth *will* turn over.

No Rock Scorns Me as Whore

Chrystos

5:32 a.m.—May

    The water doesn't breathe   No rowdy boats disturb her serenity
I dream of days when she was this way each moment   Days when no
one went anywhere full of loud pompousness self-importance   Days
when dinosaurs were not being rudely dug up for their remains   Days
when order dignity & respect were possible   Days when the proportions of things were sacred   O the moon in a dawn sky is good enough
    Where are the people who cry "I am I am" as the gulls do? They rope
themselves off with labels   They stand inside a box called their job,
their clothes, their political & social opinions, the movies or books they
read   I've never believed those items which is why I was considered
crazy   I want to know the truth   I glimpse under that malarkey
called "civilization"   Maybe people have become so stupid as a result
of having too many machines   The company we keep
    It is clear to me that the use of nuclear power is dangerous—as
is almost every other aspect of the dominant culture   Including the
manufacture of the paper on which this is written   No produce from
Vashon Island can be sold because the earth there is poisonous from the
chemicals Tacoma's paper plant produces   My life is a part of the
poisoning & cars   Alternate energy sources cannot fuel what "America"
has become   I know this way of living will not last much longer I
accept it   I will be glad if we destroy ourselves   We have made a
much bigger mess than the dinosaurs   Other ways will follow   Perhaps not   It is none of our business   I draw because I can't think
what else to do until the end   Maybe it will take longer than I
think   I'm not willing at the moment to give up the electric blanket I
am under & I do not notice too many radicals giving up their stereos, hot
showers, cars & blenders   Energy to run those machines must come
from somewhere   No protest march will alter the head-on collision
Nothing short of completely altering the whole culture will stop it
I don't think that all of the people here could be supported on an alternative culture   Well if they manage to make a revolution they'll kill
lots of people   Most could not survive adjustment to simpler life &
so they will unknowingly fight it even the radicals   Another case of
lecturing vegetarians in leather shoes
    Although it is heresy to admit it, many Indian people could not
survive either   It takes a lot of power to manufacture a can of Bud-

weiser   We have become as poisoned as the eagle's eggshell   We have fought   We still fight   Most of us have died fighting   Some of us walk around dead inside a bottle   I am ashamed   I am heartbroken   I still fight to survive   I mourn   I get up   I live a middle-class life   Sometimes

We have lost touch with the sacred   To survive we must begin to know sacredness   The pace which most of us live prevents this   I begin only now to understand faint glimpses of the proper relationships of time, of beings   I don't dig for clams because that is the main food of many birds here   I have an abundance of other food available to me   Too many humans clam this beach already   A stronger & stronger sense that I want to grow food ourselves   Probably that is not possible   I'm not thrilled about the idea of slaughter & I am not a vegetarian   We'll see   Gradually, I am taught how to behave by new teachers   By leaves, by flowers, by fruits & rhythms of rain   My mother & father were not good teachers   They are too deeply damaged by this culture which is one of obliteration   I don't know why I see differently than they do   My blessing and burden

The depth that I seek here only comes when I remove the ears in my mind   Ears discourage my honesty & because I am so isolated here honesty is absolutely essential to my survival   There is no way to "be nice" to a tree or politely endure a thunderstorm   I am stripped of pretensions as I was at nine by the wild gentle beauty of California before everybody came with stucco track houses & turquoise plastic couches   I am a child again here   A child frightened by the idea of progress, new housing, more strangers   I begin to love these lines of dark trees as I loved the hills to which I belonged as a girl   Those hills hold nothing now   Mostly leveled   Without deer, without puma, without pheasant, without blue-bellied lizards, without quail, without ancient oaks   Lawns instead   Deeply disgusted by lawns   Stupid flat green crew cuts   Nothing for anybody to eat

I am still in love with the mystery of shadows, wind, bird song   The reason that I continue despite many clumsy mistakes, is love My love for humans, or rather my continuous attempts to love, have been misdirected   I am not wise   However there is no shame when one is foolish with a tree   No bird ever called me crazy   No rock scorns me as a whore   The earth means exactly what it says   The wind is without flattery or lust   Greed is balanced by the hunger of all   So I embrace anew, as my childhood spirit did, the whispers of a world without words

I realized one day after another nuclear protest, another proposed bill to make a nuclear waste disposal here, that I had no power with those   My power rests with a greater being, a silence which goes on behind the uproar   I decided that in a nuclear holocaust, for certainly they will be stupid enough to cause one if their history is any example, that I wanted to be planting corn & squash   After there will be other beings of some kind   They'll still need to eat   Aren't the people who come to take clams like those who lobby at the airport for nuclear power? Who is not guilty of being a thief?   Who among us gives back as much as we take? Who among us has enough respect? Does anyone know the proper proportions? My distant ancestors knew some things that are lost to me & I would not have the insidious luxury of this electric heat, this journal & pen without the concurrent problems of nuclear waste storage   When we are gone, someone else will come   Dinosaur eggs might hatch in the intense heat of nuclear explosions   I will be sad to see the trees & birds on fire   Surely they are innocent as none of us has been

   With their songs, they know the sacred   I am in a circle with that soft, enduring word   In it is the wisdom of all peoples   Without a deep, deep understanding of the sacredness of life, the fragility of each breath, we are lost   The holocaust has already occurred   What follows is only the burning brush   How my heart aches & cries to write these words   I am not as calmly indifferent as I sound   I will be screaming no no no more destruction in that last blinding light

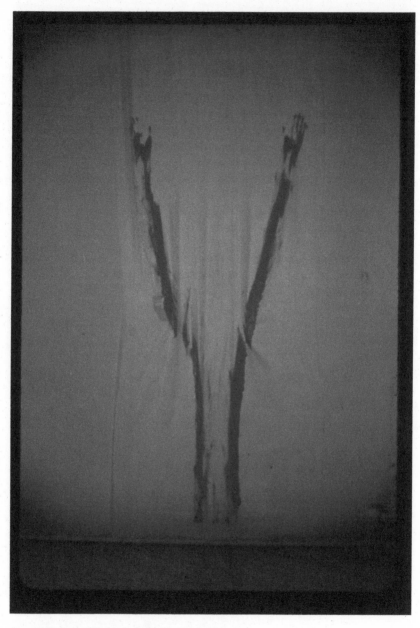

Ana Mendieta, *Untitled (Body Tracks)*, 1974
One from a suite of six lifetime color photographs, 8" x 10"
© The Estate of Ana Mendieta Collection

Appendix

The coeditors in 1981.

BOOK SUPPLEMENT

Anzaldua and Moraga: Building Bridges

by Gaye Williams

Trying to deal with racism, personally and institutionally, I have often been overwhelmed by how complex and deeply rooted the problem is. Racism takes so many shapes, faces and voices. Many women feel that the survival and growth of feminism will depend on the movement's ability and willingness to honestly deal with racism. *This Bridge Called My Back* stresses the urgency of anti-racist work for the women's movement, the challenge to and from Third world women. Reading it I was alternately relieved, jubilant and panicked. *This Bridge* contains the push needed to break the stalemate around racism, to sharpen feminism for a new beginning. I recently discussed how to use *This Bridge* as an instrument for change with its two editors, Cherríe Moraga and Gloria Anzaldua.

Cherríe Moraga (l) and Gloria Anzaldua

—*Susan Wilson*

make great political people because we're used to working ourselves to death. That's why I'm very interested in talking about relationships between us. Because that is a thing that will sustain us, that will make movement work possible. If you have a handful of friends, who are your allies, who you feel you can confide in, that will encourage you to be more, to challenge you, then it's worth being a movement person. But if doing movement work is at the expense of your own personal freedom, it ain't worth shit.

ANZALDUA: I think we're very rich in terms of having a vision, and ideals, and striving for them, and keeping on no matter what. Because we've had to confront and deal with all this and really work at developing ourselves, it's made us richer, stronger. I don't know how long we can keep it up!

What are your plans for the book?

ANZALDUA: We want to get it in as many hands as possible and have it generate discussion and other issues. I would like to see Third world women start healing themselves and start bridging the political with the psychic-spiritual. I think that's where our empow-

WILLIAMS: *This Bridge* is amazing in the variety of voices collected here and the painful honesty all the writers express. How did this project begin?

ANZALDUA: The book started with an experience I had in attending a women's retreat north of San Francisco. The treatment that I got from the people at this place was

ism.

I think the hardest thing to describe, unless you sit down and do a book, is not just racism and classism, but a whole different set of cultural values that you have because of your own cultural upbringing that never get expresses when someone says, "What's wrong here?" and you try to say what's wrong

mass of ignorant women, white women, and there were some Third world women there who were very patiently, again, trying to explain. So, I came out of there feeling so totally exhausted, like somebody had walked over me. And Barbara said to me, "It's so hard to be a bridge; that's the thing, a bridge gets walked over."

One of my favorite parts in the book is when you stand up to all the people who say you have to choose between your oppressions! The bridgework is made because of that, not in opposition to it; because you obviously you're going to be the one that says, okay, can we all get together.

From *Sojourner*—October 1981. A Boston Women's newspaper.

Afterword

On the Fourth Edition

Cherríe Moraga

Re-visioning *This Bridge Called My Back* thirty-five years later has given me great pause. I keep remembering Gloria's line: *"Who am I, a poor Chicanita from the sticks, to think I could write?"* (161). And I think about how true it was—for both of us—those self-doubts, those deeply internal questions about our "right to write." Gloria Anzaldúa and I came to the publishing project of *Bridge* as feminist activist writers, giving readings and organizing cultural events in the Bay Area, but with few publishing credits to our name. In the late 1970s, Chicanas were barely beginning to produce work in magazines and small press chapbooks. With some exceptions, the same could be said of Native and Asian American women writers at the time. But, we did have support along the way . . .

In the history of *Bridge*, Gloria has often acknowledged the artist-writer Merlin Stone as one of the book's chief advocates. (xlvi, 262.) I would like to also acknowledge a few more. The lesbian feminist writer and poet, Adrienne Rich, brought significant visibility to the project of *Bridge*. In 1979, swallowing my own timidity as a student of her work (we had never met), I sent Adrienne a draft of "La Güera" in order to announce our book plans and solicit her support. To my amazement, she invited me to publish the essay in *The Coming Out Stories* (Persephone Press, 1980), for which she was writing a foreword. Adrienne would also become an active supporter of the founding of Kitchen Table Press and its effort to republish *Bridge* after Persephone's closure in 1982.

Sally Miller Gearhart, the lesbian feminist activist and the author of *The Wanderground* (another Persephone title, 1979), was actually the first to recommend *Bridge* to Persephone Press. The manuscript was then entitled "Smashing the Myth!" (Teish, 229). A lesbian separatist in theory, Sally was my graduate studies advisor at San Francisco State University. We fought politics all the time . . . with an abiding love.

If the story of the *making of Bridge* teaches, as much as the book itself, it does so by recognizing that yes, "race matters." The support of these white women with "cultural capital" did not make or break our project. In fact, Gloria and I often laughed that we would have mimeographed the book and distributed it on street corners, if that were all that had been available to us. Still, *their* "access" brought *us* access—to a national feminist publishing and distribution network for a collection of "writings by radical women of color."

In a uniquely distinct way, Audre Lorde's and Toni Cade Bambara's presence in *Bridge* also impacted *Bridge*'s success. Audre and Toni were exemplary sister-writers, emblematic of that great surge of Black feminist writing spilling into our hands in 1970s and '80s. As "sisters of the yam" . . . they stood up in unwavering solidarity with the rest of us "sisters of the rice, sisters of the corn, sisters of the plantain" (xxxvii) and that mattered. It helped put *Bridge*, coedited by two "unknown" Chicana writers, on the political-literary map.

All in all, it was a brave moment in feminist history.

More personally, what is not known about the history of *Bridge* is the role the book played in my own evolution as a student and a public thinker. Perhaps I speak of it here for the students who hunger for "that life of the mind" to go public, to create actual testifiable change in one's life.

During the summer of 1980, when I went east to find a publisher for *Bridge*, I was completing course work in a "Special Master's" program in Feminist Writings at SFSU. Under the generous tutelage of Sally Gearhart and her then-partner, English professor Jane Gurko, I had designed my own program. (There *were* no graduate studies programs in Women's Studies at the time.) Upon my return, I was due to write my thesis, but when I came back from Boston, I came back changed. I had already come to realize that the project of *Bridge* had not only taken over my life, but also my life purpose. A standard master's thesis was no longer viable. And I made my case to my advisors.

Within the context of the late 1970s utterly white-middle-class-dominated genre of feminist writings (mediated by white instructors), *Bridge* was the logical and necessary critical outcome to my feminist studies. The book was an enormous collective "fill in the blank"—of so much that had been missing in my own education. It was what never appeared on a reading list.

Its labor *was* my thesis.

And my true teachers, Jane and Sally, concurred. With a ten-page paper to "justify" the project, *This Bridge Called My Back: Writings by*

Radical Women of Color became my (our) woman of color "thesis," stacked somewhere, in manuscript form, on the library shelves of SFSU. I honor Jane and Sally as models of an old-school feminist teaching practice, where professors were willing to "break the rules" to allow their students a "change of mind" (xlvi). I've been meaning to thank those two women in print for thirty-five years.

Having lived for several months now re-viewing, in great detail, the pages of the original *This Bridge Called My Back*, these women writers' younger voices have entered my heart (and gut) all over again; but, perhaps in an even more profound way. Because I know now, thirty-five years later, what courage it took those women to speak up—before their time—not only on the pages of *Bridge*, but all the "speaking up" they had to do *first* in order to finally get to those pages.

They are/were warrior women, to be sure, some of them more deeply than we can ever know.

. . .

"There was no body to talk to," my companion reminds me. We sit across the kitchen table.

"Yes," I say, "that's why we wrote the book."

En gratitud,
clm
26 de noviembre 2014

Notes on the Fourth Edition . . .

The year 2015 marks 35th anniversary of the making of *This Bridge Called My Back*, first published in 1981 by the feminist Persephone Press of Watertown, Massachusetts. The collection was subsequently published by Kitchen Table: Women of Color Press of New York City less than two years later. In many ways, Kitchen Table Press emerged in the effort to keep *Bridge* in print; for within a year or so after *Bridge*'s original publication, Persephone had ceased operation. The founding members of Kitchen Table Press included *Bridge* 1981 contributors: hattie gossett, Audre Lorde, Barbara Smith, and myself, Cherríe Moraga. The initial core collective also included Alma Gómez, Leota Lone Dog, Mariana Romo-

Carmona, and Susan Yung, among others. In 2002, the third edition of *Bridge* was published in a small print run by Third Woman Press of the Department of Ethnic Studies at the University of California–Berkeley, under the direction of *Bridge* contributor, Norma Alarcón.

The core writings in the fourth edition of *This Bridge Called My Back* effectively replicate the original 1981 publication of the book. What is new to this 2015 edition are the introductory materials, occasional editor notes to provide some historical contexts, and, most notably the inclusion of new artwork, and three new poems from the 1980s by Kate Rushin.

The artwork in the 2015 edition was largely collected from the Third Woman Press edition, curated by Xicana (O'dami) artist Celia Herrera Rodríguez. It replaces the original drawings by one artist, Johnetta Tinker (Gracias!), with a larger representation of eight artworks, created by US women of color during the period of *Bridge*'s inception—the late 1970s and early 1980s. The artwork reflects some of the most radical expressions of women of color resistance of its time. Of that era, Herrera Rodríguez states:

> *What had been missing in [the original]* Bridge *for me as an artist, was the visual image constructed in a similar spirit; [one] of resistance, opposition and outright revolt. In a different 'language,' but with equal commitment, the art works selected here accomplish what Gloria Anzaldúa speaks of in her foreword to the second edition. They move us to* "leave behind the defeated image" *and* "the posture as victims."[1]

In the appendix that follows, the coeditors' forewords to the 1983 second edition have been reprinted, as has Gloria Anzaldúa's 2001 foreword to the third edition.[2] Also included are the biographies of the writers and artists from 2015, along with biographies from the original 1981 edition.

They are well worth comparing, thirty-five years later.

Notes

1. Celia Herrera Rodríguez in "A Sacred Thing That Takes Us Home," *This Bridge Called My Back: Writings by Radical Women of Color* (Berkeley: Third Woman Press, 2002), 279–287.
2. Moraga's foreword to the 3rd edition is not included here, but appears in her collection, *A Xicana Codex of Changing Consciousness* (Duke University Press, 2011).

Foreword to the Second Edition, 1983

Gloria Anzaldúa

¿Qué hacer de aquí y cómo?
(What to do from here and how?)

Perhaps like me you are tired of suffering and talking about suffering, estás hasta el pescuezo de sufrimiento, de contar las lluvias de sangre pero no las lluvias de flores (*up to your neck with suffering, of counting the rains of blood but not the rains of flowers*). Like me you may be tired of making a tragedy of our lives. A abandonar ese autocanibalismo: coraje, tristeza, miedo (*let's abandon this autocannibalism: rage, sadness, fear*). Basta de gritar contra el viento—toda palabra es ruido si no está acompañada de acción (*enough of shouting against the wind—all words are noise if not accompanied with action*). Dejemos de hablar hasta que hagamos la palabra luminosa y activa (*let's work not talk, let's say nothing until we've made the world luminous and active*). Basta de pasividad y de pasatiempo mientras esperamos al novio, a la novia, a la Diosa, o a la Revolución (*enough of passivity and passing time while waiting for the boy friend, the girl friend, the Goddess, or the Revolution*). No nos podemos quedar paradas con los brazos cruzados en medio del puente (*we can't afford to stop in the middle of the bridge with arms crossed*).

And yet to act is not enough. Many of us are learning to sit perfectly still, to sense the presence of the Soul and commune with Her. We are beginning to realize that we are not wholly at the mercy of circumstance, nor are our lives completely out of our hands. That if we posture as victims we *will* be victims, that hopelessness is suicide, that self-attacks stop us in our tracks. We are slowly moving past the resistance within, leaving behind the defeated images. We have come to realize that we are not alone in our struggles nor separate nor autonomous but that we—white black straight queer female male—are connected and interdependent. We are each accountable for what is happening down the street, south of the border or across the sea. And those of us who have more of anything: brains, physical strength, political power, spiritual energies, are learning to share them with those that don't have. We are learning to depend more and more on our own sources for survival, learning not to let the weight of this burden, the bridge, break our backs. Haven't we always borne jugs of water, children, poverty? Why not learn to bear baskets of hope, love, self-nourishment and to step lightly? With *This Bridge* . . . hemos comenzado a salir de las sombras; hemos comenzado a reventar rutina y costumbres opresivas y a aventar los tabues; hemos comenzado a acarrear con orgullo la tarea de deshelar corazones y cambiar conciencias (*we have begun to come out of the shadows; we have begun to break with routines and oppressive customs and to discard taboos; we have commenced to carry with pride the task of thawing hearts and changing consciousness*). Mujeres, a no dejar que el peligro del viaje y la inmensidad del territorio nos asuste—a mirar hacia adelante y a abrir paso en el monte (*Women, let's not let the danger of the journey and the vastness of the territory scare us—let's look forward and open paths in these woods*). Caminante, no hay puentes, se hacen puentes al andar (*Voyager, there are no bridges, one builds them as one walks*).

Contigo,
Gloria Anzaldúa

Refugees of a World on Fire

Foreword to the Second Edition, 1983

Cherríe Moraga

I try to imagine the newcomer to *Bridge*. What do you need to know? I have heard from people through letters and travel that the book has helped change some minds (and hopefully hearts as well), but it has changed no one more than the women who contributed to its existence. It has changed my life so fundamentally that today I feel almost the worst person to introduce you to *Bridge*, to see it through fresh eyes. Rather your introduction or even reintroduction should come from the voices of the women of color who first discovered the book:

> The women writers seemed to be speaking to me, and they actually understood what I was going through. Many of you put into words feelings I have had that I had no way of expressing . . . The writings justified some of my thoughts telling me I had a right to feel as I did. It is remarkable to me that one book could have such an impact. So many feelings were brought alive inside me.[1]

For the new reader, as well as for the people who may be looking at *Bridge* for the second or third time, I feel the need to speak to what I think of the book some three years later. Today I leaf through the pages of *Bridge* and imagine all the things so many of us would say differently or better—watching my own life and the lives of these writers/activists grow in commitment to whatever it is we term "our work." We are getting older, as is our movement.

I think that were *Bridge* to have been conceived in 1983, instead of 1979, it would speak much more directly now to the relations between women and men of color, both gay and heterosexual. In response to a proliferation of writings by women of color up until 1980, which in the name of feminism focused almost exclusively on heterosexual relations (either by apologizing for or condemning the sexism of Third World men), *Bridge* intended to make a clean break from that phenomenon.[2] So, we created a book which concentrated on relationships among women.

Once this right has been established, however, once a movement has provided some basic consciousness so that heterosexism and sexism are not considered the normal course of events, we are in a much stronger position to analyze our relations with the men of our families and communities from a position of power rather than compromise. A *Bridge* of 1983 could do this. (I am particularly encouraged by the organizing potential between Third World lesbians and gay men in our communities of color.)

The second major difference a 1983 version of *Bridge* would provide is that it would be much more international in perspective. Although the heart of *Bridge* remains the same, the impetus to forge links with women of color from every region grows more and more urgent as the number of recently-immigrated people of color in the US grows in enormous proportions, as we begin to see ourselves all as refugees of a world on fire:

- The US is training troops in Honduras to overthrow the Nicaraguan people's government.

- Human rights violations are occurring on a massive scale in Guatemala and El Salvador (and as in this country those most hard-hit are often the Indigenous peoples of those lands).

- Pinochet escalates political repression in Chile.

- The US invades Grenada.

- Apartheid continues to bleed South Africa.

- Thousands of unarmed people are slaughtered in Beirut by Christian militiamen and Israeli soldiers.

- Aquino is assassinated by the Philippine government.

- And in the US? The Reagan administration daily drains us of nearly every political gain made by the feminist, Third World, and anti-war work of the late '60s and early '70s.

The question and challenge for Third World feminism remains: What are the particular conditions of oppression suffered by women of color in each of these situations? How have the special circumstances of their pain been overlooked by Third World movements, solidarity groups, "international feminists"? How have the children suffered? How do we organize ourselves to survive this war? To keep our families, our bodies, our spirits intact?

Sometimes in the face of my own/our own limitations, in the face of such world-wide suffering, I doubt even the significance of books. Surely this is the same predicament so many people who have tried to use words as weapons have found themselves in—¿Cara a cara con el enemigo, qué valen mis palabras?[3] This is especially true for Third World women writers, who know full well our writings seldom *directly* reach the people we grew up with. Sometimes knowing this makes you feel like you're dumping your words into a very deep and very dark hole. But we continue to write—to the literate of our people and the people they touch. We even write to those classes of people for whom books have been as common to their lives as bread. For finally, we write to anyone who will listen with their ears open (even if only a crack) to the currents of change around them.

The political writer, then, is the ultimate optimist, believing people are capable of change and using words as one way to try and penetrate the privatism of our lives. A privatism which keeps us back and away from each other, which renders us politically useless.

I must confess that at the time of this writing, however, I am feeling more defeated than optimistic. The dream of a unified Third World feminist movement in this country, as we conceived of it when we first embarked on the project of this book, seemed more possible somehow, because as yet, less tried. It was still waiting in the ranks begging to take form and hold. In the last three years I have learned that Third World feminism does not provide the kind of easy political framework that women of color are running to in droves. The *idea* of Third World feminism has proved to be much easier between the covers of a book than between real live women. Today the dream feels more remote, but this is precisely when the real work begins.

Recently, I have seen Third World women activists tear ourselves apart over the fact that we live in the most imperialist nation on the globe; and as educated people, we hold relative privilege; not only here, but especially in relation to the poverty of the Third World, engendered by the same US imperialism. (As a light-skinned woman, I must say this unreservedly.) The painful recognition of this contradiction is, I believe, the source of much confusion and strife among us as feminists and activists.

I worry about a tendency in the movement where Third World feminism becomes confused with Marxist-line party politics with a "focus on women." I worry when the most essential element of feminism, "the personal is political," begins to fade fast from our dealings with each other. Because when that happens, and history has proven this, the first to go is the right to our sexuality and with that goes lesbian rights.

Because one would not necessarily go into a Salvadoreño refugee camp espousing her lesbianism, does this mean that homophobia is not a problem in the Left, among heterosexual feminists, among Third World men, on the street? Does this mean that homophobia is not a deterrent to successful coalition-building in the US? Because families are being torn apart by apartheid in South Africa, does this mean that a Black woman should not bring up over the dinner table or in the political meeting that she has felt humiliated or mistreated by her husband, lover, or comrade? If we are interested in building a movement that will not constantly be subverted from the inside at every turn, then we build from the inside out, not the other way around. Coming to terms with the suffering of others has never meant looking away from our own.

And yet, it is true that our oppression is *not* the be-all and end-all. I worry about the tendency in the movement where women of color activists seem to be enamored with our own oppression. Where class and the actual material conditions of our lives are not taken into account even in examining the very politics we do. Who are we reaching? I worry about the tendency of racial/cultural separatism amongst us where we dig in our heels against working with groups outside our own particular race/ethnicity. This is what we have accused white people of, basically sticking to their own kind—only working politically where they feel "safe" and "at home." But the making of a political movement has never been about safety or feeling "at home." (Not in the long run, anyway.) Cultural identity—our right to it—is a legitimate and basic concern for all women of color. As Judit Moschkovich writes, "Without it I would be an empty shell . . ." (76). But to stop there only results in the most limiting of identity politics: "If I suffer it, it's real. If I don't feel it, it doesn't exist." If politics is about feeling—which feminism has rightfully politicized—then we need to expand our capacity to feel clear through and out of our own experience as well.

If my major concerns (or worries) seem in opposition to each other, they remain so only from the most superficial perspectives. What threatens our movement in each of these situations is our refusal to acknowledge that to change the world, we have to change ourselves—even sometimes our most cherished, block-hard convictions. I must confess I hate the thought of this. Change don't come easy. For anyone. But this state of war we live in, this world on fire, provides us with no other choice.

If the image of the bridge can still bind us together, I think it does so most powerfully in the words of Kate Rushin, when she states:

"stretch . . . or die."

—Cherríe Moraga

Notes

1. Alma Ayala, a nineteen-year-old Puerto Rican, from a letter to Gloria Anzaldúa.
2. *Conditions 5: The Black Women's Issue* edited by Lorraine Bethel and Barbara Smith in 1979 was a major exception.
3. Face to face with the enemy, what good are my words?

Counsels from the Firing . . . Past, Present, Future

Foreword to the Third Edition, 2001

Gloria Anzaldúa

With this edition we commemorate the twenty-first anniversary of *This Bridge Called My Back*. Despite its intermittent out-of-print status it has weathered the generations well. It validated and still verifies many of our experiences, still confirms our realities. *Bridge* created a reflective and passionate space for discussion by representing many of our diverse faces. It continues to be a refuge, linking us with each other, renewing old connections among women of color, and prompting alliances with the younger generations of women and with women and men of other tribes and continents. Social movements cross borders—ours is no different. Like a stone thrown into a pool, this book's ripples have touched people on numerous shores, affecting scholars and activists throughout the world.

We look back to the last two decades with a sense of accomplishment, of having found, gathered, or created not just one community but many—grassroots activists, scholars, teachers, queers. Some of these pueblos are not just those of color, not just those of women. It forces whites to examine their own privilege, racism, and blank (blind) spots, as well as their histories and ethnicities. Yet despite *Bridge*'s great impact on international feminisms, despite the discussions it has provoked, the theories it has inspired feminists of color to generate, the activist organizations it has motivated, despite its growing legacy, there's even more work to be done. Though the roots of contemporary feminisms of color have spread through distant soils, the struggles of some activists are still unknown to those who theorize feminist work, the voices of other marginalized peoples are still absent from this and other anthologies. Yes, collectively we've gone far, but we've also lost ground—affirmative action has been repealed, the borders have been closed, racism has taken new forms and it's as pervasive as it was twenty-one years ago. Some of the cracks between the worlds have narrowed, but others have widened—the poor have gotten poorer, the corporate rich have become billionaires. New voices have joined the debate, but others are still excluded. Lesbians feature prominently in *Bridge* but our role has been downplayed. Though it's queer folk who keep walking into the teeth of the fire, we have not been given our due.

For the past years all of us have been fired in the kiln of daily trials, traumas, raptures, and triumphs. We've surrendered to the white heat of the furnace, our bodies, minds, and souls, the clay scored and transformed by the blaze. Though wounded in the firing, bodies blistered, psyches cracked, our souls have not exploded. Emerging red hot from la lumbre we've been plunged again and again into the icy waters of adversity—fear, anger, intolerance, hatred, poverty, violence. Como salamandras we've risen from the pyre reborn, souls tempered with compassion. Among the ashes traces of our roots glow like live coals illuminating our past, giving us sustenance for the present and guidance for the future.

The seed for this book came to me in the mid-seventies in a graduate English class taught by a "white" male professor at the University of Texas at Austin. As a Chicana, I felt invisible, alienated from the gringo university and dissatisfied with both el movimiento Chicano and the feminist movement. Like many of the contributors to *Bridge* I rebelled, using writing to work through my frustrations and make sense of my experiences. I wrote an essay, with the pretentious title "Growing Up Xicana," in an autobiographical politically engaged voice rather than in the dispassionate, disembodied language of academic discourse pushed on graduate students. Much to my surprise this white man championed my writing. Later I taught a course in Chicano Studies titled La Mujer Chicana. Having difficulty finding material that reflected my students' experiences I vowed to one day put Chicanas' and other women's voices between the covers of a book. At around that time a white gay male friend invited me to guest lecture his class. The idea of el mundo zurdo—the vision of a blood/spirit connection/alliance in which the colored, queer, poor, female, and physically challenged struggle together and form an international feminism—came to me in his class. Two years later in San Francisco while attending a workshop by Merlin Stone, a working-class, spirituality-practicing, goddess-loving "white" woman, I experienced subtle and blatant forms of racism and classism from the white participants.

With Merlin's encouragement I decided to compile a book of US Third World women's voices and, before leaving the workshop, composed a call for papers. Months later I asked Cherríe Moraga to join me in editing the book. I was seriously ill part of the time and without her the project would not have been completed.

Without the writers who risked their work with two unknowns, who risked revealing their vulnerabilities, this book would not have affected so many in such deep, permanent ways. The energy generated by this collection of "stories" proved to be an alchemical one, rendering the whole greater than the parts. Without Toni Cade Bambara to "make revolution irresistible" *Bridge* could not have gotten us there-here. Persephone, a "white"/Jewish press, and later Kitchen Table Press, a woman of color press, put to use all their resources to produce the book, and with this edition, the third firing in the kiln, Third Woman Press, also a woman of color press, has picked up the torch. Without las mujeres (y hombres) of all "races" in the Bay Area, Boston, New York, and elsewhere who helped promote *Bridge* it would not have become so widely read. Without the readers who sustain the book's wide-spread, multicultural roots, the ever-increasing new generations of students, y las activistas who make our visions a reality, this book would not have become a foundational text, would not now be a site of creative dialogue and criticism.

Los consejos from the firing of the last two decades are many. The first counsel reminds us that *Bridge* has multicultural roots and that it is not "owned" solely by mujeres de color, or even by women. Like knowledge, *Bridge* cannot be possessed by a single person or group. It's public; it's communal. To exclude is to close the bridge, invite separatism and hostilities. Instead we (Third World feminists) must invite other groups to join us and together bring about social change. We must align ourselves with and support those who challenge their own inherited or acquired privileges, examine their social positions, and take responsibility for their assumptions.

To trust the other (i.e., whites) is hard when in the past they've betrayed us, and when our very lives have depended on not trusting. Though there are no longer pure victims or pure villains, differences in power and privilege are very real. When power is unequal relationships are conflicted—it's difficult for dialogue to occur among individuals of unequal power. Similarly it's naïve to automatically trust others because they're like us and "belong" to the same categories. For the past twenty years, identity politics have been extremely useful, but they too are constraining. We need new strategies, new conceptions of community.

From this vantage point of greater conocimiento we recognize otro consejo del fuego—the rhetoric of racial categories imposed on us is partial and flawed and only serves to cage us in "race" and class-bound spaces. Subtle forms of political correctness, self-censorship, and romanticizing home racial/ethnic/class communities imprison us in limiting spaces. These categories do not reflect the realities we live in, and are not true to our multicultural roots. Liminality, the in-between space of nepantla, is the space most of us occupy. We do not inhabit un mundo but many, and we need to allow these other worlds and peoples to join in the feminist-of-color dialogue. We must be wary of assimilation but not fear cultural mestizaje. Instead we must become nepantleras and build bridges between all these worlds as we traffic back and forth between them, detribalizing and retribalizing in different and various communities. The firing has bequeathed us el conocimiento (insight) that humans and the universe are in a symbiotic relationship, that we live in a state of deep interconnectedness en un mundo zurdo (a left-handed world). We are not alone in our struggles, and never have been. Somos almas afines and this interconnectedness is an unvoiced category of identity.[1] Though we've progressed in forging el mundo zurdo, especially its spiritual aspect, we must now more than ever open our minds to others' realities.

It is risky to venture outside the confines of our color, class, gender and sexuality, as it is to make alliances with others who do not fit into the categories of our self-identity. One of the biggest risks is isolation from the group with which we identify. One experience I had with this was when I was attacked by straight Chicanas at the 1984 NACS conference in Ypsilanti, Michigan and was accused of being more concerned with orgasms and the lesbian movement than with helping La Raza. Often ostracism gives us a way out of the isolation—daring to make connections with people outside our "race" necessitates breaking down categories. Because our positions are nos/otras, both/and, inside/outside, and inner exiles—we see through the illusion of separateness. We crack the shell of our usual assumptions by interrogating our notions and theories of race and other differences. When we replace the old story (of judging others by race, class, gender, and sexual groupings and using these judgments to create barriers), we threaten people who believe in clearly defined mutually exclusive categories. The same hands that split assumptions apart must also span the cracks, must wield the mutual exchange of stories. The solution is not exclusivity and dominance, but receptivity to new theories, stories, visions. We must surrender our privilege, scant though it may seem. We must hold out our manos to others and share our gains.

The primary counsel from the firing is that change, that swift-footed salamandra, is our only option. We either move or petrify. Change requires great heat. We must turn the heat on our own selves, the first site of working toward social justice and transformation. By transforming the negative perceptions we have of ourselves we change systems of oppression in interpersonal contexts—within the family, the community—which in turn alters larger institutional systems. In challenging our own negative, unconscious assumptions of self-identity we make ourselves so uncomfortable we're forced to make changes. Our images/feelings/thoughts have to be conflicted before we see the need for change. Restoring dignity and overcoming a stigmatized status changes our self-image; changes in the self lead to changes in the categories of identity, which in turn precipitate changes in community and traditions.

Using imagination (images/feelings/thoughts), love, and vision to implement change is another counsel from the firing. Imagination links us with what lives outside of us. Like radio waves our thoughts/consciousness travel on air and impact others. Imagination offers resolutions out of the conflict by dreaming alternative ways of imaging/feeling/thinking. For positive social change to happen we need to envision a different reality, dream new blueprints for it, formulate new strategies for coping in it. But because change, positive and negative, is always a source of tension, because it has no sense of closure, of completion, we resist it. We must be motivated by love in order to undertake change—love of self, love of people, love of life. Loving gives us the energy and compassion to act in the face of hardship; loving gives us the motivation to dream the life and work we want. To help me "dream" this foreword I spread the Medicine Cards and pulled horse, the power that brings visions. This book is our horse; it carries our messages, our gifts to the people.

A final counsel from the firing is that awareness of spirit, el conocimiento of the links of carne y hueso, the bonds of suffering lie behind all our acts, not just those of compassion and vision. Spiritual awareness is on the rise; humans are turning inward, looking at what's behind the eye as well as in front. A spiritual understanding of humanity's role in the universe is now required of us. Before, this radical change in consciousness, this burgeoning of a worldwide spiritual activism, this common cause among the world's peoples, this paradigm shift, was a dream—now it's a necessity. Our work of casting a spiritual light on the bridge enables us to venture into unknown territories. It prepares us to fortify the old bridges, build new ones, and cross these when we come to them. It will help us deal with new life trials, awaken the young women and men from post-feminist sleepwalking, and rouse us older folk who have become complacent and apathetic.

In this millennium we are called to renew and birth a more inclusive feminism, one committed to basic human rights, equality, respect for all people and creatures, and for the earth. As keepers of the fire of transformation we invite awareness of soul into our daily acts, call richness and beauty into our lives; bid spirit to stir our blood, dissolve the rigid walls between us, and gather us in. May our voices proclaim the bonds of bridges.

Contigo en la lucha,
Gloria Anzaldúa
November 2001

Note

1. AnaLouise Keating, ed., *Interviews/Entrevistas* (New York: Routledge, 2000), 164.

Biographies of Contributors

Writers

Norma Alarcón. Professor Emeritus, UC Berkeley. Publisher, Third Woman Press, 1979–2004. Has published multiple essays on Chicanas and other women of color in the USA, as well as a book on Mexican writer Rosario Castellanos. She currently resides in San Antonio, Texas.

Gloria Anzaldúa. Born in the Río Grande Valley of south Texas, Gloria Evangelina Anzaldúa was an independent scholar, cultural theorist, creative writer, and nepantlera spiritual activist who made lasting contributions to numerous academic fields, including Chicana studies, composition studies, feminism and feminist theory, literary studies, queer theory, and women's studies. Anzaldúa's work spans multiple genres, including poetry, theoretical and philosophical essays, short stories, innovative autobiographical narratives, and children's books. She is the author, editor, or co-editor of numerous books, including *Borderlands/La Frontera: The New Mestiza* (1987); *Making Face, Making Soul/Haciendo Caras: Creative and Critical Perspectives by Feminists of Color* (1990); *Interviews/Entrevistas* (2000); *this bridge we call home: radical visions for transformation* (2002); and two bilingual children's books: *Friends from the Other Side/Amigos del otro lado* (1993) and *Prietita and the Ghost Woman/Prietita y la Llorona* (1997). Her posthumous publications include *The Gloria Anzaldúa Reader* (2009) and *Light in the Dark/Luz en lo oscuro: Rewriting Identity, Spirituality, Reality* (2015). Anzaldúa died in May 2004 from diabetes-related complications.

Toni Cade Bambara was born March 25, 1939. She edited two anthologies, *The Black Woman* (1970) and *Tales and Short Stories for Black Folk* (1971); wrote the short story collections *Gorilla, My Love* (1972) and *The Seabirds Are Sill Alive* (1977); and the novel *The Salt Eaters* (1980).

Bambara succumbed to colon cancer December 9, 1995, and her collection of essays and interviews, *Deep Sighting and Rescue Missions* (1996), and novel *Those Bones Are Not My Child* (1999) were published posthumously.

Barbara Cameron (Lakota, 1954–2002) was a photographer, poet, writer, and a nationally recognized political activist. She was born in Fort Yates, North Dakota and was raised, primarily by her grandparents, on the Standing Rock Reservation. Barbara attended the American Indian Art Institute in Sante Fe, New Mexico, majoring in photography and film and then moved to San Francisco in 1973 where she became fully immersed as an organizer around Gay and Native concerns. In 1975, she cofounded Gay American Indians, and she co-produced the Lesbian/Gay Freedom Day from 1981 to 1985. In 1986 she traveled in a women's delegation to Sandinista Nicaragua and in 1988 served as a Jesse Jackson delegate to the Democratic National Convention. Her four years as the Executive Director of Community United Against Violence, among many other organizing efforts, garnered her the Harvey Milk Award for community service in 1992. Barbara will also be remembered as a human being of humble heart and of the highest integrity.

Andrea Ruth Ransom Canaan holds an MFA from the University of San Francisco. She is completing a memoir, *The Salt Box House on Bayou Black*. It tells of generational transmission of trauma passed from a mother to daughter and so on. It is her journey of being raised in a close, loving, spiritual, and activist community in New Orleans, Louisiana and her passage through madness during and after being sexually molested and abused by a very powerful minister during the heart of the civil rights movement. She is a full-time writer and resides with her partner in San Francisco, California.

Jo Carrillo, JD/JSD, is a professor of law at the University of California, Hastings College of the Law, in San Francisco, where she is the first woman of color to have joined the tenured faculty. She is also: a former research fellow at The Center for the Study of Law and Society at UC Berkeley; a former visiting professor at Stanford Law School; and a past recipient of the UC Hastings Research Chair. Her contribution to *This Bridge* was written when she was an undergraduate at Stanford University. As an interdisciplinary scholar, Carrillo is interested in how artists discuss and incorporate law into their creative work and, more generally, in how literature serves as a public record of the oppression individuals experience in society. As a literary writer, she is ever interested in improving her vision and her craft.

Chrystos. My books are: *Not Vanishing*; *Dream On*; *In Her I Am* (Lesbian Erotica); *Fire Power* (available from my PO Box 4663 Rolling Bay, WA 98061); *Wilder Reis* (German translation); *Red Rollercoaster*; *Fugitive Colors* (order from Cleveland State Poetry Center). Gloria Anzadúa's support of my work continues to sustain me.

Cheryl Clarke. (b. 1947) is the author of four books of poetry, a critical work, *After Mecca: Women Poets and the Black Arts Movement*, and a volume of her collected writing, *The Days of Good Looks: Prose and Poetry 1981 to 2005*. Her writing also appears in *Signs: A Journal of Women in Culture and Society* (Summer, 2010), celebrating the 25th anniversary of *Some of Us Are Brave: Black Women's Studies*, another iconic women of color text. Clarke retired from Rutgers University in 2013 after 41 years. She and her lover, Barb Balliet, co-own Blenheim Hill Books in Hobart, NY, the Book Village of the Catskills. They are organizers of the annual Hobart Festival of Women Writers.

Gabrielle Daniels received her MFA in English from the University of California, Irvine in 1999. She's been the recipient of a Ludwig Vogelstein grant in 2004, and the Carl Djerasi Fellowship from the University of Wisconsin Creative Writing Institute in Madison in 2005. Gabrielle was a witness to the first stirrings of what has become the Wisconsin Uprising. She's currently at work on a memoir of growing up in New Orleans and the San Francisco Bay Area, and hopes to return to California to live and to write. Gabrielle also writes a news commentary blog— "This Black Sista's Page"—that will soon branch out to feature book reviews.

doris davenport. i am still a writer, educator, and literary & performance poet from the Appalachian foothills of Habersham County (Cornelia) Georgia. i have earned degrees from Paine College (B.A. English), SUNY Buffalo (M.A. English), and the University of Southern California (Ph.D. Literature). Presently, i am an Associate Professor of English at Stillman College in Tuscaloosa, Alabama. In December 2001, i published my eighth book of poetry, *ascent*. i still think THIS BRIDGE is an important work and i do "stand behind" my essay—i only regret that it is not more analytical, longer, and stronger. Contact information: zorahpoet7@gmail.com. More information: http://www.redroom.com/author/doris-diosa-davenport,

Mary Hope Whitehead Lee. "I was born and raised in san diego California/the last big town before the mexican border." She currently lives in Phoenix, Arizona where she works for migrant rights, connecting African Americans to this shared and common cause.

Aurora Levins Morales is a Puerto Rican Jewish writer, historian, artist & activist. She's the author of: *Kindling: Writings on the Body; Medicine Stories;* and *Remedios: Stories of Earth & Iron from the History of Puertorriqueñas;* and two books with Rosario Morales: *Getting Home Alice* and *Cosecha and Other Stories.* She works with Sins Invalid and Jewish Voice for Peace Artists' Council, and lives with chronic illness in Cambridge, Massachusetts. Still here, still writing, still radical. Blogging at http://www.auroralevinsmorales.com/main-blog.

Genny Lim served in the San Francisco Art Commission from 1991 to 1995 on the Visual Arts Committee, as Chair of Community Arts and Education Committee, and as Chair of the Advisory Board for the San Francisco Writers Corps. She has performed in live and recorded poetry/music collaborations with jazz greats—Max Roach, Herbie Lewis, Francis Wong and Jon Jang. She has performed at jazz festivals from San Francisco, San Jose, and San Diego—to Houston and Chicago. She has been a featured poet at World Poetry Festivals in Venezuela (2005), Sarajevo, Bosnia-Hercegovina (2007), and Naples, Italy (2009). Her play "Paper Angels" was performed in San Francisco Chinatown's Portsmouth Square to packed audiences in 2010 and won the San Francisco Fringe Festival Top Ten Award for Best Site Specific Work. Her performance piece "Where Is Tibet?" premiered at CounterPULSE in San Francisco in 2009 and was also performed at the AfroSolo Arts Festival in 2010. She is author of two poetry collections, *Winter Place* and *Child of War,* and co-author of *Island: Poetry and History of Chinese Immigrants on Angel Island 1910–1940.*

Naomi Littlebear Morena. We were all just kids drawing our lines in the sand, which time has predictably erased. I work as I've always done. I raise my [young] son. Mama is old but is good at sports. She plays guitar and drums and sees the world through his eyes. I am grateful.

Audre Lorde (1934–1992), leader among women of color, was a well-known essayist and poet who described herself as black, lesbian, feminist, poet, mother and warrior. Through her writing and activism, she fought for African-American and Lesbian/Women's rights. Her work is lyrical and socially aware, infused with lesbian consciousness. Her writing on the topic of poetry challenges that it should not be a sterile word play, but a "revelatory distillation of experience." She produced ten volumes of poetry, five books of prose. Among these are *The Black Unicorn, The*

Cancer Journals, The Collected Poems of Audre Lorde, Our Dead Behind Us, Sister Outsider: Essays and Speeches, Zami: A New Spelling of My Name. She was the New York State Poet Laureate from 1991 to 1993 and co-founder of Kitchen Table: Women of Color Press. Audre Lorde died in 1992 after battling cancer for fourteen years.

Cherríe Moraga grew up two blocks from the San Gabriel Mission, just east of East Los Angeles. Her Mexican elders have all passed on, as she continues to write in their name. Moraga's published writings include: *Loving in the War Years: lo que nunca pasó por sus labios* (1983); *The Last Generation* (1993); *Waiting in the Wings: Portrait of a Queer Motherhood* (1997); and, *A Xicana Codex of Changing Consciousness: Writings 2000–2010.* Throughout the last twenty-five years, she has also written, directed, and published for the theater, most recently, *New Fire—To Put Things Right Again* (2012) and *The Mathematics of Love* (forthcoming). In 1980, Moraga cofounded Kitchen Table: Women of Color Press of NYC, with Audre Lorde and Barbara Smith (herein) and others. Twenty years later, she became a founding member of La Red Xicana Indígena, a national network of Xicanas working in the areas of social justice, education & culture, and Indigenous rights. Since 1996, Moraga has served as an Artist in Residence in the Department of Theater and Performance Studies and in Comparative Studies in Race and Ethnicity at Stanford University. She calls Oakland, California—and the family she raises there with her partner of nearly two decades—"home."

Rosario Morales (1930–2011) was a New York Puerto Rican living in Massachusetts. She was a feminist independentista and communist since 1949. Over thirty years ago she broke a lifetime silence with her work in *This Bridge Called My Back: Writings by Radical Women of Color.* With her daughter Aurora Levins Morales she co-authored *Getting Home Alive.*

Judit Moschkovich is Professor of Mathematics Education in the Education Department at the University of California at Santa Cruz. Her research focuses on mathematical thinking and learning. Her publications examine algebraic thinking, classroom mathematical discourse, and language issues in learning mathematics. Originally from Argentina, she moved to the US in high school. Her mother tongue is Spanish, her mother's mother tongue was Portuguese, and her grandmother's mother tongue was Yiddisch.

Barbara Noda is a writer of Japanese ancestry born in Stockton, CA, and raised in the Salinas Valley. Her first book of poetry was *Strawberries,* published by Shameless Hussy Press. She lives in Northern California.

Pat Parker (1944–1989) was born in Houston, Texas. She moved to Oakland, California in the early '70s to pursue work, writing, and activism. She worked from 1978 to 1987 as medical coordinator at the Oakland Feminist Women's Health Center, which grew from one clinic to six during her tenure. Parker also participated in political activism ranging from early involvement with the Black Panther Party and Black Women's Revolutionary Council to formation of the Women's Press Collective. She was engaged in gay and lesbian organizations and held positions of national leadership regarding women's health issues, and domestic and sexual violence. She published several poetry collections including *Child of Myself*, *Pit Stop*, *Womanslaughter*, *Movement in Black* and *Jonestown and Other Madness*. Her work is included in many anthologies.

Mirtha N. Quintanales was born in Havana, Cuba, and immigrated to the United States early in 1962 at the age of thirteen. She received a PhD in Anthropology from Ohio State University. She teaches in the Latin American, Caribbean and Latino Studies Program at New Jersey City University in Jersey City, where she served as the director of the program for nearly twenty-five years. Her work—short fiction, essays, letters, poetry, and literary translations (from Spanish to English) have appeared in a wide variety of publications. She is co-editor of and contributor to the award winning *Telling to Live: Latina Feminist Testimonios* (Latina Feminist Group, 2001, Durham, NC: Duke University Press). Current projects include: research on the US Latino boom in media and the performing arts; co-editing a book on home and the Latin American/Latino experience, "Hogar, Dulce Hogar: Ideologies of Home and the Latin American and Latino/a Experience" (working title, forthcoming 2014–2015); and little by little, work on an original screenplay-turned novel, "Fan" (working title).

Kate Rushin grew up in Camden, NJ, and the African-American town of Lawnside, NJ. She holds degrees from Oberlin and Brown Universities and has received fellowships from The Fine Arts Work Center in Provincetown and the Cave Canem Foundation. Rushin has read her poems on NPR and her work has appeared in *New Worlds of Literature* (Norton) and *Callaloo*. She has taught at MIT and Wesleyan University.

Barbara Smith. Through nearly four decades of work as a writer and the editor of visionary collections of Black Feminist writings, now documented in *Ain't Gonna Let Nobody Turn Me Around* (SUNY 2014),   Smith has played a groundbreaking role in opening up a national, cultural, and political dialogue about the intersections of race, class, sexuality, and gender. Her titles include: *All the Women Are White, All the Blacks Are*

Men, but Some of Us Are Brave: Black Women's Studies (with Gloria T. Hull and Patricia Bell Scott); *Home Girls: A Black Feminist Anthology; Ain't Gonna Let Nobody Turn Me Around: Forty Years of Movement Building;* and, a collection of her own essays, *The Truth That Never Hurts: Writings on Race, Gender, and Freedom.* A resident of Albany, New York, Smith also served two terms as a member of the Albany Common Council. In 2005 she was nominated for the Nobel Peace Prize.

Beverly Smith was one of the authors of The Combahee River Collective Statement in 1977. She has worked as a college instructor and a women's health advocate; and has written several articles on racism, feminism, and Black women's health, including reproductive rights.

Luisah Teish is the author of *Jambalaya: The Natural Woman's Book of Personal Charms and Practical Rituals.* She is an Elder/Womanchief in the Ifa/Orisha tradition and founder of Ile Orunmila Oshun. She teaches at the Institute for Transpersonal Psychology and the California Institute of Integral Studies. Teish is a ritual theater director and global community activist. www.luisahteish.com. www.ileorunmilaoshun.org.

Anita Valerio is now **Max Wolf Valerio**, having transitioned from female to male in 1989. Published work includes a memoir, *The Testosterone Files* (Seal Press, 2006), and poetry in *Troubling the Line: Trans and Genderqueer Poetry and Poetics,* edited by TC Tolbert and Tim Trace Peterson (Nightboat Books, 2013). Burned out on identity politics, Max now identifies primarily as an individual, and a classic liberal. A book of poems, *The Criminal,* is forthcoming in 2015 from EOAGH Books.

Nellie Wong. Author of four books of poetry, Nellie Wong's latest is *Breakfast Lunch Dinner,* Meridien Press Works, San Francisco, 2012. Two of her poems are inscribed in public sites in San Francisco, where she lives. A native of Oakland, her alma mater, Oakland High School, named a building after her in 2011.

Merle Woo is the daughter of a Chinese immigrant father and an orphaned Korean mother. She is a retired lecturer in Women and Asian American Studies. Fired from UC Berkeley because she is a socialist feminist lesbian and staunch supporter of student democracy, Merle won both a union arbitration and an out-of-court settlement. She is a longtime leader of the Freedom Socialist Party and Radical Women, a published writer and breast cancer survivor.

Mitsuye Yamada. Shaped by her wartime concentration camp experiences during World War II, her activities as a writer, educator, and political activist are interrelated by human rights, peace, and gender issues. She is author of *Camp Notes and Other Writings*, a combined edition of her first two books of poems and short stories (Rutgers University Press, 1998). She was formerly board member of Amnesty International USA and served on the Committee of International Development, which promotes and funds development of human rights work in Third World countries. She is a board member of Interfaith Prisoners of Conscience, an organization that works to support and free political prisoners in the US. She was formerly Adjunct Associate Professor of Asian American Studies at the University of California, Irvine. Now in her nineties, she is in the enviable position of simply enjoying life with her large family that includes seven grandchildren and a newly arrived great-grandson, Asher Philip Yamada-Harivandi.

Artists

Theresa Hak Kyung Cha (1951–1982) was born in Pusan, South Korea. Her family immigrated to the US in 1962 and settled in Hawaii. In 1964, they moved to San Francisco, and the Bay Area became Theresa's home. Theresa Cha studied Comparative Literature, French film theory and performance, and conceptual art during her ten years' of study at the University of California, Berkeley. She made her first return trip to Korea in 1979, and returned there again in 1981 to begin shooting the unfinished film, *White Dust from Magnolia*. In 1980, she had moved to New York City where she worked as an editor and writer for Tanam Press. She produced *Dictee* and *Apparatus*. On November 5, 1982, Cha was murdered.

Celia Herrera Rodríguez (Xicana/O'dami) is a two-spirit visual, installation, and performance artist, who teaches in the Chicano Studies Program at the University of California, Berkeley. She is also an Adjunct Professor at California College for the Arts. Herrera has shown her work throughout América and Europe—from The Institute of American Indian Art Museum to international conferences in Belgium, Ireland and Turkey. Her work is housed in several private collections and museums throughout the country. Herrera's work is notable for its intricate conceptual conversation with Mesoamerican and American Indigenous thought and imagery. Since 2005, Celia Herrera has collaborated as the designer for the premiere productions of Cherríe Moraga's plays, including: *The Hungry Woman*; *Digging Up the Dirt*; and *New Fire—To Put Things Right*

Again. Her drawings are also featured in Moraga's *A Xicana Codex of Changing Consciousness*.

Happy/L.A. Hyder is a fine artist working in color photography, mixed media and installation. She is also a performer and writer. Visiting Lebanon for the first time in 2010, her images hold a mythic quality of place with a reality of resilience. The envisioning to production of *New Country Daughter/Lebanese American* (herein) brought a great sense of understanding and freedom to her exploration of racial identity, embracing of feminism in theory and practice, and claiming a lesbian identity.

Yolanda M. López emerged from the Chicano Civil Rights movement in the late 1960s. In the decade of the 1970s, she reconsidered the images of women in popular Chicano culture, la Virgen de Guadalupe being one of the most often cited. As a Chicana artist, feminist and critical thinker, her work, often tinged with mild satire, proposes a critique of our visual environment. She sees Chicano culture as fluid and negotiable.

Ana Mendieta (1948–1985) was born in Cuba and came to the US in the early 1960s. She was a feminist minimalist and performance artist who used her body, earth, water, fire, sand and blood in her art. Elements of Santería were also transformed and integrated into her performance and installation works, especially in Cuba. In speaking of her work, Mendieta states in the documentary, *Fuego de Tierra*, "It is always about the search for origins." She died in 1985 after a tragic and suspicious fall from her husband's 34th floor apartment window.

Betye Saar was born in Pasadena, California in 1926. Her diverse background includes African-American, Irish, Native American, Creole, German and Scottish heritage. She calls her works "assemblages": three-dimensional, free-standing wall hangings made from natural or constructed objects. Saar reclaims African-American history by restoring derogatory or stigmatized images and enshrining them. Her goal is to show cultural differences and universal similarities. Her interests in art and the context of her work draw from personal experiences, historical events, and politics.

Hulleah J. Tsinhnahjinnie was born into the Bear Clan of the Taskigi Nation, and born for the Tsinajinnie Clan of the Diné Nation. Exhibited nationally and internationally, Tsinhnahjinnie claims photography and video as her primary languages. Creating fluent images of Native thought, her emphasis is art for Indigenous communities. She has been a recipient of the Eiteljorg Fellowship for Native American Fine Art, a Chancellor's Fellowship at the University of California-Irvine, the First People's Community Artist Award, and a Rockefeller artist in residence. She is currently Director of the C. N. Gorman Museum and Associate Professor in the Department of Native American Studies at University of California Davis.

Liliana Wilson was born in Valparaíso, Chile where she began drawing at the age of eight. As a young woman, she studied law, but quickly became disenchanted after Chile suffered a military coup that lasted 25 years. She immigrated to the United States in 1977 and pursued formal studies in art. The drawing that appears in this volume, *Los desaparecidos en el cielo* (*The disappeared in heaven*) represents the bodies of two people who washed ashore in 1975 after they were tortured and thrown overboard from a ship called "Lebu." The military used the ship as a place to torture men and women after the overthrow of Salvador Allende's government. The two drowned, but their appearance on a beach became proof of the atrocities of the military.

Biographies of the
Original Contributors, 1981

Norma Alarcón was born in Monclova, Coahuila, Mexico and raised in Chicago. Will receive Ph.D. in Hispanic Literatures in 1981 from Indiana University where she is presently employed as Visiting Lecturer in Chicano-Riqueño Studies.

Gloria Evangelina Anzaldúa. I'm a Tejana Chicana poet, hija de Amalia, Hecate y Yemaya. I am a Libra (Virgo cusp) with VI—The Lovers destiny. One day I will walk through walls, grow wings and fly, but for now I want to play Hermit and write my novel, *Andrea.* In my spare time I teach, read the Tarot, and doodle in my journal.

Barbara M. Cameron. Lakota patriot, Humkpapa, politically non-promiscuous, born with a caul. Will not forget Buffalo Manhattan Hat and Mani. Love Matri, Maxine, Leonie and my family. Still beading a belt for Pat. In love with Robin. Will someday raise chickens in New Mexico.

Andrea R. Canaan was born in New Orleans, Louisiana in 1950. Black woman, mother and daughter. Director of Women and Employment which develops and places women in non-traditional jobs. Therapist and counselor to battered women, rape victims, and families in stress. Poetry is major writing expression. Speaker, reader, and community organizer. Black feminist writer.

Jo Carrillo. Died and born 6,000 feet above the sea in Las Vegas, New Mexico. Have never left; will never leave. But for now, I'm living in San Francisco. I'm loving and believing in the land, my extended family (which includes Angie, Mame and B.B. Yawn) and my sisters. Would never consider owning a souvenir chunk of uranium. Plan to raise sheep, learn to weave rugs and blankets, and write in New Mexico.

Chrystos. Last year I moved to Bainbridge Island. I am living in a house overlooking the water. I have chickens and a big vegetable garden. Prior, I lived in the San Francisco Bay area, with the last four years in the Mission barrio. I will be 34 this November (double Scorpio, Moon in Aries). I've been writing since I was 9 and this is the first time I've been paid.

Cheryl Clarke. A lesbian-feminist writer who lives in Highland Park, NJ. She has published poetry in *Lady Unique Inclination of the Night, Second Cycle* (1977), a feminist journal of the goddess. She has published reviews in *Conditions V: The Black Women's Issue* (1979) and *Conditions VI* (1980). Her poetry also appears in *Lesbian Poetry: An Anthology* (Persephone Press, Inc., 1981).

Gabrielle Daniels was born in New Orleans, LA, but has lived most of her life in California. She doesn't miss gumbo as she used to, but "cooks" as a member of the Women Writers Union of the Bay Area,

doris juanita davenport is a writer who lives in los angeles. she is a lesbian and feminist, a devotee of yemaya and a believer in tequila. she was born in cornelia, georgia; has a ph.d. (black literature) at the university of southern california. moreover, she is obsessed with truth, period.

hattie gossett born: central new jersey factory town lives: northern harlem enjoys: thinking conversating reading jazzing and opposing patripower work herstory: mother's helper maid cook wife barmaid waitress forthcoming book: *my soul looks back in wonder/wild wimmin don't git no blues.*

mary hope whitehead lee i am/at heart/a gypsy recluse/who for the moment/is a poet and a blues lyricist/i was born and raised in san diego california/the last big town before the mexican border.

Aurora Levins Morales. I was born in Indiera Baja, Puerto Rico, in 1954 of a Jewish father and a Puerto Rican mother, both communists. I have lived in the US since I was thirteen & in the Bay Area for five years, where I work as a teacher's aide for pay & as a writer and performer at La Peña Cultural Center for sanity and solidarity.

Genny Lim is co-author of *Island: Poetry and History of Chinese Immigrants on Angel Island 1910–1940*, published by Hoc-Doi, July 1980. She is the author of *Paper Angels*, a full-length play produced by the Asian American Theater company of San Francisco in September 1980. She has been a contributing editor to *Bridge* magazine, a national Asian American quarterly, and a contributor to *East/West* newspaper. Her writing has been published in *California Living, Y'Bird, American Born and Foreign* (Anthology by Sunbury Press), *We Won't Move* (International Hotel Anthology by Kearny St. Workshop), *Networks* (Anthology of Bay Area Women Poets by Vortex), *Beatitude, Women Talking, Women Listening,* and *Plexus,* among others.

Naomi Littlebear. This has been no fairy tale. I hated gang fights, street life, stumbling on dope, actin' tuff, being poor, wearin' second hand inferiority complexes, smart-mouthed cholos and their Gabacho counterparts. I rebuild my broken dreams in Portland, Oregon.

Audre Lorde. "I was born in the middle of NYC of West Indian parents & raised to know that America was not my home." Most recent work: *The Cancer Journals* published by Spinsters Ink. She is also the author of *The Black Unicorn,* a book of poems published in 1978 by Norton, along with many other works of poetry and prose.

Cherríe Moraga. I am a very a tired Chicana/half-breed/feminist/lesbian/ writer/teacher/talker/waitress. And, I am not alone in this. I am the first in my family to ever be published in a book. Of this, I am proud for all for us. Los Angeles born and raised, I recently moved to Boston after three hardworking and transformative years in the San Francisco Bay Area. (Gloria convinced me to further note that I am a libra/virgo cusp with the #6 [the lovers] destiny, just like her.)

Rosario Morales. I am a New York Puerto Rican living in Cambridge, Massachusetts—a feminist independentist & communist since 1949. I married, farmed in Puerto Rico, studied science and anthropology and raised three children. I now break a lifetime "silence" to write.

Judit Moschkovich. I was born and raised in Argentina. My grandparents were Jewish immigrants from Russia and Poland. My parents and I immigrated to the United States when I was fourteen. My greatest struggle has been to be all of who I am when confronted with pressure either to pass for American or to choose between being Latina or Jewish. I have been a feminist for as long as I can remember.

Barbara Noda. A writer of Japanese ancestry. Born in Stockton, raised in Salinas Valley. First book of poetry is *Strawberries,* published by Shameless Hussy Press. Wrote a play called *Aw Shucks (Shikata Ga Nat).* Writing a novel. Likes to climb mountains.

Pat Parker is a "revolutionary feminist because (she) wants to be free." A Black Lesbian Poet, her writing spans over fifteen years of involvement in liberation struggles: the Civil Rights movement, the Black Liberation movement, Feminism, and Gay Liberation. She is the author of four books of poetry, including *Movement in Black* (Diana Press) which contains her collected works. Pat lives and works in Oakland, CA.

Mirtha Quintanales. I immigrated to the United States on April 2, 1962 when I was thirteen years old, a Cuban refugee. Eighteen years later I'm still struggling with the after-effects of this great upheaval in my life, always wondering where is home. As a latina lesbian feminist, I am one with all those whose existence is only possible through revolt.

Donna Kate Rushin lives in Boston, Massachusetts and works as a Poet-in-the-Schools through the Artists' Foundation. Her work has appeared in *Conditions 5*, *Small Moon*, and *Shankpainter*. She believes that the fight is the struggle to be whole.

Barbara Smith. I am a Black feminist and Lesbian, a writer, and an activist. I was born in Cleveland, Ohio in 1946 and was raised by a family of Black women. I have been a member of the Combahee River Collective since its founding in 1974. My writing has appeared in many Black and feminist publications. I co-edited *Conditions V: The Black Women's Issue* with Lorraine Bethel and *All the Women Are White, All the Blacks Are Men, but Some of Us Are Brave: Black Women's Studies* (The Feminist Press) with Gloria T. Hull and Patricia Bell Scott. I am now dreaming of making a film about Third World feminism.

Beverly Smith. I am a 33-year-old Black lesbian. I grew up in Cleveland, Ohio, in a family which included my twin sister Barbara, my mother, grandmother, aunt, and great-aunts. Sometimes I get sick and tired of trying to be a grown-up lesbian feminist which is why I still maintain cordial relationships with my teddy-bears.

Ms. Luisah Teish is a writer, lecturer, teacher, performer and political activist. Her most recent work is a collection of poems, *Don't Kill Is Fattening*. She is presently teaching Afro-Cuban Ritual Dance and Culture in the Bay Area and working on a book on Women's Spirituality. She is a native of New Orleans, Louisiana.

Anita Valerio is a Poet. One woman attempting Reality in an increasingly static delineated environment & the continuous bulwark of privilege, etc.

I don't really believe in the goddess. Born Heidelberg, Germany, 1957—my father was in the military so we lived all over the country. I grew with a mish mash of rich cultures—very confusing. I am now learning to celebrate the discontinuity of it all. Most pressing current concern: saving the earth from nuclear & other destructions.

Nellie Wong is poet/writer/socialist/feminist/cheong hay poa born Oakland Chinatown, thlee yip/American style year-of-the-dog-woman whose feminism grows out of *Dreams in Harrison Railroad Parks*/1st Organizer/ Women's Writer Union founding member/ Unbound Feet/ secretary to the spirit of her long time Californ' forebears.

Merle Woo is a writer of drama and fiction, is a humanities lecturer in Ethnic Studies/Asian American Studies at the University of California, Berkeley. She is a feminist and the mother of Paul, 13, and Emily Woo Yamasake, 17. Her work has been published in *Bridge, An Asian American Perspective*, and *Hanai*, an anthology of Asian American writers.

Mitsuye Yamada is a second generation Japanese American teacher and poet whose book of poems *Camp Notes And Other Poems* was published by the Shameless Hussy Press in 1976. This collection includes poems written during the World War II years in a concentration camp in Idaho, but her later writings deal with issues concerning the Asian Pacific woman in the US. She is a member of the Asian Pacific Women's Network and is currently teaching Creative Writing and Children's Literature at Cypress College in Orange County, CA.

Credits